Last Hand

A Suburban Memoir of Cards and the Cold War Era

Tom Price

iUniverse, Inc.
New York Bloomington

Last Hand
A Suburban Memoir of Cards and the Cold War Era

iUniverse books may be ordered through booksellers or by contacting:

iUniverse
1663 Liberty Drive
Bloomington, IN 47403
www.iuniverse.com
1-800-Authors (1-800-288-4677)

ISBN: 978-1-4401-3619-1 (sc)
ISBN: 978-1-4401-3620-7 (e)

Printed in the United States of America

iUniverse rev. date: 4/7/2009

Contents

Introduction

Where Are You From?

I looked at my watch as I waited at O'Hare International Airport for my flight to Germany. It was almost time to start boarding the plane. It was the 17th of November, 2000. The presidential election, which was held ten days before on the 7th, was still unresolved as a result of multiple recounts and lawsuits. The United States stood on the brink of a constitutional crisis—the country was completely polarized by politics. I stood up to board my plane. I was flying coach, as I always did for the long journey overseas. Computer bag over my shoulder and garment bag in hand, I joined the line filing onto the plane. I didn't particularly enjoy long flights. I picked up a newspaper and made my way down the aisle toward the back of the plane.

After finding my seat, I stowed my garment bag in the upper compartment and my computer bag under the seat in front of me, thus ensuring that I would have no room to move during the nine-hour flight. I took my seat by the window and began watching other passengers locate their seats. Some struggled with their luggage; some appeared cool and calm, as if they travel every day. Others seemed relieved that they made it onto the flight at all.

I enjoy observing people when traveling. Train stations and airports always intrigue me in that way. Each person walking past me or sitting near me has a story entirely their own. Where have they been? Where are they going? As with every flight I catch, I was curious as to who would sit next to me. I can usually spot him or her as they search for their seat. Time would reveal soon enough whom it would be.

A woman in her midforties approached my row. As her eyes scanned the row numbers along the aisle, there was a look of recognition in her eyes when she arrived at my row. She identified a spot in the upper compartment to deposit her bags, and squeezed into the seat next to me. I began to read my newspaper, which detailed the election debacle. I allowed the woman to have the armrest, which won me a smile. I returned the smile and looked back down at my paper.

There are generally two types of travelers you'll be seated next to on a plane: outgoing and talkative, or quiet folks who keep to themselves. When I heard her say, "It's crazy, isn't it?"—referring to the newspaper, I knew which type was sitting next to me.

"Yes, it is," I said, as pleasantly as possible.

"I'm Kim, by the way."

"Tom, nice to meet you."

"Nice to meet you, too. So, where are you from?"

I'm not one for small talk usually until I get to know the person a little better. There were two ways I could answer her question. I could answer with a simple generic location, or go into some detail about where I really came from. I opted for the easier of the two, and let her do most of the talking. Besides, I was always curious about other people's stories, and I never gave much thought to my own story. For some reason, however, her question remained in my thoughts, especially as I looked at the newspaper.

Where am I from? Not from this damn place, certainly, I thought.

A Forgotten Place

I come from a place that still exists in name, although it's changed enough that it's only a distant relative of its former self. Some of my contemporaries have assimilated well into their "new" country and surroundings. Not unlike the case for any new immigrant that comes here, it's taking time for me to adjust, as well. Every day it seems like I have to adapt to something new—I believe I'm adjusting well, but there are times when I long for the "old country." That country disappeared, along with the cold war and the emergence of a new world order. Most of my family didn't make it through that transition.

The place I came from was a land of proud people. Geographically and politically speaking, we were separated from the other half of the world, so the populace had a tendency to look inward. We didn't have as many distractions then as we do today—we didn't have cable TV or the Internet. There weren't any cell phones or Palm Pilots. You could speak your mind more freely—it was a time before political correctness made people hypersensitive about offending anyone. Communities were tight, and people were—for the most part—friendly. Because there weren't as many distractions, many families spent more time together than we do now. Mine did.

One thing my family used to do together was play cards. Once fairly common, it's a pastime hardly anyone enjoys anymore. Sometimes, if we had enough players, we'd have multiple games going at once. Almost all my relatives played the game, but none so passionately as my immediate family. I really wish I could play one last hand with them. But, that time has passed.

Because I live in a country of constant change, it has become a different place today than it was when I was young. As time passes, it will continue to change. I'm still here, and the place where I grew up has the same name as when I was born. However, it's most certainly a different place today. The landscape is different. The people are different. The culture is different. The community is different. The clock can't be turned back. And in some ways, I guess that's a good thing.

Before my memory fades and I forget how things used to be, I want to describe the place where I came from, as I remember it. Someone else will probably come along and write their own version of history, but this one is mine. And my story is a story of family, community, country, and a forgotten game of cards.

CHAPTER 1

Welcome to the Family

Playing the Cards You're Dealt

I guess, I should start at the beginning, my name is Tom Price. I was born in the city of Chicago just days before the great blizzard of January, 1967. While I was technically born in the city, I was raised in the suburbs. I was the last member of the family—the youngest of three boys. The suburbs were different in those days as were the families that resided there. My family, for instance, was a card playing family. The game we played was pinochle. It's what kept us together over the years regardless of whatever little conflicts that arose between family members. I could always take comfort in the fact that we always had the game. Today you'd be hard pressed to find someone playing pinochle anywhere but the local retirement home. But when I was growing up it was a common occurrence at our house. On any given Saturday night, back when I was six, I could be found sitting next to one of the "big" people, watching them play out their hands and picking up the finer points of the game. Pinochle was once a very popular game in the United States dating back to the mid-nineteenth century. It's quite possible that several generations of Prices learned the way I did. At least that's how my brothers and I learned how to play.

When most people think about cards, they think about poker. Often poker is more about the people playing than the cards on the table. If the stakes are high a player can bluff or buy the pot. In pinochle, as in life, it's all about the cards and making the most of them. You can't bluff your way to a win but if you play your cards right you can still move closer to a victory even with a bad hand. I'm not the first one to recognize that relatives are a lot like the cards one might receive. Even though I wasn't born into wealth and privilege, God dealt me a good hand when it came to my family.

That Saturday night in 1973, my grandparents were visiting and as always cards were on the agenda. Each card game was like a study in Price family dynamics. It was the setting for the great struggle for the soul of the family between Dad and Grandpa Hinesley. I went and sat next to my dad, Dick Price. Growing up, I always felt Dad embodied the American dream. He started his own business, bought his own home at a young age, and did things his own way. The Dick Price way of doing things

A game of four-handed pinochle in the early '70s. Visible are from left to right, Jerry Hinesley, Grandpa Hinesley, and Dad, who has his back to the camera.

wasn't haphazard but methodical and regimented, whether it was the art of making a peanut butter and jelly sandwich or how to arrange the dishwasher. While Dad's habitual personality could get on your nerves, it made him a great teacher when it came to cards. No matter what kind of cards you were dealt, you could always rely on Dick Price's rules of thumb when it came to the game of pinochle. Dad's confidence wasn't the only thing that made him convincing, his appearance also provided an air of credibility to his words. That's because in 1973 Dad's hair was silver-gray giving the impression of years of card playing experience. And so it was that I normally watched and learned the game from my dad. Of course, I learned more than pinochle from him.

Father and Son

On the night of Saturday, October 17th, 1992, I stood in the living room of apartment 902, Columbus Plaza, at 233 East Wacker Drive in Chicago. I was waiting to go out with several friends who were visiting the city with me that autumn weekend. My father and his partner, Fred Anderson, had turned the apartment into an art studio. Dad had been working as a self-employed commercial artist since 1960. The apartment was used for work during the week, and relaxation on the weekends. Dad would trade off weekends with Fred. This was Dad's weekend, but he was finishing up a project with a Monday deadline.

Dad came out of the small kitchen to join me in the living room. His hair was snowy white as ever, and he was still struggling with his weight. He had a jovial personality and would typically joke around with me. I had come to expect it. He found it humorous that after studying overseas in Germany for two years I would return to the United States to wrap up my degree, only to befriend a group of Germans studying in the U.S.

"You could have saved yourself the trouble of living in Germany," he joked.

When I told Dad I'd like to bring some friends to Chicago in October, he offered to get a guest apartment in Columbus Plaza for them. Dad loved playing host and guide to people visiting from out of town, so he was excited about having four new people to whom he could show off the grandeur of Chicago. That Saturday night, we discussed what I should show them.

I grew up in the suburbs, but Dad was my connection to the city. While growing up Dad lived all over the city, from the southeastern edge at 11700 South Buffalo Avenue to the most northern edge in Rogers Park, at 2711 Jarvis. He loved working downtown the most. He could have worked out of his suburban home and acquired suburban clients; instead, he focused on his most important clients downtown. Over the years, many of the large companies he did work for, such as Kraft, Abbot Laboratories, Motorola, and the National Safety Council, moved to the suburbs, but Dad maintained his Chicago office. I first visited him at his office on Wabash. It was an older-style office building, with wooden doors and mahogany paneling that lined its narrow hallways. The building used to have an elevator operator who would take you to your desired floor. After exiting the elevator, I remember turning right and heading down the narrow hallway, at the end of which stood the entry to Dick Price and Associates. The mahogany door had a large frosted glass window with the company name painted in gold and black lettering. It reminded me of Sam Spade's door in the Maltese Falcon. Inside, there were several offices occupied by different artists who worked with Dad. When my brothers and I visited Dad's office, we went outside and climbed up the rickety fire escape. In the fall of 1981, Dad moved to a new office space. He and Fred Anderson, who had shared space with him on Wabash, settled on Columbus Plaza.

Columbus Plaza became a second home of sorts. The Plaza belongs to the Illinois Center development, which is a mixture of residential and commercial buildings on what's called the New Eastside. The New Eastside is a great location for enjoying downtown Chicago. It's situated just north of Grant Park and Millennium Park, and just east of the Magnificent Mile. I loved going there. Dad and Fred didn't usually work on the weekends, unless they were backed up with work. They alternated weekends as to who would use the apartment. For that reason, I became very familiar with the downtown area, but Dad was an expert. He was always keeping me apprised as to the new buildings that were going up and local events, and he knew all of the restaurants in the area. The area of New Eastside began to boom during this time. He enjoyed it when I brought in visitors because he loved to show off his city.

I had arrived with the Germans the night before. On the morning of the 17th, I got up early, assuming they would want to get an early start. I was wrong. I waited more than two hours before they were ready to go. I recounted this story to Dad, and told him I planned to stay in the guest apartment with the Germans so I could sleep in and get up when they did. Dad suggested I stay in our apartment to avoid having to fight for a shower, and if they came by early, he would wake me up. I agreed.

"Do you know what you're doing tonight?" he asked.

"I figured we'd go to North Pier and eat at Dick's Last Resort, then go to the nightclub there. After that, who knows?"

"Do you need money?"

"No, I think I'm good, actually," I replied, somewhat unprepared for the question. Then he said something else I didn't expect.

"Tom, I love you," he said in an odd way.

"Yeah, Pops, I love you too," I replied, in a way that we both understood it to mean more than a simple "you too" statement.

Whether it was picking me up from the airport or the bus station, driving me to college, giving me some money if I needed it, or picking me up if the car broke down, he was always there. I learned from an early age that I could always count on Dad. If he said he'd be somewhere at a certain time, it was like money in the bank. He was always willing to help a person in need, and it's something I always loved about him.

Then there was a knock on the door.

"I need to get going, is it a problem if I come back late? Will it bother you?" I asked.

"No, I'll shut the bedroom door," he said, and then added, "Have a good time."

"Thanks, Pop. We will," I said on my way out.

That was the last time I ever saw Dad alive. It was also the beginning of the end of my family. It wasn't long thereafter that we didn't even have enough players for a single game of three-handed pinochle. But I'm getting ahead of myself.

In 1973, sitting in a kitchen full of cigarette smoke, I observed Dad's hand as he chose the next card to play. "Ok, Buddy, when you take the bid and have a strong trump suit and a long second suit, you want to draw out your opponent's trump to make your second suit good, like this," he said, as he laid down an ace of diamonds, which was trump, and then picked up his cigarette from the ashtray to take a drag.

"Why do you do that?"

"So your opponents can't trump your second suit and you'll be able to make those cards good. Do you understand?"

I nodded even though I wasn't completely sure of what he meant. The process of learning how to play would take some time but I'd get plenty of opportunities in those days.

The Overlooked Generation

As with most families, my family was shaped by my parents and their life stories. My parents' generation arrived during a time that was unique in American history. They were born during the Great Depression, grew up during the Second World War, and came of age during the Cold War. The United States thrived, and established itself as a global superpower as they grew up. Everything that seemed to be great about America, they experienced firsthand. We overcame the Depression. We defeated the Axis powers, using American industrial might and determination. We stood in the way of Communist world domination. The United States had the best cars, the best food, the best water, the best way of life. It was clear to my parents that it was destiny for the U. S. to be the leader of the free world, a frame of mind that never left them.

Loyalty to the family also played a prominent role in my parents' lives. They stuck together through thick and thin-it was uncommon for a family to break up. That's simply how it was. God and religion were also very important to them-neither of my parents went to church on a regular basis, but it seemed they accepted that God determined your fate. Because they overcame so much during the first half of their lives and witnessed the shaping of the global community, it also seemed apparent to them that the United States had God on its side.

Although their generation was unique in many ways, it lacked a defining moment in history by which it could be categorized. Though they were born during the Depression, they were too young to have experienced the brunt of the economic disaster. Many of them were lucky enough not to have to fight in the Second World War, as they were still too young. They experienced and benefited from the postwar boom, and many happened to fall squarely between the Korean and Vietnam Wars with regard to military service. (My father joined the army at nineteen, and had to serve in neither). Serving in the army during a time of peace, however, didn't guarantee a long life. Despite not having fought in the war, the "overlooked generation" of the late 1920s to early 1940s played a great role in the economic growth that followed the Second World War.

The Price Side of the Family

Dad's side of the family always seemed to be clouded in mystery for me. I was lucky enough to know my grandparents, although I didn't see them all that often. I have aunts, uncles, and cousins on the Price side whom I see rarely, if at all. Periodically, we would go to some family function, stick to ourselves and then get the hell out of there. When I was young, about four or five, the Price gatherings were torturous because I didn't know anybody. It felt like having a cookout with fifty strangers. I was the youngest of all the grandchildren, so many relations had an idea of who I was, but I didn't know them from Adam. Most of the kids at such gatherings were much older than I was, and the games people played, such as volleyball or billiards, were too advanced for me. For whatever reason, our family was never close with the Price side of the family, yet it was the Prices who put the most emphasis on the philosophy that "a family that plays together stays together." Grandma Artie was the glue in the Price family.

My grandparents loved their children. A year after they got married, in 1928, my Aunt Nancy was born. Next came two uncles: Tedford in 1930 and Milton in 1932. Finally, on the 21st of August, 1934, my father, Richard Price, was born. God and family meant everything to Grandma Artie. When my father was only two years old, tragedy struck the Price family. My father's older brother Tedford (Teddy) became very sick. His sickness was said to have been misdiagnosed as whooping cough—it was,

The Prices in 1958 (left to right) Uncle Milt, Aunt Joy, Dad (kneeling), Mom, Grandpa George, and Grandma Artie.

Aunt Nancy and Uncles Teddy and Milt, Christmas, 1935.

in fact, diphtheria. Uncle Teddy died on September 9th, 1936. He was six years old.

It was 1936, and my grandparents didn't have a lot of money. A neighbor, saddened by Teddy's death and sympathetic to the financial strains of the young couple, offered to pay for the funeral and burial. Teddy's death changed Grandma Artie forever. Her bitterness for and skepticism of doctors would leave its mark on our family—my brother and I still have little faith in the medical profession. Years later, still conscious of how fragile life can be, Grandma Artie helped my mother take care of us after each of us was born. She told my mother how hard it was to lose a child, and how she never got over it. My mother was deeply affected by Grandma Artie's sorrow, and never forgot it.

My grandmother was always a bright light of optimism, despite having lost her first son and despite the financial difficulties her family faced during the Great Depression. She believed that things would always work out for the best. The Depression affected people in different ways—some people became very conservative when it came to money and savings. Grandma Artie took more of a "live for today" approach—she believed in spending money on those close to you, even if times were tight. Dad adopted this carefree view of life and money. This proved to be helpful later on, when he was self-employed. He wasn't overly stressed if business was slow, because he always believed things would work out. Grandma Artie was the opposite of a selfish person, hell-bent on self preservation. She maintained a strong faith in God throughout her life, and her optimism and faith strongly influenced my father.

Artie Price wasn't a pretty woman. In fact, from a kid's perspective, her appearance was downright frightening. Remember the witch from the tale of Hansel and Gretel? That was Grandma Artie. She had a large nose, steel blue eyes, and snow white hair that didn't quite reach her shoulders. She stood five foot two inches tall and had a stout build, with a light, raspy voice and a little chuckle that sounded like a witch's cackle. She also had the "Price Stare"—a penetrating look that made you feel like she was about to tear your heart out. Dad had The Stare, my brother Steve had it, and I have it. We look that way naturally, regardless of our mood—with the exception of my brother Scott, who has to work at it. Most of the time, Grandma Artie always looked angry in pictures, even though she usually wasn't. Although she looked the part, she never really acted like a witch. She did have a temper, but I made sure I never tested it.

Grandma Artie loved to play games, and hated to lose. She especially enjoyed pinochle. Artie was a fierce competitor, full of determination when she sat down at the card table. Like a hawk, she watched all the cards in play on the table. Her reading glasses hovered over her nose while she played, giving her the appearance of a bookkeeper hard at work while she kept score. Between deals she rehashed the previous hand, periodically dipping her fingers in the obligatory snack bowl for peanuts or popcorn. Dad adopted Grandma Artie's passion for competition and handed it down to my brothers and me.

"You're under the gun HL, the bid is twenty-nine to you," said Dad giving Grandpa Hinesley the Price stare.

Grandma Artie playing pinochle.

"That's a dime if I go set, so I'll pass," answered Grandpa Hinesley.

"Devil hates a coward," Dad mused as he grabbed the three cards in the kitty and placed the newly acquired cards in his hand and discarded three before laying down a run in spades.

A Family That Plays Together Stays Together

We played pinochle on all occasions—birthdays, holidays, anniversaries, vacations, or even just routine visits. We always had a pinochle deck handy. My family played two types of pinochle: three-handed and four-handed games. In the three-handed game, you played as an individual, trying to beat the other two players. In the four-handed game, you played with a partner and tried to beat the other team. When my grandparents came over, we normally played two tables of three-handed pinochle. One table would be the winner's table, and the other was called—well, let's just call it the "second" table. We'd play for hours. The player with the lowest score at the winner's table would move down to the second table, while the winner at the second table moved up.

My brothers and I learned the game at an early age. We started playing before we could hold the cards by ourselves. We had plastic card holders, with two plastic disks held together by a spring in the middle. We stuck our cards in the holder, fanning them out and sorting as we went.

The game of pinochle is played to one hundred points. You get points in two ways: with special card combinations in your hand, called meld, and by taking tricks during game play. Examples of meld would be a king and queen of the same suit—called a marriage and valued at two points. The game's namesake, pinochle, the combination of the queen of spades and the jack of diamonds, is worth four points and so on. The game is played with a deck of forty-eight cards. It is essentially a double deck of ace through nine. Each suit has twelve cards. If you pay attention during the game, you always know, more or less, what each player has in their hand. Not everyone paid attention. Both Mom and Grandma Hinesley could throw you off your game because they played erratically. One moment they acted like they had never played the game before, and screwed up easy plays. The next moment they ran away with the game. Across the table from Dad sat someone who watched every card very closely, my grandfather, Herbert L. Hinesley.

The Hinesley Side of the Family

Although we were somewhat detached from the Price side of the family, it was the polar opposite with my mom's side of the family, the Hinesleys. We spent a lot of time visiting my grandparents. They lived close by, in the village of Mount Prospect, Illinois. We'd go over to their house for almost any occasion. If we weren't visiting them, they were often visiting us. On those occasions, we almost always played pinochle. I felt at home with my grandparents, and they were always kind and generous with me. I wasn't spoiled, because nothing came for free at the Hinesley's, but they were fair and loving.

Just as the Prices were led by Grandma Artie, the Hinesleys were headed up by Grandpa Hinesley. We used Grandpa Hinesley's surname, because he demanded respect—and I didn't disappoint. My mother's life was dominated by my grandfather. Grandma Artie may have helped shape Dad's personality, the characteristics of which he made his own. But Mom's personality was not merely shaped by my grandfather—she spent her life trying to meet with his approval, and remain in his favor. While I spent most of my time watching Dad play, Grandpa Hinesley was my other pinochle mentor. It would be hard to find two more different men. In many ways their personalities were reflected in how they played cards.

I was reminded of their differences by a small indentation in the otherwise indestructible Formica kitchen table top. While Dad was very competitive he was also very gracious when it came to games. For example, in pinochle, if you misplay you renege. You go set if you took the bid, which means

Grandpa Hinesley and Grandma Artie—both had strong personalities. Artie influenced my father, whereas Grandpa Hinesley affected my mother.

you lose the hand and the amount of points you bid. It's not a misplay until the trick is turned and the next card is led. Dad would call his opponent's attention to the mistake before the trick was turned, giving him a chance to correct his error instead of going set. Grandpa Hinesley, on the other hand, would watch quietly and force the set once the trick was turned. Technically, Grandpa Hinesley's way was correct but less gentlemanly in a friendly game of cards. Dad didn't want to win because of an honest mistake—he wanted to win by out-playing the other player. As far as Grandpa Hinesley was concerned, catching a mistake was part of the game.

You couldn't find a more honest player than Dad nor a more suspicious player than Grandpa Hinesley. It was that combination (and Dad's temper) that put the dent in the table. One night, before my card watching days, amid a heated game Grandpa Hinesley accused Dad of cheating. Dad flipped. Dad had a slow burn temper but Grandpa Hinesley knew how to stoke the flames. On this evening Dad reached his limit. He slammed the tumbler glass in his hand down so hard on the table that he left an impression from the bottom of the glass. It served as a reminder to my brothers and me not to test his temper nor challenge his honesty.

One reason Grandpa Hinesley wanted to be sure everything was on the up-and-up when playing cards, or any other time, was that he always had to fight for what he got in life. Even after getting it, he felt he had to keep fighting to keep it. One thing's for sure, Grandpa Hinesley was a fighter.

Perseverance

I entered the lobby of Friedrich's Funeral Home that November morning with my wife, my seventeen-year-old stepdaughter, and my nine-year-old son. I had been there a number of times before, either arranging or attending services for Grandma Hinesley, Dad, or Mom. This time it was for Grandpa Hinesley. The atmosphere was hushed, and the foyer deserted. I could just make out the sign outside the visitation room, straight ahead of where I stood. In white letters was the name "Herbert L. Hinesley." I entered the visitation room, my family toddling along behind me. Uncle Herb and his wife, Aunt Delores, were already sitting there, along with two of my older cousins: Herbie the 3rd, and Maryellyn. As I bent down to whisper to my son Spencer to behave himself, I could see the open casket at the far end of the room, past several rows of chairs. With my family, I made my way to the casket. There he was. He looked peaceful, eyes closed and hands neatly folded together. Spencer, startled by the reality of it, broke into tears. Mine would come later.

Funeral visitations were always awkward for me, the bodies seem so artificial, like wax figures. I suppose I have become somewhat numb when it comes to funeral homes and the whole funeral process—the first couple of times one makes the "arrangements," it's easy to be caught off guard as to what is reasonable and necessary. A scene from the movie *The Big Lebowski* always enters my mind, in which John Goodman's character; Walter Sobchak, says, "Just because we're bereaved, doesn't make us saps!"

Herbert L. Hinesley in 1966.

At ninety-eight years old, Grandpa Hinesley was one of the more consistent characters in my life. He was always there. If someone told me he would live to be one hundred and ten, I would have believed it. But he didn't, because in his mind, there wasn't any point. His second wife had passed away about a month before—but Grandpa Hinesley didn't die out of grief for his widow. It was closer to spite.

Grandpa Hinesley and Lorrie had been separated for a number of years—when they married, he was eighty-something and she was twenty years his junior. She had managed to outlive several husbands, thus accumulating some wealth. They signed a prenuptial agreement, but my grandfather sensed she might contest the will if he died before she did. In true Hinesley style, he hunkered down for the long haul. As he became more difficult to live with, due to his deteriorating physical condition, Lorrie moved out. Unfazed, Grandpa Hinesley was determined to outlive her. A month after learning of her passing, Grandpa Hinesley was finally able to die in peace, knowing he had persevered and won out. One thing Grandpa Hinesley tried to teach me as a kid was the importance of perseverance—to follow through, despite any hardships or obstacles you may face. When I learned of her death at his funeral, everything fit together. I could see Grandpa Hinesley in my mind's eye, giving me a wink and a chuckle, as if I were a kid again, watching him get double pinochle in the last hand of the game. As Dad would say, "Now that's an I-gotcha!"

Down on the Farm

Grandpa Hinesley was born in October of 1907, and came from a long line of Hoosiers. Grandpa Hinesley grew up on the family farm, the second of six boys. His father Arville was a farmer with a sizable farm outside of Muncie, Indiana, in the rural town of Sulfur Springs. The boys grew up doing farm work to help their father. Their main crop was corn, but they also had some livestock and chickens.

Hard work was commonplace on the farm, and Grandpa Hinesley developed a great work ethic. He also realized he didn't want to spend the rest of his life working on a farm. Although he left Indiana, he always remained a proud Hoosier at heart.

The farm also left its mark on my mother. Because her family didn't have a great deal of money, when she was growing up, they spent their vacations down on the farm. Although a good portion of the 166 acres was used for crops, a significant area was undeveloped, and could be used for hunting. A creek ran through the property, where they were able to fish. Life on the farm took place in a male-dominated environment. Daisy Hinesley, Mom's grandmother, had to raise six boys while working the farm. Although small in stature (she stood about five feet tall), she was a really hard-working woman. She didn't take any grief from her boys, either. Mom was always a little afraid of her grandmother.

During one visit as a girl, Mom sat with her grandmother in the kitchen, preparing food for dinner. Suddenly Daisy sneezed, causing her teeth to fly out of her mouth and skid across the kitchen floor. Unbeknownst to my mother, Daisy had false teeth—but my mother had no knowledge of such things as a girl. Another time, Daisy went down to the chicken coop to pick out a couple of chickens for dinner. Without any warning, she cut their heads off and let the chicken bodies run around the yard. Uncle Herb couldn't eat chicken for a long while after that. Daisy may have seemed gruff compared with Mom's other grandmother, due to living on

The Hinesley Family down on the farm in June 1942: (left to right) Eugene (partially cut off), Paul, Lester, Daisy, Arville, Carl, Herbert and Roland.

a farm and raising six boys, but toward her grandchildren she was always very loving. Mom loved going to the farm, and became very close with her grandparents.

Head West, Young Man

After graduating from high school, Grandpa Hinesley set out for Iowa State University in Ames, Iowa, in the summer of 1926. He had decided to study electrical engineering. No stranger to hard work, Grandpa Hinesley worked at an apple orchard near the university at the beginning of the hot summer of 1926, filling bushels of apples. Work started early in the morning, and continued until sundown, with only a lunch break in between. Many students worked at the orchard, so the owner was never shorthanded. Using this circumstance to his advantage, the owner didn't pay much for the amount of work required. As a result, Grandpa Hinesley learned a valuable life lesson—watch out for employers who use someone's hard work ethic to their advantage, without providing fair compensation.

Grandpa Hinesley soon discovered a number of people with electrical engineering degrees working at the apple orchard. "What good is an electrical engineering degree, if all you're going to do is work in the fields?" he thought. "Anyone can do that." He decided to transfer to Boyles College in Omaha, Nebraska, to study business administration instead. It seemed a more practical course of study that could be applied in any industry.

While searching for a place to stay in Omaha, Grandpa Hinesley found a boarding house run by a Danish bricklayer, Hans Nielsen, and his wife Rasmine (a.k.a. "Min"). Hans and Min were from Denmark, but remarkably they didn't meet or marry until after their arrival in the States, shortly after the turn of the century. After getting married in New York, they moved out west to Omaha. It was lucky that Grandpa Hinesley found Hans Nielsen, because Hans also needed workers to help with his bricklaying business. A grateful Herbert Hinesley began work for Hans Nielsen as a "hod carrier" (a person who keeps a bricklayer supplied with cement and mortar.)

While living at the boarding house and attending Boyles College, Grandpa Hinesley met Hans's daughter, Marna Nielsen. Marna, born in 1911, also began taking classes in stenography at Boyles College in 1927. Their friendship turned into romance. Things

The newly married Mr. and Mrs. Hinesley.

seemed to be going his way, and in the summer of 1927, Grandpa Hinesley landed a job with the Hartford Insurance Company. As time went by, his relationship with Marna Nielsen grew more serious. It was an exciting time in their lives as the Roaring Twenties came to a close, and they decided to marry. They were married on October 15th, 1929. Nine days later, on "Black Thursday," the stock market crashed. The newlywed couple now had to cope with the Great Depression.

The Meaning of Money

Grandpa Hinesley continued to work hard when the Depression hit. He was fortunate to retain his job during the economic crisis. Later, he said it was difficult to turn down claims during that time, because a great number of people were struggling to make ends meet. My grandparents wanted to start a family, but knew it was a risky thing to do. They witnessed other people who were less fortunate than they were act irresponsibly by having children when they didn't have the means to provide for them. This really aggravated my grandfather, who lectured us about fiscal responsibility for the rest of his life. When he and Marna felt they could afford it and had a home of their own, they would start a family. By 1932, they were able to do just that.

In April 1933, their first child, Herb Jr., was born. Little more than a year later, on December 26, 1934, they gave birth to a daughter, Maryellyn. Mom was a cute, chubby redheaded toddler, earning the nickname "Chubby." It was a nickname that would stick with her for the rest of her life. Everyone who knew her called her "Chubby," despite having lost all her baby fat by the time she went to high school.

My grandparents stopped having children for a while. The family had to scrimp and save to make things work out. This meant repairing shoes and patching pants instead of buying new clothes. As my mother grew up, she was constantly reminded of the value of money—and in turn, Grandpa Hinesley's frugality had a lasting affect on my mother. Her outlook on money and security could not have contrasted more with that of my Dad. Dad seemed cool and calm when things got tight. Mom, on the other hand, became increasingly stressed when money grew scarce.

Social Stature

Grandpa Hinesley was always sensitive to how others perceived him. The cards were stacked against him in many respects. He had something of a complex about his height (he stood about five foot six). He always believed that short people had to work harder to get noticed. He also lost his hair at an early age. Coming from a simple rural family that didn't have a lot of money, he didn't want people to perceive him as a short, balding hayseed. So, he made an effort to stand out in other ways. For instance, he always dressed professionally, and was quite stylish. He paid attention to quality when it came to the type of suit or shoes he wore. He was also quick to notice the quality of dress on others.

Another way he stood out was with impeccable manners. He was very careful about the words he used and the topics he talked about in mixed company. He also judged others by the way he assumed he was being judged—he could become quite judgmental at times. He believed it was important to preserve one's social stature, which he impressed upon my mother.

Social organizations give people a sense of belonging and can provide a feeling of enhanced self-worth. This could be the reason Grandpa Hinesley became very active in the Masons in the early 1940s, ultimately achieving the status of Master Mason. My grandmother also became involved in the sister organization, the Order of the Eastern Star. My grandparents remained active with the Masons off and on for the rest of their lives.

Despite the stress Grandpa Hinesley put on himself about money, social status or any other hang-up he may have had, he remained at all times on an even keel. He never showed signs of great stress. My mother, on the other hand, was a different story.

The Other Game

After observing Dad and Grandpa Hinesley play for a while, I became restless. I went downstairs in the family room to where the other game was taking place. This was where the players with the low hands were banished. At the round card table sat my oldest brother Steve, Grandma Hinesley and Mom. Mom had made sure everyone was supplied with a full drink and a nearby snack bowl filled with popcorn. I had come downstairs to see who was winning more than to pick up playing tips from watching the players. I didn't aspire to play at the downstairs table. It could be fun to watch though, since there was always a chance to see someone play a ten into an ace. That way I could laugh as if I would have known better. I think Mom paid more attention to her duties as a hostess than the hand that was being played. While in a game, she'd elicit my help.

"Tommy, can bring down some more popcorn?"

"Sure," I said, happy to have a task to complete.

I ran upstairs and grabbed the big bowl of popcorn on the kitchen counter. I helped myself you a handful or two before returning downstairs to replenish the bowls on the table. It was getting late and my time of watching cards was coming to an end. After they finished the game, Mom turned to me, "Go upstairs and brush your teeth, I'll be up in a minute to tuck you in."

I went upstairs and gave my teeth a quick, insufficient brushing, a habit that would lead to great dental bills and hours of pain in later life. I hopped into bed and waited for Mom. I was followed shortly by Scott who shared the room with me. After a short while Mom tucked us in with a short story and a quick prayer.

"Now I lay me down to sleep…"

From the door way Mom shut off the light, "Sleep tight."

That was the Mom I'd like to remember.

A Little Drama

One evening when I was home from college, I heard the car door slam. I was sitting in the kitchen, eating dinner and watching TV. The door swung open, and Mom, dressed in her white winter coat and beige knit cap, quickly entered the house. Her white purse bulged oddly under her arm, and I knew instantly what was inside it. She cradled the purse like a running back headed for the end zone.

I greeted her with a simple, "Hey!"

Mom didn't acknowledge me as she made a beeline for her room. Confronting her would do no good—I gave her time to hide it. After a few minutes, I entered her room. She was lying in bed.

"Not feeling well?" I asked.

"Go away," she said, in an overly dramatic tone.

People say the nice thing about vodka is that you can't smell it. Well I can. I know when it's in a glass or a mixed drink, on someone's breath, or even in someone's sweat. Frankly, I wish I couldn't smell it at all, but my nose underwent years of training. "Fine, you won't let me help you, anyway," I said as I turned to leave.

"Just get out and leave me alone. No one loves me!" She hissed.

What drama! She really could have been an actress when she was half in-the-bag. Unfortunately for me, there were extended periods of time when I'd be the only one privileged enough to witness it. Although sometimes, Dad, Uncle Jerry, and my brothers were also treated to an occasional alcohol-inspired performance.

Her artificial smile, exaggerated gestures, or overly pleasant demeanor were always a good tip-off that a grand show was about to begin. On this day, I had a private showing. I was convinced her long-term bout with alcoholism would kill her, but, much to my surprise, in the end she overcame it single-handedly. My relationship with Mom encompassed more than those dark times, but the impact of those hard-learned lessons never left me. It couldn't have been easy for Mom, being a woman during a time when the role of women in the United States was changing forever. It was like she was lost in the shuffle. I can only try to understand.

Another Place

My parents first met as students at Nicholas Senn High School on the north side of Chicago back in the late 40s. The paths open to each of them at that time were very different than they would be when I went to school. Senn had a number of established traditions and customs. The school had a large number of clubs and activities, in addition to traditional sports offerings. During Dad's four years at Senn, there were approximately forty non-sports-related extracurricular groups and activities. Each enjoyed healthy participation by the student body. My high school had fewer than half as many such activities. At Senn, these clubs played a large social role in the lives of the students-they were good forums in which to meet people and socialize. This may have been the case in my school as well, but to a lesser degree. I went to a German Club meeting at my school once. Nobody wanted to do any serious fund-raising or promotion to gain additional members. Of the seven people at the meeting, five of them would rather have adjourned the meeting to play Dungeons & Dragons. Senn, however, was different.

Mom's extracurricular activities differed greatly from Dad's. Like many schools of the time, Senn was a gender-segregated environment in many respects. Senn offered a number of sports—however, there were few official girls' sports. There was the Senn Girls' Athletic Association—the SGAA was almost more of a club than a sports entity, but participation could earn a girl school letters and pins. The SGAA met after school on Tuesdays to play sports or participate in other various activities. All girls were eligible to join, and they played basketball, volleyball, and baseball, and went hiking, picnicking, and horseback riding. For incoming freshmen, they organized a "freshie tea" party. For graduating seniors, they staged a mother-daughter tea. The result was an odd mix of sport and social club in the SGAA.

Additionally, there were two popular clubs back then that you would be hard-pressed to find in any school today. The first was the Gourmet Club, which, according to the 1953 yearbook, "...helps the girls with all the problems facing a modern homemaker." The Gourmet Club wasn't solely for cooking, but also dealt with budgeting, household management, and the "etiquette of entertaining," as well. The second club was the Senn Hostesses. The hostesses were girls who were selected, based on their dependability and character, to represent the school to guests and parents who visited the campus. Each hostess wore a green badge that identified her as a hostess. The expectation was that they were to be pleasant and ready to serve if needed.

Senn also offered something unique, in that there were social clubs not affiliated with the school, similar to social fraternities and sororities you would find on a college campus today. They used Greek letters, staged "rush week" and "hell night," and generally resembled a fraternity in every way except for having a fraternity house to call home. I'm not sure how Dad found the time to do it all, but he joined one of these organizations—the

Mom having dinner at a sorority event.

"Delta" fraternity—his freshman year. It was here that he started a long-lasting friendship with Joel Schimpf, who later married my mother's best friend Gayle Jarl, and become my godfather. Delta held their meetings at the local park district field house. They organized fundraisers throughout the year to pay for their various activities and parties. Once a year, they also organized a dance. Mom was involved with Gayle's sorority, which commingled with Dad's fraternity. Mom and Dad socialized often during high school, even though they didn't date until long after they graduated.

Dick Price and Associates

Besides sports and history, Dad's next-greatest passion was drawing and painting. He began to develop his art skills at an early age. He did a postcard sketch on a trip to Iowa in 1940, which spurred Artie to encourage his artistic pursuits. In junior high school, he started making a comic strip in the style of Dick Tracy. Soon Dad was developing into an artist.

Postcard sketch drawn by Dad in November 1940 at age six.

Shortly after starting high school, Dad entered his work in several local contests and won his first "official" recognition. Building on this success, Dad entered other contests and won more awards. At school, he gained a reputation of being a skilled artist. He began to study art formally at Senn, achieving high marks. He employed his talents in the drama department, working on set design and backgrounds for plays. In his free time, Dad also drew and painted. Dad seemed to enjoy the fact that he could differentiate himself and gain a special identity within the family through his art. His sister Nancy established herself in high school with top grades. Her academic stature was so good, in fact, that she received a full scholarship to Northwestern University when she graduated. Dad wasn't interested in going to college—he said the people he knew from high school who went to college seemed immature and not serious about their futures. Dad wanted to move on with his life, and was preparing to do just that. He knew his grades wouldn't get him a scholarship anywhere, so he planned a future as a commercial artist.

As high school graduation approached, Dad began to investigate art schools where he could further his dream of becoming a commercial artist. Shortly after graduation, he signed up to take the scholarship test at Ray-Vogue school (today, the Illinois Institute of Art), and was awarded a 10-week scholarship to study commercial art. This was the jump-start Dad needed to begin his studies.

Ray-Vogue's curriculum consisted of everything one needed to develop the all-around skills required by a professional. Before Photoshop, Illustrator, PowerPoint, or any other publishing software, newspaper ads, business presentations, and graphic design work had to be done by hand. Various font styles had to be learned, and layout skills and drawing techniques perfected. Ray-Vogue was one of the best places to perfect those skills, with a reputation and a network of graduates recognized by advertising firms across Chicago as being top-notch.

After a year of intensive study, Dad joined Bob Amft and Associates, a commercial art firm, in 1953. The year Dad worked for Bob Amft and Associates, the Korean War came to an end. Knowing he was still eligible for the military draft, Dad decided the time was right to serve voluntarily. Having learned much about the commercial art trade, he left Bob Amft and Associates in 1954, and joined the army.

After leaving the military, Dad went back to being a commercial artist, and started to think about his future. He began where he left off with Bob Amft. After a while, Bob Amft wanted to concentrate on his painting. So Dad started his own business, Dick Price and Associates.

Early handmade Dick Price business card.

At first, Dick Price and Associates was a loose association of commercial artists who worked independently, and Dad outsourced work that required specific skills to the best-suited artist within the group. Each artist might also do his own independent work, but being a part of Dad's business added credibility and stability.

Graduation and a New Life

Mom graduated a year after my father, in the summer of 1953. She continued doing office work at Hibbard, Spencer, and Bartlett and then, later, AB Dick. It wasn't Mom's ambition, however, to be an office worker for the rest of her life. My mother grew up in a time when many women expected to get married, settle down, and raise a family. It was a social norm—it wasn't seen as a restriction of one's freedoms, nor an obligation set forth by law. There also wasn't any shame associated with getting married and raising a family. Mom shared the expectation to get married after high school with many of her female contemporaries. She didn't realize it at the time, nor did any of her friends, but the social perception of the role of women was about to change, and she would be caught right in the middle of it. In 1953, however, that change was still some time away.

It's easy to assume that anyone can be successful at staying home and raising a family. Thinking back on it now, I'm amazed at the number of skills Mom seemed to innately possess. As a kid, I assumed she was born with these skills. She was a good cook. (She was a significantly better cook than my grandmother, in my opinion.) She could sew. She was great with clothes—she knew the qualities of different fabrics, and how to wash and care for them. She maintained a nice garden. She was knowledgeable about all sorts of arts and crafts. Only later did it dawn on me that she wasn't born with these gifts, but rather, she worked hard at everything she did. Her knowledge came with life experience—and by the time Mom was ready to get married, she was a great catch.

That Day in May

In the mid-1950s, Mom began to think about marriage. Her older brother, Herb Jr., was the first one to take the plunge. My grandfather wasn't happy about it. Uncle Herb had a streak of independence—having a knack for motors and machines, but not academics, he left high school after his junior year. His girlfriend, Delores, rubbed my grandfather the wrong way. Herb was in love with Delores, and, despite his father's misgivings, decided to marry her. Herb Jr. was wise enough to realize that Grandpa Hinesley would make his life miserable if he stayed in Chicago. While together on a trip to Wyoming, Herb and Delores found the place where they wanted to settle down. Herb was able to get a printing job and begin his own life out west.

My parents on their wedding day, May 29th

In the early months of 1956, Mom began dating Dad, her former Senn acquaintance. They hit it off. They had a great deal in common: interest in art, common friends from school, and, most importantly, their love of cards. Soon they were engaged. It may seem funny that a love of cards could help bring a couple together, but it did. They were great partners, and played well together. What added to the relationship was that both sets of in-laws loved to play pinochle. This not only made it easy to get along with their future in-laws, but also meant that both sets of in-laws got to enjoy each other's company over a game of cards.

As the big day grew closer, Mom's excitement and stress grew. It wasn't a huge wedding, and included only close friends and relatives. Mom's grandparents came, excepting Daisy Hinesley, who passed away in 1954. Mom's maid of honor was, of course, Gayle Schimpf. Dad picked his brother Milt to be his best man. The date was set for the 29th of May, 1957, at the St. James United Church at the intersection of Rockwell and Albion. The wedding went well, and, most importantly, to Mom's satisfaction. In later years, Mom and Dad always skipped town to celebrate their anniversary alone. My brother Scott and I made the best use of that time to celebrate their anniversary in our own way.

Time to Move

Shortly after they married, Mom and Dad moved into an apartment on Newgard Avenue, on the North Side. Over the course of the next three years, they enjoyed their lives as a newly married couple. They spent quite a bit of time with their in-laws in those days, having dinner and playing cards. They even traveled with them. They went out west, along with Grandma and Grandpa Hinesley and Uncle Jerry, in 1958 to visit the Nielsens in Omaha and Herb Jr.'s family in Cheyenne. While out west, they saw the major sights in Wyoming, like Yellowstone and the Grand Tetons, as well those between Chicago and Cheyenne, such as the Badlands and Mount Rushmore. The following year, Mom and Dad went to Canada, this time accompanied only by Grandma Hinesley. It was during this trip that Dad discovered Grandma Hinesley walked in her sleep. Welcome to the family! All in all, everyone got along and they established a strong family bond.

On April 18th, 1958, Arville Hinesley, Mom's grandfather, passed away. The future of the Hinesley family farm was uncertain. Grandpa Hinesley had hoped Uncle Herb would take over the administration of the farm before he moved away to Wyoming. Without anyone to run the farm, it was decided to sell the 166 acres, and split up the proceeds among the six brothers.

Mom and Steve in front of Grandpa Hinesley's house during construction.

With the money from the farm in hand, Grandpa Hinesley decided it was time to buy a home. The Hinesleys began to look to the northwest suburbs-it was a period of tremendous growth there. Many new homes were being built throughout the area. Grandpa Hinesley wasn't the type of person to rush into buying a home on impulse—the Hinesleys had been renting a three-bedroom flat on North Campbell since moving to Chicago in 1943, so they were under no pressure to make a hasty decision. On the weekends they drove out to where new houses were being constructed to have a look around, similar to the way we might drive around looking at Christmas lights today.

Grandpa Hinesley finally found a builder whose work and reputation for quality met his expectations. In 1960, Miller Builders was finishing up a subdivision project called Brentwood in Des Plaines. They had some lots in the bordering village of Mount Prospect, where they were building the same models. Grandpa Hinesley soon made a down payment, and construction began. The house was completed in 1961. My parents were also in the market for a home—Dad's business was going strong, and, as of November, 1960, they had a brand new baby, my brother Steve. My parents observed the construction of the home and visited my grandparents when the house was completed. They were impressed, with the home and with the builder. Soon, they too had "suburbia fever."

CHAPTER 2

The New Suburbia

Going to School

I took my surroundings for granted as I walked to school that sunny day. As I strolled past seemingly perfect green lawns, trimmed bushes, and silver maple and white ash trees, I joined the other Greenbrier kids on their way to school. The houses were still relatively new, as were the asphalt streets. The wide streets that stretched thirty feet across seemed huge to me at the time. It was common for kids in the neighborhood to walk to school during the 1970s. We flowed down the winding streets like leaves floating and drifting down a stream toward their final destination.

Verde Drive was the route I took to school, a common one for many of the Greenbrier kids. It is a long, winding street that runs north and south down the middle of Greenbrier. Many of the streets in Greenbrier connect to it at some point. The elementary school itself was strategically placed at the corner of Verde and Roanoke Drive. This made the school easily accessible for people living in Greenbrier but far enough from the dangers of busy streets and highways.

When comparing Greenbrier with other neighborhoods in the area and other places I've been, I've come to realize how well the community was designed from the start. Apparently I was not the first person to make this observation. The Arlington Herald (today called the Daily Herald) reported that a delegation of fifty—seven Swedish government officials looking for insight into the planning and development of American subdivisions toured Greenbrier in July of 1963. In

1966, the Chicago Tribune's October 8th Builder's Briefs section reported on twenty-four French government delegates who visited Greenbrier to learn more about how American single-family homes were produced and planned. According to the story, a member of the French delegation indicated that "French home buyers could do nothing but envy the Americans for the space and luxury they get for their money." The delegation also seemed impressed by the fact that some of the appliances, such as gas countertop stoves and gas ovens, were included in the house. However, you didn't have to be European to appreciate Greenbrier.

Miller Builders' Vision: The Creation of Greenbrier

After the Second World War, a large number of people began to move out of larger cities into the surrounding suburbs. Many of these people were veterans taking advantage of new Veterans Affairs (VA) loans. This wasn't limited to World War II veterans, but included later veterans, as well.

Widespread growth in the Chicago suburbs continued throughout the 1950s and 1960s. One such suburb was the Village of Arlington Heights, some twenty-five miles northwest of downtown Chicago. In the fall of 1961, Miller Builders, the company that built Grandpa Hinesley's house in Mount Prospect, announced that it was going to build a 700-home subdivision in Arlington Heights, called Greenbrier.

Greenbrier ("Greenbrier in the Village Green," as the original plats call it) was built over the course of five years, from 1961 to 1966. The subdivision was built in twelve sections, or "units." Miller Builders was owned by Albert J. Miller, who started the company in Skokie in 1953, building several houses in the

Advertising for the new Greenbrier subdivision.

Skokie area. As time went on, Miller's business began to grow, and Miller Builders began to take on larger projects. During the late 1950s and early 1960s, they were involved in subdivisions in several Chicago suburbs, including Morton Grove, Wilmette, Mount Prospect, Des Plaines, Buffalo Grove, and Arlington Heights.

When it came time for the Greenbrier development, it seems that Miller Builders was at the top of their game. By the time Greenbrier came along, Miller Builders had gained a reputation for building quality homes with quality materials. They were juggling multiple projects at the time, but focused a strong marketing effort on the Greenbrier project, touting "unsurpassed value" and a "total community." In the Greenbrier Development, these claims actually rang true.

Miller Builders Ad from October 1961.

When developing the subdivision, Miller Builders hired Carl L. Gardner and Associates of Chicago to design the "total community." Carl was a former executive director of the Chicago Plan Commission who started a consulting company, specializing in planning, in 1953. In the 1960s, his firm worked on a number of consulting projects in the Chicago suburbs, often working with cities and villages to create a comprehensive master plan for their community. They also did smaller projects, such as planning subdivisions like Greenbrier. Another such subdivision was University Hill Farms in Madison, Wisconsin.

In an article titled "University Hill Farms: A Project for Modern Living," which was written for Wisconsin Magazine of History, Daina Penkiunas describes how Gardner incorporated parcels of land to be used for churches, parks, and a school. The result was that University Hill Farms became a "total community," as did Greenbrier a few years later. When a builder develops a subdivision, it is typically required to dedicate a certain amount of money (or land) for schools and parks to serve that community. The amount to be dedicated is based on the number of houses and projected occupants. Many builders might opt to dedicate money instead of land, in order to get the maximum value out of the land. Gardner chose to lay out Greenbrier to include the dedicated land for the school and parks in the design, as was done for University Hill Farms. Gardner's Greenbrier design allowed children to easily walk to school and to the parks from almost any house in the subdivision. Miller Builders used the fact that land was dedicated for parks, a school, and a swimming pool with a field house as selling points in their ads for Greenbrier. In addition to the large amount of land dedicated for recreational use, the Gardner design incorporated curvilinear street designs, as opposed to a chessboard layout, allowing the community to flow better.

Miller achieved "unsurpassed value" in Greenbrier in several ways. The first and most obvious way was in the cost of the homes. When the subdivision originated in 1961, the models in Greenbrier cost between $21,900 and $24,900. In two other Miller Builders projects of the time, Brentwood and Devonshire (both located in Des Plaines), the prices were somewhat higher. Devonshire homes ranged from $22,900 to $28,750, while Brentwood homes ranged from $23,900 to $29,900. The Greenbrier houses were of newer design and, more significantly, had a much better location. The timing and location of the Greenbrier subdivision couldn't have been better.

Roads to the Future

In the late 1950s and early 1960s, the population of the Chicago suburbs was on the rise. The number of people living in Arlington Heights grew 640%, from its 1950 population of 8,768 to its 1970 population of 64,884. To meet the transportation needs of this staggering population boom, new highways and shopping centers were built. Most of the Chicago expressways were started in the 1950s and were completed by the early 1960s.

In 1961, however, the far northwest suburbs weren't yet linked into the system. Around the same time that Miller Builders announced their plans for Greenbrier, the Illinois Highway Commission announced plans to expand Illinois Route 53 and create a superhighway that would run north and south along the western rim of the Chicago metropolitan area. The new six-lane superhighway would stretch from Rohlwing Road in Addison up to Dundee Road in Arlington Heights. The new expansion would continue to use the name Route 53 to the north of Addison.

View of Greenbrier and key bordering roads in 1963.

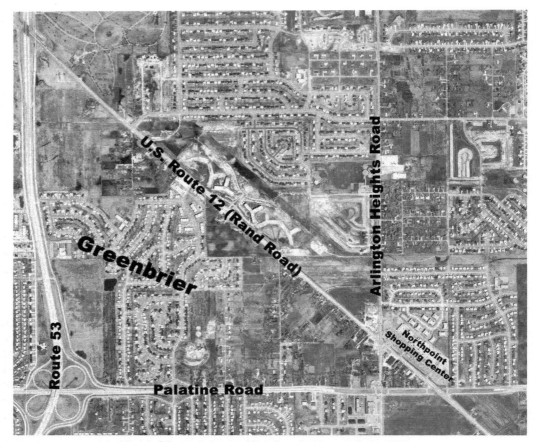

View of Greenbrier and key bordering roads in 1970.

According to the plan outlined in the announcement, the Congress Expressway would be extended to Addison and would merge with the new Route 53. The Congress Expressway would later become I-290 today, and would be renamed the Eisenhower Expressway in 1969. The Northwest Expressway (later named the Kennedy Expressway) and the Northwest Tollway (I-90) created a direct route into the city from the Northwest Side.

Construction for the Route 53 expansion began at the Northwest Tollway interchange. This was a great development for the people in Greenbrier because the new Route 53 would have a full interchange at Palatine Road, essentially right at Greenbrier's doorstep. The highway improvements would take a number of years to complete, but, when they were completed, they provided an easy commute into the

Chicago Loop by using either today's I-90 (Northwest Tollway/Kennedy Expressway) or I-290 (the Eisenhower Expressway).

The new Route 53 also provided a simple route to the "world's busiest airport," O'Hare International Airport, as well as the largest shopping mall in America (at least at that time)—Woodfield Shopping Center. In addition to easy access to Route 53, Greenbrier was also bordered by two key roads: U.S. Route 12 and Palatine Road. Both roads offered various options for getting to shopping and other businesses.

Shopping Boom

What would shopping be like without the giant shopping mall? I'll never know, because shortly after Miller Builders began finishing the first houses in Greenbrier, Randhurst Mall opened in the neighboring village of Mount Prospect in 1962. Randhurst's name was derived from its location, at the corner of Rand Road and Elmhurst Road. At the time it opened its doors, it was the largest shopping center under one roof. It had three main anchor stores when I was growing up—Carson Pirie Scott, Wieboldt's, and J. C. Penney.

Randhurst was also a selling point in the later half of the building of Greenbrier. Getting to Randhurst was relatively easy for the new residents of Greenbrier by simply taking Rand Road southeast to Elmhurst Road. Randhurst was especially convenient for us because it was located halfway between our house and Grandpa Hinesley's house. Randhurst also played host to events such as art shows, fashion shows, and even children's theater in the open mall area. These events connected Randhurst with the community in ways other than shopping.

Randhurst's role as the leading shopping center in the northwest suburbs was somewhat short-lived. In September of 1965, the Daily Herald reported that a 262-acre shopping center complex was being planned close to the intersection of the Northwest Tollway and Route 53. The project was being spearheaded by Sears, Roebuck and Company. The shopping center complex mentioned in the article would become Woodfield Mall, named after former Sears, Roebuck and Company board chairman General Robert E. Wood and Chicago retail legend Marshall Field. However, the mall didn't open in 1967, as the Daily Herald article originally anticipated. Instead, the project first broke ground on October 9th, 1969. The final plan used a 191-acre site for the giant shopping center. Woodfield opened its doors on September 9th, 1971, with fifty-nine stores, and much of the mall still under construction.

The foundation of a dream in early summer, 1962

As more stores opened, Woodfield claimed to be the world's largest enclosed shopping center. By 1973, the mall had one hundred eighty-nine stores, a movie theater, and an ice rink. When the mall opened it had three anchor stores, each of which was planned to be the biggest store of its respective chain-Sears, Roebuck and Company; Marshall Fields; and J. C. Penney. Woodfield continued to grow as it became one of the most popular tourist attractions in Illinois. For the residents of Greenbrier, Woodfield was just a few exits away, south on Route 53.

First on the Block (Well, Almost)

Dad seemed to have a plan to live the American Dream. After having served in the army, he realized he didn't want to work for someone else, so he became self-employed and made his own way. Being a person who really valued family, soon after he married Mom, they had their first son in late 1960. The next step was to own their own home.

Construction of our house in midsummer, 1962

One of the key factors in Dad reaching this dream was the VA guaranteed loan. Having served in the army between 1950 and 1955, he was eligible for the Korean GI Bill. The VA didn't actually provide the home loan, but guaranteed the lender protection against loss in the event the veteran failed to repay the loan. It was better than having a great credit rating, because it protected the lender. Even though my father didn't fall in love with the army, he was still smart enough to realize it pays to serve your country.

Our house near compleation in late summer, 1962

Like many people of the time, my parents decided to leave the city for the suburbs. Chicago was changing, but not for the better. As people began to leave the city, established neighborhoods began to change. The more the neighborhoods changed, the more the remaining residents decided to move. There were various reasons couples like my parents wanted to leave. Concerns about crime, deteriorating infrastructure and quality of schooling, increasing taxes, lack of space, and other changes in the community were all issues that motivated people to migrate to the suburbs. My parents were impressed with the work Miller Builders had done on Grandpa Hinesley's house, so they decided to take a look at the new Greenbrier models.

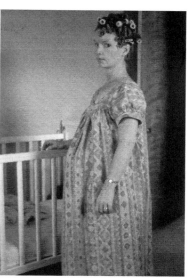

Mom, looking very pleased with my father and very pregnant with my brother Scott, in late summer of 1962—this picture was taken while my parents were staying with my grandparents before the house was complete.

The first models for Greenbrier were completed in mid-September, 1961. Pleased with what they saw, Dad made a down payment on a home by the end of October. This made our family one of the first families to settle in Greenbrier. Mom and Dad chose a "Martha Washington model" with a May 1st completion date. The house was situated in the center of the subdivision.

The houses in Greenbrier consisted of ranch styles and bi-level styles, with a traditional colonial appearance. During the course of the development, families could choose from eighteen or so house designs in various colors. All homes included wall-to-wall carpeting, aluminum siding, landscaping, built-in ovens and ranges, and tiled bathrooms, as well as other features popular at the time.

My parents visited the construction site periodically during the summer of 1962. There were some minor construction delays, forcing my parents to live a short while with the Hinesleys while awaiting completion of the house. Mom was seven months pregnant with my brother Scott when they closed on the house in September of that year.

Shopping with Mom

One carefree Indian summer day, I played outside in the green grass of our backyard. I'd already completed my time at preschool, which was held at the same park district field house and pool promised by the Miller Builders Ad years before.

Besides finger-painting or making hand impressions in plaster of Paris, I spent my hours there trying to secure playtime with the cool wooden trucks they had on hand. Free of the burden of preschool I climbed the red wooden fence in the backyard. It was a cool fence to have as a kid because you could walk the perimeter of the backyard on top of the fence as if it were a balance beam, due to planks Dad secured on top. Dad designed and built a wooden fence for our backyard to keep my brothers away from the construction still underway in Greenbrier. Nobody else in the neighborhood had a fence like it. In the warm sun I was walking the planks when I heard Mom call out.

"Tom, time to come in!"

I'd ignore Mom sometimes if I was in my play world. So much so that my parents had my hearing tested. This time I ran inside to see what joy awaited me.

Before I was old enough to go to school, Mom dragged me along with her to do her shopping. When I walked into the kitchen, Mom was already to go. Looking at me through her horn rimmed prescription sunglasses; she still managed to spot my dirty hands. After she helped me wash up we were on our way. During those days, there were two main places close to Greenbrier to do your grocery shopping: Jewel and the A&P. We frequented the A&P, and collected the Sperry and Hutchinson Company (S&H) green stamps there. The green stamp program was basically a rewards program—you'd receive a certain number of green stamps depending on how much you spent in the store. Then, you saved them in your S&H book (which held twelve hundred stamps) and redeemed them later for some item in the S&H "Ideabook" or at the S&H Redemption Center. At the Redemption Centers, you could buy almost anything under the sun, if you had enough stamp books saved up. Mom took pleasure in collecting the stamps and redeeming them for an appliance or a gift. The one appliance that I recalled getting with the S&H was the electric skillet that she often used for our family dinners.

The Greenbrier Civic Association

There were elements of life in the "New Suburbia" that have since disappeared that go unnoticed until you wish you had them. There are times that I feel that way about the Greenbrier Civic Association.

One nice thing about moving into a new subdivision is that everyone is new to the neighborhood. This allowed my family to get to know almost everyone in the neighborhood. Shortly after Greenbrier was built, residents formed the Greenbrier Civic Association in early 1963. The main purpose of the civic association was to provide a link between the community and the village or town. The

1976-77 Greenbrier Directory, produced by the Greenbrier Civic Association.

Greenbrier Civic Association performed that function, but also went a step beyond that.

The first function the Greenbrier Civic Association held was a "getting to know you" gathering, where Greenbrier residents were invited to attend a cocktail party with dancing. The underlying theme of the civic association over the years was to inspire community participation in a positive way. Another service they provided was a Greenbrier Directory. The directory listed every resident in Greenbrier. The benefit was that you knew or could find out who your neighbors were and contact them if needed. This, of course, occurred during a time before everyone was hypersensitive about privacy issues.

The civic association also was very active in village politics that had anything to do with the Greenbrier subdivision. For instance, they were successful blocking the unwanted development of land bordering Greenbrier. They also invited politicians to speak on the issues of the day. During the 1968 campaign, they invited the Representative of the 13th District, Donald Rumsfeld, to speak at Greenbrier School. According to a Daily Herald report of the meeting, Donald Rumsfeld believed the Johnson administration should be more transparent in handling the Vietnam War, and is quoted as saying, "We operate more effectively for the public's interest if we perform in a goldfish bowl."

Now there's some food for thought.

The civic association performed functions a park district might offer today. They organized a 4th of July Bike Parade for the elementary school children of the neighborhood-kids decorated their bikes in a patriotic way and lined up on the morning of the 4th at Verde Park. Their bikes were then judged for best decoration, while they did laps around the two tennis courts behind the school. One lucky kid from each group won a prize. Another activity the civic association organized (and in which Dad played an active role) was the Greenbrier Boys Softball League. It was a great way to get to know other boys, and make friends with kids in other grades. It was the little things, outside its normal charter, that the Greenbrier Civic Association organized that kept the community close.

The Face of the Community

Even when all of the ingredients are in place, things don't always go as planned. In the case of the Greenbrier development, one might say things went better than planned. The subdivision's layout incorporated features that lent themselves to a thriving community. Its location made it easy to enjoy the benefits of the growing Chicago metropolitan area for entertainment, business, and commerce. The most important ingredient, however, was the people that made up the community.

During the early years of Greenbrier, from 1962 to 1968, the people in the community were proactive in creating a family environment. During this time, the Herald would print the "goings on" in Greenbrier. These social columns were titled "Greenbrier Patch" or "Greenbrier Gleanings," and written by several authors. Whoever wrote the article lived in Greenbrier and reported on all types of social activities, from birthdays to people having guests in from out of town.

The new suburban Dad in the spring of 1963.

It was written like a Christmas letter you might receive from a friend or relative recounting what he did throughout the year, except these stories detailed the various families in your neighborhood and were updated every two weeks or so. Our family made the "Greenbrier Gleanings" a few times. In one instance, the highlights of our 1967 vacation to the East Coast and then Florida were detailed. Being listed in the newspaper made you feel like you were important to the community and it created a stronger bond with your neighbors.

One reason people seemed to fit in well in Greenbrier was that the homes in Greenbrier fell in the middle of the price range and drew people from a wide range of professions. The residents represented a cross section of both white- and blue-collar workers. The houses themselves reflected the community in that they were nice homes, but still modest and functional. In 1968, the Greenbrier Apartments were added to the community for smaller families.

Many residents of Greenbrier came from neighborhoods in the city and were looking to have a close-knit neighborhood in the suburbs. As a result, a kid growing up in Greenbrier during the 1960s and 1970s experienced an environment essentially free of class warfare. At that time, there weren't any "snobs" in Greenbrier. No one seemed to flaunt their money if they had it, and kids didn't seem to take notice or care if someone didn't. Money or status didn't seem to be an issue for the kids in Greenbrier—that is, until they moved to other schools or came into contact with other subdivisions. Sometimes, the middle of the road is a nice place to be.

CHAPTER 3

Through Thick and Thin

Steve, Scott, and Tom

I sat crouched against the stone-lined embankment, waiting for the enemy to attack. Rifle in hand, I peered over the edge of the embankment for some sign of the approaching enemy. My ears were tuned to any sound that might give away his position while I made sure not to give away my own. Suddenly I heard rustling feet on the grass on my right flank, and I waited for the right moment to spring the trap. Then, he came into my sights.

"Bang, bang, bang! I got you!"

"Oh, man!" said Doug, "I didn't even see you. How did you know I was there?"

"I heard you running around and just waited," I said.

It was the summer of 1974, and my close friend Doug Brooks and I were playing a war game in his backyard. At the age of seven, I had already known Doug for two or three years. He was a little taller than me, with short brown hair and a friendly face. Doug's house stood kitty-corner to my own in back, allowing me to go there whenever I had the chance. We didn't have any cool toy guns, so we used baseball bats as rifles. The handle of the bat was supposed to be the muzzle. We used square bean bags from a Toss Across tic-tac-toe game as grenades. The bean bags were better than tennis balls because they didn't bounce, and preferable to baseballs in the event you got hit with one. As we sat discussing the best tactic for the next attack (as well as two seven-year-olds can), Mom's voice rang out into the evening air.

"Steve, Scott, Tom—dinner!" she belted out like a song.

Mom's five o'clock "Dinner Call" had an unforgettable ring to it, too. I said my quick goodbyes to Doug and took off running. I cut through our neighbor's yard to get home quickly. My brothers and I were almost always within shouting distance. As I entered the house, I could smell the familiar scent of spices and hamburger meat.

Frisky, our dog, greeted me as I entered. He wagged his tail so hard his back feet slid around the linoleum floor. Frisky was a smallish mutt, a mix between a collie and a German shepherd. He was like my little brother, and for thirteen years of my life, we grew up together. Frisky was just another member of the family, with his endearing personality and particular character flaws. Until I went to school, Frisky and I were inseparable.

Although Frisky was a great companion for a kid like me, he wasn't the best-behaved dog. He drove Dad crazy at times. Dad was the one who wanted a dog, but he originally wanted a German shepherd. However, Dad wasn't the one who got him. When I was just a year old, my mom took the three of us out, and we came across someone selling puppies. Undoubtedly, my brothers started begging for one, and Mom caved in. She bought Frisky for something like five dollars.

Handling the new puppy became a challenge. It took some time before he was housebroken. Actually, he was never entirely so. If we left for several hours to go to a movie or to Grandpa Hinesley's house, oftentimes Frisky just couldn't hold out. He had a strong bond with the family, and when we left him by himself, he had a tough time. He chewed on shoes, toys, and furniture, and tore them up. When we were away, anything was fair game.

He also ran away a lot. Somehow he figured out how to escape our backyard, and off he went. One night when I was returning home from grocery stopping with Dad, a dog ran across Kennicott Drive, right in front of our car.

"Was that Frisky?" I asked in disbelief.

Sure enough, we stopped the car, only to discover Frisky out for a night walk by him-

**Mom with a young Frisky—I'm
the toddler in the doorway.**

self. Although he was mischievous at times, he was good at tricks and was well-behaved around other people.

As I entered the house for dinner, Frisky was happy to see me, as he always was.

"Wash your hands!" Mom called out.

I headed upstairs to the bathroom as my brothers filed into the house. I was the youngest of the three boys, which meant I became very adept at self-defense from an early age. My older brothers were Steve and Scott. Steve was just over six years older than me, and Scott was four years older. Soon we were all washing our hands in the upstairs bathroom. There was a large mirror, and fluorescent lighting. Although there were two sinks, it was still crowded. Being the youngest, I always had to push my way in, but not too hard, so as not to get hit. After washing our hands, the three of us bounded down the steps to the kitchen.

The kitchen had a distinct 1970s look. The kitchen was dark despite the sunlight shining through a large window. The maroon appliances sat beside our chestnut brown cabinets, topped with white marbled laminate countertops. The lower half of our walls was covered with dark paneling. Atop that was the stylish gold, brown, and olive green wallpaper. My mother had hung an array of rustic antique knickknacks on the walls, similar to what you'd see in a Cracker Barrel.

In the center of the kitchen dangled a wagon-wheel light fixture with frosted glass lights around it. In the center of the wheel was an additional light that shone down onto the table to spotlight our dinner. It was Sunday night, and we were having Rice-a-Roni Spanish rice with big chunks of ground beef, a staple of any good 70s diet ("The San Francisco Treat").

There was a set number of dishes on the Maryellyn Price dinner menu The most frequent offerings included spaghetti and meatballs, hot dogs and macaroni, fried chicken (she made the best fried chicken ever), rump roast, pot roast, salmon patties, hamburgers, tuna casserole, chicken casserole, and, of course, Spanish rice. I will say that I appreciate her efforts to rotate the selections, so at least we didn't always have to eat the same thing.

The three of us—Scott, Steve, and I in December 1967.

My brothers and I made our way to our usual positions at the table. What can I say; we were a family of habit. Both of my parents smoked, so there was always an ashtray on the table. Mom was almost never without a cigarette, and mealtime was no exception. Today, most people consider smoking in the presence of children unacceptable, but the fact that my parents smoked was probably the most significant reason I never took up the habit.

A Family Dinner

As Mom served dinner, the TV on the kitchen counter blared away. It wasn't unusual for us to eat while watching TV. I'm sure this is why my brothers and I have such difficulty making small talk—we never had to. However, my brother Scott has never been short for words on any subject, whether he knows anything about it or not. But then again, he was the middle child, and they're almost always the gregarious type.

Back in 1974, there was no cable TV in the Chicago area. Each house had a TV antenna on the roof, which was typically attached to the chimney. More significantly, nobody paid a dime to watch TV then, it was absolutely free (someday, younger generations may find this shocking). The quality of the reception varied depending on the weather and the location of your antenna, but the signals at that time were pretty strong, and reception in our area was generally good.

There were two frequency types used for TV broadcasts: VHF (very high frequency), which was used for channels two to thirteen, and UHF (ultra high frequency), for channels higher than thirteen. All of the main channels in 1974 were broadcast in VHF. TV sets used to have knobs and dials for changing channels, and for tuning in the station. It may sound crazy, but people had to actually approach the television and change the channel by hand. The UHF stations were more low-budget stations, and reception wasn't usually as good as for the VHF stations. In order to even watch a UHF channel, the main TV dial had to be set on UHF, and then you had to turn a specific UHF dial to get the stations. It may seem primitive by today's standards, but it was free, and the only game in town.

Dad at the kitchen table in 1973 (note the unintentional "Price Stare).

Mom at the kitchen table with her ever-present cigarette.

There were eight TV stations that broadcast regularly in 1974 in the Chicagoland area. CBS, NBC, ABC WGN, and WTTW (the PBS station) were broadcast in VHF. WGN broadcast syndicated shows, as well as a good number of locally produced shows, most notably *The Bozo Show*. There were three UHF channels at the time, WCIU-TV, which broadcast mostly ethnic shows and a stock market review on weekday mornings; WFLD-TV, which broadcast syndicated shows, old movies, and some local programming; and WSNS-TV, which, like WFLD, had mostly syndicated shows, old movies, and some local programming, like White Sox baseball.

On Sunday evenings at five, our Sunday-night routine began. First we watched *60 Minutes* on CBS, then Wild Kingdom on NBC at six o'clock, a popular nature show funded by Mutual of Omaha in the 1960s and 70s. Marlin Perkins hosted *Mutual of Omaha's Wild Kingdom*. My family and I couldn't resist a good documentary-style animal show. Marlin Perkins didn't actually interact with any dangerous animals, however—he had a partner, Jim Fowler, for that. When traveling around the African bush, Marlin Perkins stayed in the jeep and narrated, while Jim Fowler was sent out to wrangle the dangerous animals. "Watch as Jim sneaks up on the one hundred and fifty-pound hyena," and so on. It made for great TV. By this time we had finished eating dinner, so we either asked to be excused or stayed to watch the next show, *The Wonderful World of Disney*.

The Wonderful World of Disney was a crap shoot, it could basically be anything Disney had produced, from a Davy Crockett story or Kurt Russell movie to a narrated program about a bear cub growing up. By no means as entertaining as *Wild Kingdom*, we typically headed upstairs to play football in Mom and Dad's room (the real deal, not a video game). We always checked with Steve first to see if he wanted to play.

Steve, the Older Brother

There have been some things in the course of my life that I've taken for granted. One such thing is the bond between brothers. For the longest time, I assumed that siblings in most families were like us. Over the years, when I talked to people about their siblings, I discovered—much to my surprise—that they weren't all that close. This was something I didn't understand, because the connection between me and my brothers was like cement. It was an unspoken understanding between us that we would be there for each other through thick and thin. Both of my brothers played a strong

My brother Steve at the age of six.

Big brother Steve loved both Scott (top) and me (bottom) so much that he could hardly let us go.

role in shaping the person I am today. My older brother Steve was my very first role model.

Because Steve was quite a bit older than me, we never had to compete for anything at home, like toys. I felt a special bond with Steve because we were both lefties in a house of righties. I think Steve liked being a role model. He enjoyed showing me new and cool things. Once he took me to a carnival someone had set up in their yard. It was summertime, and I was maybe four or five. We walked a block or so to get there. There were games where you could win candy, and they even had some small rides. It wasn't anything extravagant, but still, he must have thought I'd enjoy it. So he took me of his own free will, and I've never forgotten it.

While growing up, I imitated Steve at times by choosing the same things he did, like his favorite color, sports team, and music. While Scott and I were like a pair running a three-legged race, complimenting each other's skills in order to win, Steve, as the oldest, represented the lone ground-breaker, setting the stage for us to compete. Our collective goal was to be the best at what we did. From an early age, Steve was a perfectionist, who raised the bar for the rest of us.

Steve was born on November 9th, 1960. On the morning he was born, the Chicago Tribune announced the results of the 1960 election between Kennedy and Nixon. With Chicago's help, Kennedy took the election, and ushered in the era of the "New Frontier." Like the election, my brother's birth was also tense and full of complications. Steve was a breech baby, and the doctor was forced to deliver him by cesarean section. That was his first groundbreaking move, as Scott and I would also be delivered in the same fashion. Because the use of obstetric ultrasound technology was still in its infancy (no pun intended), they took an x-ray of my mother to determine the baby's position. I have always wondered what kind of long-term effects that may have had on Steve's health. As Steve grew up, he always seemed to be plagued by some minor illness. He often suffered from hay fever. This gave him a miserable disposition at times.

Physically, Steve never seemed threatening. He was a medium-sized kid-not tall, but not short, either. In 1974, all of the Price boys had messy hair. Then again, the 1970s weren't known for illustrious fashion or hairstyles, so we didn't really stand out. Steve had the darkest hair of us all, almost black. While not outwardly menacing, Steve did have a nasty temper, and a clear mind when he was mad, which was considerably more dangerous than being blinded by rage. It was best not to push him over the edge.

Like Dad, Steve demonstrated artistic talent at an early age. What better family to support his skills, than one devoted to art? We were surrounded by all types of artistic materials, from drawing pads and pencils to paint and animation cels. Dad had built a small art studio in our downstairs family room by erecting a wall and splitting the room in two. Since Dad was self-employed, work could come at any time, and might have tight deadlines. This meant working late downtown or at home over the weekend, or at other odd times. Steve had all the tools he needed at home to advance his skills. Not only did he have talent, he had passion and creativity to boot.

When I was old enough to sleep in a regular bed, I moved into a larger room that I shared with Scott, while Steve moved into his own room. Steve got all-new furniture, including a desk, two sets of drawers, a matching bookshelf that sat on the longer of the drawer units, and a cool trundle bed. Most of his room was painted gold, similar to the kitchen, but the wall behind his desk was covered with thick, one-foot-square cork tiles. Mounted to the wall was a swing-arm desk lamp. Almost all of the items in Steve's room were an extension of his personality in some way, but the swing-arm desk lamp was completely Dad's influence. All of us had a swing-arm light. They were great. Dad had a combination fluorescent-and-regular-light swing-arm lamp on his own drafting table. As he did with many other things, Dad assumed we would find these lamps as useful as he did. He was so methodical that it was self-evident to him that we needed the same style of lamp for our desk to do our homework or draw. "How can you see what you're doing?" he would ask, adjusting the lamp to ensure there was enough light. I think this annoyed us all equally, but Steve showed it more. In order to maintain any sense of privacy, Steve usually disappeared into his room and shut the door.

Steve remained locked in his room like a hermit for great stretches of time, to read, do homework, or draw. When he was twelve in the summer of 1973, Steve began creating his own comic books. His main character was Super Fuzzy. He created a whole world of characters based on movies, television, and books. He used characters like Dr. Fuzz for Dr. No and Wolf Fuzz for the Wolfman, and so on. He used pads of drawing paper to make the comic books, and drew lines for the cartoon boxes, stapling them together when he was finished. He ended up making between fifty and a hundred comic books.

Steve gained a reputation with his friends and acquaintances at school for being a great illustrator. When he wasn't drawing Super Fuzzy comics, he was working on some other project. In addition to art, Steve loved to read. I remember him reading Charles Dickens, H. G. Wells, Sir Arthur Conan Doyle, Jules Verne, and

Steve reading in his "cave".

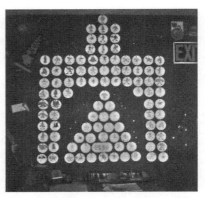

Steve's work area, complete with character disks pinned to the cork-panelled wall.

Ian Fleming the most, but he read other classics as well. Of course, he loved the book *Jaws*, by Peter Benchley, which everyone seemed to read in the early 1970s. Steve was a big movie buff, and when *Jaws*, the movie, came out he went shark crazy. He even made homemade *Jaws* T-shirts using Dad's permanent markers. *Jaws* was the first movie that got Steve interested in film as an art form. He began to buy books like *The Making of Jaws* and *The Making of King Kong*. The movie also inspired him to experiment with film and animation. He used Dad's 8-mm and Super 8 cameras to make short films. He always seemed to be creating something—he simply loved it. I don't think I've ever met another person quite like him in that way. Little did he know, one day he would wind up working for Steven Spielberg.

When Scott and I went to ask Steve if he wanted to play football with us in Mom and Dad's room, he was working on a character disk. Each time Steve introduced a new character into his comics, he created a reference drawing on a paper disk cut out of Dad's heavy-stock paper. Each disk was then tacked up on the cork wall behind his desk with a pushpin. Soon the wall was covered with disks. I snuck up there every now and then just to marvel at his work. I showed his drawings off to my friends as well, but I had to be careful—Steve was very fastidious. He seemed to know if any little thing was out of place, and he hated anyone trespassing in his room.

Steve looked up from drawing and gave us a mischievous smirk. "Is it clear?" he asked.

"Yeah, Mom and Dad are in the kitchen watching TV," Scott responded.

"OK, I'll be there in a minute," he said, as he picked up a colored pencil to make some finishing touches on his drawing.

Scott, the Middle Child

While Steve was the brother who served as the role model I admired, Scott was the brother in the trenches by my side. Scott and I shared the same room for more than

A sampling of Steve's Super Fuzzy character disks.

ten years. We played sports and cards together, and went places together. It wasn't so much that Scott and I were alike, but we knew each other so well.

Two years after Steve was born, Scott arrived on November 17th, 1962. Scott was the textbook middle child. Overshadowed by Steve's academic and artistic achievements, Scott looked for ways to differentiate himself. Two such ways were sports and his outgoing personality.

From the time he could walk, Scott was prone to injury. Shortly after taking his first steps, he tripped over one of Dad's shoes and bit though his lip, requiring several stitches. It was an omen of things to come. Give Scott a ball, and he will create a game to play in the space available. At the age of six in our front yard, diving to catch a baseball, Scott tore his left knee open on a water main sticking out of the

Scott and Mom in early 1963.

ground. Again, stitches were needed. Scott was always a little more hyperactive than the rest of us. It must have been difficult for him not tear the stitches out before the doctor could remove them, but he managed. The following day he tore his knee open again playing soccer.

Despite having a tendency to get hurt, Scott remained undeterred from pursuing his love of sports. He always played sports with a passion and determination to win. That's what made him good at a wide range of sports, despite any physical or athletic shortcomings he may have had. Not only did Scott have a great love for sports, he was a huge fan of professional sports. Being from Chicago, Scott could follow just about any sport, and enjoyed them all.

Maybe Next Year

Being a sports fan as a kid growing up in Chicago definitely tested your ability to handle frustration. Chicago has a long history of suffering sports fans. Our city is represented in the four main professional sports: baseball, football, basketball, and hockey. And from 1960 to 1980, Chicago sports teams enjoyed little success.

Neither of Chicago's two major-league baseball teams, the Cubs and the White Sox, even made the playoffs. Traditionally, people from the north side of Chicago support the Cubs, and citizens from the south side support the White Sox. No one in my family disliked the White Sox, because at that time, the two clubs

Two views of Scott Price, the athlete: (top) the healthy baseball player (bottom) the injured football player.

would never play each other unless they both made it to the World Series. I knew full well that was never going to happen.

Although the Cubs didn't make the playoffs, they did have some good players during those years, who made the games enjoyable. Just as they are today, Cubs' games were regularly broadcast on WGN, which was like a fourth major network in Chicago. One thing the Cubs had going for them was the "Voice of the Cubs," Jack Brickhouse. Jack Brickhouse was the model sportscaster. He had a perfect broadcasting voice, and an aura of credibility. There was a time during the early 1960s that he was the White Sox and Chicago Bears announcer, as well as the Cubs announcer. By the mid-70s, he was only announcing at Cubs games with his partner, Hall of Famer Lou Boudreau. Jack got excited by great plays, and the audience ate it up. During a home run, he would cheer his trademark "Hey, hey" or "Wheeew boy." He made the games more entertaining to watch when the Cubs had a mediocre team. When Jack Brickhouse retired in 1983, WGN hired another great broadcaster, Harry Caray, to announce the Cubs games. Harry's style was very different from Jack's. Jack had the presence of a newscaster, reporting a great story as it transpired. Harry was more like a fellow baseball fan, kicking back, enjoying the game, and having a beer. Ironically, before announcing Cubs games, Harry Carey broadcast games for the White Sox, along with former baseball player Jimmy Piersall. The Sox weren't worth watching at the time, and I found Harry Caray irritating. The funny thing was that when he joined up with the Cubs, I didn't mind him so much anymore.

Chicago's football team, the Bears, had a little more success than the two baseball teams, but not too much more. In 1963, in the days before there was a Super Bowl, Chicago won the NFL championship. Although the Bears wouldn't have many great teams until the 1980s, they were blessed with some of the greatest players to play the sport. In the 1960s, the Bears had Hall of Famers—tight end Mike Ditka, running back Gale Sayers, and linebacker Dick Butkus. Not long after Gale Sayers left football over a serious knee injury, the Bears signed another great running back, and maybe the best all-around football player of all time (not that I'm biased), Walter Payton. The Bears had some tough seasons, where the only thing they had going for them was Walter Payton. He really made football worth watching during that time.

Because the Bears and other Chicago teams weren't contending teams for most of the 1960s and 70s, many of the kids around Greenbrier had "back-up favorite" teams they supported. This was most evident with football. Additionally, it was easy to show your support for the various teams because stores like Sears and J. C. Penney all carried loads of official NFL-licensed products. They sold sheet sets, drapes, sleeping bags, towels, bathrobes, sweaters, sweatshirts, hoodies, socks, watches, pajamas, winter coats, rain coats, pile-lined parkas, mittens, knit caps, and anything else you can imagine. All of the items were priced like every other product, and didn't cost a mint. I'm sure I had just about every NFL item available, at one time or another. The most popular teams at the time were those who played in the Super Bowl, like the Pittsburgh Steelers and the Dallas Cowboys. Some kids also liked the Miami Dolphins. In our house, Steve liked the Los Angeles Rams (which I also adopted as my alternate team), and Scott liked the Minnesota Vikings. For me, the best thing about Scott's preference for the Vikings was that they lost four Super Bowls. Of course, the Rams didn't fare any better, so it didn't matter that much. Ironically, regardless of how well our alternate teams played during those seasons, it would be the Chicago Bears who first win a Super Bowl.

Basketball became Scott's favorite sport. The Chicago Bulls were an expansion team in the 1966-67 season. The Bulls actually started out very well—they had the best record for their first season of any expansion team. Although they had some good seasons, basketball fever hadn't taken hold in Chicago just yet. As kids, the player who inspired the most awe was Julius Erving, a.k.a. "Dr. J." Julius Erving started his professional basketball career in 1971 in the ABA (American Basketball Association). The ABA was a professional basketball league that competed with the NBA from 1967 until it folded after the 1976 season. Dr. J changed basketball. He was the first one to turn the slam dunk into an art form. He abused players by blowing past them and making an awesome dunk. When he went to the NBA in 1976, the sport began to change. How couldn't you like him? He was a highlight film in human form. Chicago was later blessed with Michael Jordon, who surpassed Dr. J and every other basketball player before him, and turned Chicago into a basketball city.

The one Chicago team that seemed to have the best chance at winning a championship from 1960 to 1980 was the Chicago Blackhawks. One of the original six hockey teams of the National Hockey League, the Blackhawks had a mixed history of highs and lows. Although the Blackhawks haven't won the Stanley Cup since 1961, between 1960 and 1980 they made it to the Stanley Cup finals four times (in 1962, 1965, 1971, and 1973). In 1969, they signed my favorite Blackhawk, Hall of Fame goalie Tony Esposito. We used to play floor hockey in our hallway on the tile floor. I always played goalie, and emulated "Tony O's" style. We played a lot of sports indoors, where we probably shouldn't have (for instance, playing football in Mom and Dad's room).

That ill-fated evening, Scott turned to me and said, in a hushed voice, "Go get the football and meet me in Mom's room."

"Where is it?" I whispered back.

"I think it's in our room by the closet."

"Great," I mumbled, meaning, "How the hell am I going to find it in there?"

The Two Oscars

Scott and I began sharing a room when I was three and he was seven. I received a used foam "big boy" bed and old mismatched bedroom furniture. Hand-me-downs from my older brothers were commonplace. It didn't bother me, because it meant I was BIG! Rooming with Scott could have been worse. Although he bullied me every now and then, he was always there for me, even if Steve was mad at me for whatever reason. Our room generally appeared as if a tornado had struck, and we were not unlike the characters from the show *The Odd Couple*, except we were both Oscar. This meant that we were excessively messy. You wouldn't know it at first glance, but underneath all of the clothes and toys were hardwood floors. And I was supposed to find a football in all that mess?

Our room was at the end of the upstairs hallway. I opened the door, pushing clothes out of the way as it swung open.

"Here goes nothing," I thought.

After I entered the room, I turned left to search by the closet, which had two slatted folding doors inevitably left open due to the layer of clothes blocking the doors. No football.

This was no traditional football I was hunting for. When we played inside, we used a pillow football from Sears. Each of us received one the previous Christmas. Although they weren't official NFL football pillows, they came in colors that matched NFL teams' colors. Steve had a blue and gold Los Angeles Rams ball, Scott had a purple and gold Minnesota Vikings ball, and I had a blue and orange Chicago Bears ball. Frisky had destroyed Scott's ball, and Steve kept his belongings under lock and key.

I had to pick up the pace—we were running out of time to play. My par-

Roommates: By the time this photo was taken, Scott and I had been roommates for seven years (this photo was taken on the day Scott graduated from Rand Junior High

ents would be checking in on us anytime now. I glanced over at the bookshelf next to the bed. No football. I knew better than to waste much time looking under my bed, because I ran out of storage space under there the last time I "straightened up" my room. I dove onto my bed to look by the nightstand between Scott's bed and mine. Nothing. I glanced under Scott's bed, which was flush against the back wall of the room. It wasn't there, either. I was run-

Our bedroom in 1972, before my beloved NFL sheets from Sears.

ning out of places to look. The wall to my right was a common wall with my parents' room. Along that wall were two dressers separated by a desk (illuminated, of course, by a swing-arm lamp mounted on the wall). And there, under the chair by the desk, was the football! Let the games begin.

Scott stuck his head in and said, "What's taking you so long?"

"Got it," I said, showing him the ball, which he plucked out of my hands.

"Let's go."

We Were No Angels

Scott and I snuck into Mom and Dad's room.

"Where's Steve?" I asked.

"He'll be here in a minute. Let's play the Quarterback Game until he gets here," Scott said, getting into position.

The Quarterback Game was pretty simple. Mom and Dad had a king-sized bed, with the head of the bed against the back wall. The closet was on the opposite wall. The Quarterback Game was a two-part game. First, the quarterback threw the football into the closet (with his back to the bed) before getting sacked onto the bed. When the pass made it into the closet without being blocked or the quarterback getting sacked, the second part of the game came into play. Both players lined up, facing each other at the closet. The player on offense threw the ball toward the bed with one hand, then both players tried to catch the ball. When the offensive player got the ball and made it to the bed, it was a touchdown. If the defensive player got the ball, he tried to get to the closet and then go back to the bed. If he managed that, it would be a defensive touchdown. If he didn't make it, he was then the offensive player, and the process started over again. As you can imagine, we created a great deal of noise, and got pretty rough. This was particularly the case with Scott and me, because we always played as hard as we could.

Steve hated to get into trouble. When Scott and I played indoor sports, we had a tendency to break things and then work as a team to fix it or cover it up. Steve, on the other hand, was skilled at disappearing when trouble came. If we played the Fumble Game, the idea was for the other two players to make the third player drop the ball. All of a sudden, Steve would disappear. A moment later, Mom or Dad would appear at the door, and Scott and I got into trouble.

When Scott and I broke something, it was usually a window. One summer, when I was about twelve or so, I was sitting on my bed when Scott threw a basketball at me. The ball bounced off my knee, and crashed through the window. We knew better than to throw a basketball in the house, but we decided to make up a story to make it seem more like an accident (other than simply being careless). On closer examination, we discovered that it looked more like a shoe had broken the glass, than a basketball. We told my parents that Scott broke the window accidentally while kicking off his shoe. It was a freak accident that the shoe flew at the window. It seemed unlikely, but if you saw the window, it wasn't entirely unbelievable. Two days later, we were goofing off in the living room, tossing a baby shoe around that Mom had bought as a gift for a coworker (leave it to us to make a game out of any object). One of my sidearm tosses got past Scott and—you guessed it— the shoe broke a small triangular window in our front door. Now we had a dilemma: We had already used a shoe story. It would sound pretty far-fetched to say we broke another window with a shoe. Since the window had a round hole in it from the shoe, we said we were playing outside and a tennis ball got away from us and broke the window.

To avoid getting in any trouble, Scott and I would usually try to fix the problem ourselves such as replacing a window or patching drywall. If we couldn't fix it we'd end up paying for it with allowance or extra chores but since no one was typically home when something broke, we usually avoided getting in more serious trouble from Dad.

In any event, Steve hadn't shown up yet for our football game.

"What's taking him so long?" I asked.

"Who cares? It's your turn," Scott replied, tossing the ball to me.

It was my turn to be quarterback. I knew as soon as I hiked the ball, Scott would come flying at me for the sack.

"Hike!" I yelled, dropping back for the pass.

Scott was just about on top of me when I got the ball into the air. He hit me good, though, and sent me flying across the corner of the bed and off onto the floor with a loud thud. The pass was good, but we both froze, and listened for approaching footsteps. We knew that that much noise could attract unwanted attention. Then, out of the corner of my eye I saw a figure in the doorway. It was Steve, thank God. I got up, my hip hurting slightly from the contact with the floor.

"Want to play the Fumble Game?" Scott asked.

"Sure," said Steve.

We started the Fumble Game by simply tossing the football to someone and then going after him and the ball. Normally, it was wise not to hold onto the ball too tightly—if you did, the other two players would whack at you with all their might until you dropped it. As luck would have it, Scott whipped the ball at me. I grabbed it and tried to make it to the bed. If you made it to the bed, it meant a break in play, then restarting the game from the beginning. I didn't make it far before the ball was hammered out of my arms and onto the floor. Scott took a stride toward the ball and bent down to pick it up. I dived across the floor with an outstretched arm to knock the ball away. That's when I heard it. The floor shook from below. Dad's home office was directly beneath the bedroom, and he was pounding on the ceiling—the jig was up. Steve had already magically disappeared. Scott and I looked at each other, and the nonverbal message was clear—every man for himself! I headed for the bathroom, Scott ducked into our room and grabbed a book, and Steve sat behind his desk, working on his newest Super Fuzzy comic.

Our indoor sport wasn't limited to football—we also played Nerf basketball in our living room, using two lampshades as hoops. Scott emulated Dr. J, flying through the air with his arm outstretched for a tomahawk dunk. It wasn't long before we destroyed the lamp shades, to the displeasure of my parents. We were no angels. If it was summertime, we might start a bottle-rocket war or swing on the school flagpole. In the wintertime, we threw snowballs at cars or skitched on the school bus. If you're not familiar with skitching, skitching comes from ski + hitching. In the winter time, as kids, when the streets were snowy or icy you could hold on to the bumper of a car or bus and skitch. I wouldn't recommend it. I guess we were always up to something mischievous, but that's boys for you.

We even boxed a little when I was young. When I was five or six, we had two pairs of boxing gloves. It amused my brothers to see if I could take them on. I didn't like to lose, and the more they beat me down the harder I came back. After a while I had no more to give, but they continued to taunt me. It reminds me of Paul Newman fighting George Kennedy in *Cool Hand Luke*. The fights inevitably ended the same way as in *Cool Hand Luke*, as well with me fighting until I could no longer stand. My training paid off, though, during the summer of 1975, when we held a neighborhood "Olympics" in our yard. We competed in the high jump, long jump, twenty-five-yard dash, obstacle course, and boxing. We separated the boxers by size. I made short work of my competition, even though one boy was a couple years older than me. Wisely, I retired after that fight.

Our World of Music

When my brothers and I weren't tearing down the house playing a made-up game, we shared another passion that has stayed with us for the rest of our lives—music. The 1960s and 70s were great years for popular music, and I was fortunate to have people around me who enjoyed all types. On the nightstand I shared with Scott, we had an old combination radio-record player, with a built-in speaker. At one time it had had a snap-on cover, which was long since lost. It was cheap, but it worked. We listened to that radio every night when we went to bed, but didn't get much use out of the record player because the needle was trashed.

In 1974, AM radio was what you tuned into to listen to music—FM radio was still in its infancy. We listened to station 890 on the AM dial. The "Big 89" offered quite a line-up in those days, with Bob Sirott, John Records Landecker, and Larry Lujack. The format was Top 40 rock and contemporary music—typically, you heard the same songs over and over again during the week. Although the music was generally very good, you still might hear something like "One Tin Soldier," by the band Coven, ten times.

When we went to bed, Scott and I listened to John Records Landecker. We loved his show. He did a segment called "Boogie Check," where listeners would call up and comment on the topic of the day, or just shout out something over the air. We lay in bed at night waiting for the "Boogie Check" jingle: "Boogie check, boogie check, oooh aaaah, boogie check, boogie check, oooh aaaah."

Then, John Records Landecker would announce, "'Boogie Check,' you're on the air!"

Some stoner would pipe up, "Hey, man, is this John Records Landecker?"

"Yeah, you're on 'Boogie Check!'"

"Great, man, I love your show and I got a joke for you."

"Go ahead."

"Ah, man, I forgot it."

Click.

The segment went on for about ten minutes or so, running through callers in rapid succession. On those nights, the silliness put smiles on our faces as we drifted off to sleep, listening to a classic song like "Stairway to Heaven."

During waking hours, my brothers and I listened to the family stereo downstairs .It was a Voice of Music Stereo Console, with record player and record changer. Technology has changed so much since that time, that a twenty-year-old today would probably believe me if I told him the stereo console was purchased by my great-great-grandfather just after the Civil War. The record changer feature allowed multiple records to be stacked on the spindle while held in place by a little latch. When the record came to an end, the arm returned automatically to its starting position while the latch released the next album. The arm then automatically moved that album to play position, and slowly lowered the needle to the album. To a four-year-old boy, it was very clever and impressive. (I don't know that it would impress anyone today.)

Before we had our own albums, my brothers and I played Mom and Dad's records. They had all kinds, including popular classical music—we listened to Mozart, Beethoven, Wagner, and various other composers. They had a large selection of folk music, featuring artists like Burl Ives, The Brothers Four, and Peter, Paul, and Mary. We also listened to musicals like West Side Story, but what I enjoyed most was Allan Sherman.

Allan Sherman was a comedian who did song parodies. His musical success came in the early 60s, but his success had faded by the time I listened to his music. We had a couple of his albums, and the best by far was *My Son, the Nut*, which came out in 1963. It contained Allan Sherman's biggest hit, "Hello Muddah, Hello Fadduh!" The whole album was good, and we listened to all the songs over and over again. Our favorites were "Eight Foot Two, Solid Blue" and "Hungarian Goulash No. 5." Many times, the parodies were done so well that if I hear the original tune today, I'll automatically think of the Allan Sherman lyrics.

Over time, my brothers and I began to acquire our own music. Steve bought his own stereo and began to separate his albums from Scott's and mine. Steve was very particular when it came to his records (and everything else he owned). He assembled a collection like no other. By the time he graduated from high school, he had more than one thousand records, and by the end of college, he had close to eighteen hundred. His collection included all types of music, from movie soundtracks to classical music, and from rock and roll and blues to new wave and punk songs. He loved the Beatles from the start. When Steve was interested in a group, he didn't buy one or two singles or an album here or there, he bought the group's entire catalog. He acquired all of the Beatles albums first, then the solo albums as they came out. I can't hear a Beatles song without thinking of Steve. By 1979, Steve's collection was basically a who's who of classic rock. The Rolling Stones, Jimi Hendrix, the Who, ELO, Eric Clapton (and every band he played in or joined), the Yardbirds, Led Zeppelin, Pink Floyd, and much more. He even had albums from bands like UFO. It was an impressive collection, and I would have been taking my life in my hands if I ever risked touching any of it.

Because Steve successfully guarded his albums, it forced Scott and me to get our own records. There were a couple of albums in my Uncle Jerry's collection that found Scott's ear: the official Broadway recording of *Hair the Musical*, *A Hard Day's Night* by The Beatles, and, most importantly, *Led Zeppelin II*. As roommates, Scott and I knew how to rock in the double room! Although I must admit I misunderstood the opening lyrics to "Whole Lotta Love." Instead of "You need coolin," I thought they sang, "You need Kool-Aid." But, then again, I was about three years old when I first heard the song. Scott's early collection also included an eight-album set called *K-Tels Super Hits of the Sixties*. The best thing about that set was that it contained all of the hits by the one-hit wonders of the 60s, as well as hits from bigger artists. It was great stuff.

After Scott got his own stereo, we combined our albums, unlike Steve. Our collection also included 45s, which were smaller records with a single song played at 45 rpms. After a while, some of the singles got scratched or didn't appeal to us anymore, so every now and then Scott and I cleaned out our collection. Always coming up with some way to compete, we developed a unique way to get rid of our old 45s—chucking them onto our neighbor's roof from our bedroom window. Making it across our own backyard was a challenge in itself, but getting it on their roof was almost impossible. Many attempts never cleared the bedroom window—in order to get any velocity, you had to have full arm movement, which meant standing several feet back from the window.

Scott could be such a bad influence on me at times. I won't say if we ever got a 45 on the neighbor's roof, but I will tell you that later, when Scott and I played "ultimate frisbee" in college, we won every championship

Scott, in the process of ruining another lampshade.

CHAPTER 4

Growing Up in Greenbrier

Life as a Kid in Greenbrier

Growing up in Greenbrier during the late 1960s and throughout the 1970s was special. Prior to the development of the subdivision, the area north of Palatine Road was all farmland. In its first five years, Greenbrier may have seemed more rural than urban, but that changed by the late 1960s. By that time, the area had been developed enough so the residents felt like they belonged to the metropolitan area—like Chicagoans—without the negative aspects of living in the city, such as limited space and busy streets. Additionally, the area had not yet become overdeveloped. There was plenty of open space, which, for a kid, provided the illusion of being in the countryside. The result for the kids in Greenbrier was a happy medium of space and community life.

During that time, there was never a dull moment. In the Chicago area, there are seasonal extremes, with bitterly cold winters and hot and humid summers. Many houses in Greenbrier didn't have air

Greenbrier kids marching during the school's Halloween parade, 1966.

Aerial view of Greenbrier in April of 1975.

conditioning, and ours was no exception. During the summer months of the 1970s, we placed electric fans strategically throughout the house. Scott and I had a metal dual fan in our window that brought in fresh air. It reminded me of a dual-engine bomber from the Second World War because of its dual props. It sounded like a bomber, too, which added to the effect. Even so, the summer heat inside the house was unbearable, so we spent much of our time outside, wandering the neighborhood.

Greenbrier offered a number of outdoor options, depending on what you wanted to do. On hot summer days, Frontier Pool was a popular place to go. It had three swimming pools: a baby pool, a twenty-five-yard regulation swimming pool, and a twelve-foot-deep diving pool. The diving pool had three diving boards, including a high dive if you felt daring. I usually didn't, because I never managed to enter the water properly and wound up smacking my belly or my back against the water. Do that a couple of times, and you tend to lose enthusiasm for the high dive. For us, Frontier Pool was a short walk to the southeast corner of the neighborhood. Since I spent a lot of time there already for swim team, I wasn't often in the mood to go swimming.

If you felt like fishing, you could grab your rod and reel and head down to the reservoir behind Verde Park. It wasn't exactly sanctioned fishing—the reservoir was surrounded by a tall fence with barbed wire at the top. As far as I know, it was a sewage and runoff reservoir for the neighborhood. It wasn't made for swim-ming—that's for sure—but it was pretty good for catching bluegills and bullheads. Besides, sneaking in and out was half the fun. There was a section of the fence where two of the barbed wire strands were missing. The trick was to climb to the top, drop your rod over, then hold down the one strand while swinging your leg over. You might get snagged, but it was the risk you took.

If fishing wasn't your thing but you still wanted some outdoor adventure, you could go to what was known as the "nursery." The nursery was a large section of undeveloped land just west of Greenbrier and east of Route 53. Miller Builders had attempted to build a sixteen-building apartment complex called Greenbrier West on the site. The Arlington Heights Planning Commission

My swim team photo, taken at Frontier Pool in the summer of 1976.

voted it down, primarily because of strong opposition from the Greenbrier Civic Association. As a result, the land lay vacant for a number of years. Their loss was our gain, because it was like having a forest preserve close to home. The nursery was divided into two sections: One section had large trees and bushes, along with paths you could wander. The other section was essentially an open field with tall grass.

Smear the Queer in action—Scott was *it*.

If you wanted to play a pick-up game of baseball, football, or "Smear the Queer" (so named simply because it rhymed), there were three parks with plenty of space. Smear the Queer used a football, and the object was to hold on to the football as long as possible while the other players tried to tackle you or take the ball. It was a challenging game. During the late 60s and early 70s, it wasn't unusual to get a group of kids together to play a pick-up game of football, soccer, Smear the Queer, or baseball, because there were so many kids in the neighborhood. The three parks in Greenbrier were Greenbrier Park, located on the northern edge of Greenbrier close to the school; Frontier Park, an open field on the eastern edge of Greenbrier, just south of Ladd Street; and Verde Park, a smaller park in the center of Greenbrier, at the intersection of Champlain Street and Verde Drive. Verde Park was the closest option for me, because it was located at the end of my street.

Going to the White Hen

On a June day in 1975, a time when kids rode their bikes freely around the neighborhood unescorted, my friend Doug and I headed to the White Hen Pantry. Located in a strip mall called Greenbrier Plaza, at the entrance into Greenbrier, it was an ideal destination for kids in the neighborhood because you didn't need to cross any busy streets to get there. It was our main source for candy, and they had a broad selection. If we didn't find what we wanted at White Hen, we went to North-gate Pharmacy in the same strip mall.

Today, I was on a mission. Over the last several years I had started to collect "Wacky Packs," and I heard that White Hen had them. Wacky Packs were trading cards, only each card was a sticker with product spoofs on it. For example, there was "Skimpy Crummy Beanut Putter" instead of Skippy Peanut Butter and "Cap'n Crumb...tastes cruddy even in milk" instead of Cap'n Crunch cereal. The artwork on the cards was top-notch, which added to the appeal. To a seven- or eight-year-old, this was humor at its best. They were packaged just like baseball cards, and came with a stick of bubble gum. They sold out pretty quickly, so they were a hot item when they were in stock. Doug didn't collect Wacky Packs, but he loved Hostess Suzy Qs, so he was more than happy to accompany me to the White Hen. While I waited in my room for Doug to arrive, I looked over my Wacky Pack collection, which I kept in a shoebox.

Me, in my Cap'n Crumb Wacky Pack T-shirt.

Although Doug and I were close friends, we were different in many ways. Doug was clean-cut and neat. He always kept his room clean. His hair was always neatly cut and was pretty much the same year-round. He didn't watch too much TV and was even tempered. I was a little more free spirited. My clothes were always clean (when I left the house), but often less orderly than Doug's. My hair was almost never orderly, for two reasons: First, Grandpa Hinesley always cut my hair—from my first haircut until I went off to college. (For this reason, I tried to keep haircuts to a minimum.) Second, during the 1970s, just about everyone in the United States had bad hair, thereby making it easy for me to slip through the cracks.

Frisky began barking downstairs, so Doug must have arrived. He waited patiently for me out front.

"I'll be right there, I just need to grab my bike," I yelled, on my way to the garage. "Mom, Doug and I are going to White Hen!" I shouted, attempting to duck into the garage before any negative response came.

"Be back in time for dinner!" Mom hollered from downstairs.

I opened the garage door, and I saw my bike leaning against the far wall. It was a Schwinn Stingray, a hand-me-down from Scott after Steve and Scott received brand new Schwinn three-speeds. I was grateful to have it, and even though it was an older bike, was still pretty cool. It had green tires, which were great for making skid marks on the sidewalk.

"How's it going?" Doug asked as I led my bike out of the garage.

"Pretty good. What do you think you'll get from White Hen?" I asked.

"I don't know—I wanna look around, see what they got."

"OK, let's go!"

I sped off down the driveway and into the street. Doug and I reached coasting speed as Champlain Street curved to the left. From there the street sloped downward, so you could see a good distance down the street. About two hundred yards down, I could make out a group of kids playing touch football. I knew a number of kids in that area—Tom Dobleske, Jim Kluka, Scott Dittmer, Mike Stuertz, and Rob Wall. It was most likely those guys, and maybe some older kids I knew around the neighborhood. As we got closer, Doug and I rode up onto the sidewalk, so as not to interrupt their game. Sure enough, it was Dobleske, Kluka, and the rest. We waved and shouted that we were headed to White Hen. As we came to the end of Champlain Street, we checked Alleghany Drive for cars, then crossed the street.

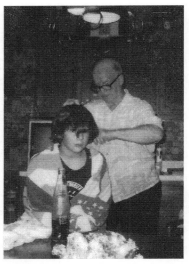

Grandpa Hinesley cutting my hair during the summer of 1975.

Across the street stood two buildings from the Greenbrier Apartments. We rode our bikes between the two buildings toward the back parking lot. A tall fence stood on the border of the Greenbrier Apartments parking lot and the rear of the Greenbrier Plaza strip mall. A large gap in the fence made a nice shortcut to get to White Hen. We walked our bikes through the gap and got back on to ride to the front of the building. The strip mall itself was shaped like a box, except for the White Hen portion of the building. White Hen jutted out from the rest of the building in a half-circle of tall glass windows. This was ideal for a kid biking to the store, because you could park your bike right outside the store and keep an eye on it while you were inside.

We parked our bikes and went inside. Like all convenience stores, the White Hen had a number of aisles for food and other goods—but we were focused only on the candy. The candy racks were connected along the service counter, which stood in the middle of the store like an island surrounded by a candy covered coastline. I scanned the White Hen's vast selection of candy for the Wacky Packs box. My eyes skimmed over the Paydays, Zero bars, Oh Henry! bars, Bounty bars, Almond Joy and Mounds bars, 100,000 dollar bars, and Chunky bars. It was neverending. My eyes lingered on the long shape and red wrapper of the Marathon bar, which I loved—it was an eight-inch bar of braided, chocolate-covered, caramel goodness. However, I was on a mission, and couldn't let myself get distracted.

The chocolate bar offering changed often as manufacturers tested out different products, and it was tempting to see if there was anything new. There was also a large quantity of boxed candies, like Milk Duds, Sno-Caps, Good & Plenty, Lemonheads, Atomic Fireballs, Junior Mints, Dots, Goobers, and Raisinettes. I continued to scan the racks. Next to the boxed candies were the two-packs of cake products like Hostess Twinkies and Ho Hos. Beyond those were the Topps sports trading cards.

The Wacky Packs weren't with the sports trading cards either! My heart began to sink. I was just about to ask the man behind the counter if they had any when I noticed a box on the countertop that was slightly obscured from view by a jar of Dubble Bubble Gum. There, to my relief, was a half-full box of Wacky Packs! I bought four packs, and also a bag of Gold Rush bubble gum. Gold Rush was little nuggets of yellow gum that came in a cloth pouch tied with a string. The gum itself was barely a mouthful, but the nuggets tasted good and looked cool, and the pouch was a neat touch. I learned from an early age that it's all about the presentation.

Once I bought my Wacky Packs I started getting antsy, and wanted to leave the store as quickly as possible so I could check out my newly acquired cards. Doug was ready to go, so we cheerfully left White Hen with our loot and sped back to my house. As we biked up to my house, I noticed Grandpa Hinesley's brown Buick sitting in our driveway.

"Isn't that your Grandpa's car?" Doug asked.

"Yeah, they must be having dinner with us tonight."

It wasn't unusual for my grandparents to visit us on the weekends and play cards, so I wasn't surprised to see their car.

We parked our bikes on the sidewalk and sat down in my front yard. Doug started in on his Suzy Qs, while I tore open the Wacky Packs. There weren't many cards in a package, so if you got doubles you always felt gypped. Soon my mouth was packed with a good-sized wad of gum.

I was admiring some of the stickers I got when Doug asked, "You're playing in the softball championship tomorrow, aren't you?"

"Yeah, are you coming for hot dogs and ice cream after the game?" I mumbled, as best I could with a mouthful of gum.

"I don't know, I think we are." Doug answered.

Just then, Mom's voice rang out into the evening air, "Steve, Scott, Tom—dinner!"

"Well, I guess that means I have to go," I said, as I gathered up my Wacky Packs. I discarded my wad of gum in the empty wrapper. "Thanks for going to White Hen with me," I added, as Doug got on his bike.

"No problem. Good luck tomorrow!" he said, as he rode away.

I hadn't thought about the big game much until Doug mentioned it. It still seemed like a long time away. Steve was right behind me when I walked in the door—he had been at his friend Rob's house across the street when Mom called us.

"Go wash your hands," Mom bellowed as we entered the house.

As I washed my hands, Scott came bursting in covered in dirt, from playing catch with Dad. Scott, of course, was pumped up for championship game.

Greenbrier's Big Game

Saturday afternoon was the 1975 championship game for the Greenbrier Boys' Softball League. The league was organized in 1967 by the Greenbrier Civic Association. The first couple of seasons were only roughly organized. Greenbrier boys between the ages of six and twelve were eligible to play. In order to give the league parity, each team received an equal distribution of players from each age group.

The original teams wore hand-dyed T-shirts as uniforms, and brothers could play for different teams. Steve and Scott played for different teams in 1969, and Scott's team won first place. In following years, brothers played for the same team. Soon, all the teams had standardized T-shirts, with different team colors. The front of the shirt had the Greenbrier Boys' Softball icon printed on the front, along with the season's year in the center of the ball. Each team had its own sponsor, so a logo or sponsor name was printed on the back of the shirt.

In 1970, the local paper began publishing the results of the game. In the early years, the top three teams received a felt patch. From 1971 on, there were organized team photos, mostly in black and white. By 1975, teams received trophies for first place. There was even an organized all-star game, with trophies for the all-star players, as well. The end of the season brought a championship game between the "American League" and the "National League," along with the trophy ceremony, followed by a cookout and ice cream party.

The 1975 season was a special season. Unknown to anyone at the time, Greenbrier Boys' Softball had peaked. In the seasons that followed, interest and participation dwindled down. Although the end-of-season celebration continued for several years, its size diminished, along with the number of eligible players in the neighborhood. Soon only a few teams remained, and by the late 1980s, the league faded away.

1975 was Scott's last season of eligibility. He had become a powerhouse for hitting home runs, averaging four per game and gaining a reputation among the teams in the league. Not to detract from his glory, but hitting a home run was relatively easy, because there weren't any walls to stop a ball. If any ball got past an outfielder, it was a guaranteed home run, as long as you weren't slow running the bases. Dad coached the team with one of the other dads, Mr. Novesel. By 1975, Dad had been coaching for four years. He could really teach kids how to catch. The way to win was to reduce the number of errors to a minimum. Steve helped out as an assistant coach. It was my second season, and I was becoming a decent player. This year our team was the Blacks, and we were sponsored by Kunkel Realtors.

Our team had dominated that season, going 13 and 0 and ending the season as "American League" champs. After winning a game, we usually went to the local pizza joint—Barnaby's—for a victory celebration. Located in Greenbrier Plaza close to White Hen, Barnaby's was a sponsor for one of the softball teams. Despite trouncing the Barnaby's team that season, they still let us into the restaurant. We were grateful. In addition to the good food, we could watch the pizza being made in the kitchen.

As the big game approached, we practiced during the week. We had to be ready, knowing we were going to be without a couple of players who were on vacation, including our first baseman. There were ten players per side, which included the extra position of short center field. During practice, Dad sent me out into short center field. We had been working on catching all season, and Dad wanted to test my skills to make sure I was ready. He hit a long hard drive out to me, and I made a fantastic jumping catch. All in all, the practice went well. We were all looking forward to the game on Saturday.

Scott at bat during the 1975 Greenbrier softball season.

Living Dangerously

After washing my hands, I hurried downstairs to see what there was to eat. Mom was outside in the backyard grilling hamburgers. Grandma and Grandpa Hinesley were out back relaxing on the porch. Grandma Hinesley sipped a glass of wine as I joined them. I gave them both a hug. Frisky was running around the back yard, excited by Grandpa Hinesley feeding him dog biscuits. Once the burgers were done, we moved to the long redwood-stained picnic table. It was always a challenge to get seated properly because of the long detached benches that went with the table. Any time someone needed to get up, it required a team effort to let them out. The table was covered with a plastic table-cloth, held on by white clasps in the shape of a letter G. On the table were baskets of buns potato chips, and burger toppings.. I took a bun and some chips. Mom passed burgers, and I took a cheeseburger while Mom poured me a glass of 7 Up ("The Uncola"). I was in heaven. After the meal, Grandpa Hinesley and I challenged Steve and Scott in a game of Jarts.

Jarts was similar to horseshoes, with two plastic rings set about twenty-five feet apart. You tossed the Jart underhand, into the rings. The Jarts themselves were twelve-inch darts with dull but weighted metal tips. It had three plastic wings that slid to the back of the Jart on its descent, so it looked something like a rocket. Each player got two throws—a hit in the ring got you three points, and getting closest to the ring earned one point. The winner was the first team to reach twenty-one points.

Jarts, also known as lawn darts, were banned in 1988, due to the potential danger of getting hit with one. According to the Consumer Product Safety Commission, three children died from injuries resulting from Lawn Darts. Around the time the ban took effect the U.S. population was about 250 million people, I guess you can never be too careful. In 1975, however, Grandpa Hinesley and I played Jarts, and we may have lost the game, but at least we escaped with our lives.

The mosquitoes began to bite, so we all decided to go inside. As always, when we got together with my grandparents, we ended up playing cards. Although sometimes we played poker, we almost always played pinochle. On this night, we played two tables of three-handed pinochle. After a while it was time for me to get ready for bed, so I said goodnight and went upstairs. After changing into my Chicago Bears pajamas and brushing my teeth, I got comfy under my NFL blanket while Scott turned off the light. The radio played David Essex's "Rock On." We waited for Boogie Check, and fell asleep.

I started playing Jarts at a young age. I was a dare-devil from the start.

Saturday Morning Cartoons

I woke up the next morning and made my way downstairs to the family room (a.k.a. our playroom). The steps and floor were covered with thick, red shag carpeting. Dad had divided the room into two rooms, half for us and half for his home office. The wall that divided the two rooms had a hole in it, where the TV sat inside a cabinet. That way, if Dad was working, he could reverse the TV so it faced his office.

Saturday morning was one of my favorite TV times. In the days before cable, a kid would live or die by the Saturday morning schedule. Each season you hoped the networks didn't screw up and eliminate your favorite shows. The Saturday morning cartoon schedule also got a great deal of preview coverage at the beginning of each season, the same way primetime TV did. Each season we perused the TV guide to see what new shows were coming out. Much like candy manufacturers tested out new candies on the market, the TV networks tested out new cartoons or kids' shows. Steve was already old enough not to care as much about the cartoons, but Scott watched some cartoons with me. The one show we never missed was *Bugs Bunny*, which was on early, at 7:30. Then came *Hong Kong Phooey*, a Hanna-Barbera cartoon in which a janitor turned into a kung-fu master crime fighter when trouble arose. Although the character was pretty weird, Scatman Crothers did his voice, which made him sound cool and likeable. The show had a catchy tune for its introduction, which roped me in to watch it. Of course, there wasn't really anything else worth watching at eight o'clock in the morning.

Hanna-Barbera cartoons dominated the cartoon market during the 1960s and 70s. In addition to Saturday mornings, Hanna-Barbera had done some primetime cartoons as well, most notably *The Flintstones*. Shows that ran during the late 1950s and the 60s went into syndication and could be seen on stations like WGN and WFLD in the after-school timeslot. Even though they were reruns in syndication, these shows became part of a kid's everyday life, because you only had a small number of stations from which to choose. There were comedies like *Huckleberry Hound, Quick Draw McGraw, Yogi Bear, Magilla Gorilla, The Jetsons, The Flintstones,* and *Wacky Races*. Hanna-Barbera made some action shows, too, such as Space Ghost and Jonny Quest. Saturday mornings was where Hanna-Barbera really dominated in 1975, with shows like *Hong Kong Phooey, Speed Buggy, Super Friends,* and *Scooby Doo, Where are you?*, as well as various spin-offs of their syndicated shows.

There were some weird shows from Sid and Marty Krofft that seemed LSD-induced. In 1975, it was *Sigmund and the Sea Monsters* and *Land of the Lost*. Before that there were shows like *H.R. Pufnstuf.* "Pufnstuff" says it all. I might watch one of those shows on any given Saturday, just because they were so weird. But who needed that when you had cartoons?

Hong Kong Phooey was on ABC, and after the show ended, I was treated to some musical education in one of the most influential cartoons on Saturday mornings: *Schoolhouse Rock! Schoolhouse Rock!* cartoons featured little educational topics set to music. The music and lyrics were very catchy—you couldn't forget them. Reciting the preamble to the U.S. Constitution is a piece of cake thanks to *Schoolhouse Rock!* The cartoons ran between the morning shows on ABC. The main subjects tackled by *Schoolhouse Rock!* during the early 1970s were grammar, social studies, science, and math. So I watched, "I'm Just a Bill," (which dealt with how a bill becomes a law) just before going up to the kitchen for a bowl of Super Sugar Crisp Cereal. I needed my strength for the big game.

Greenbrier Boys' Softball Championship IX

The rest of the day before the game went by pretty quickly. It wasn't long before I was looking for my "75 Blacks" team T-shirt. Before I knew it, we were loading our equipment into the trunk of our blue 1972 Pontiac Catalina. We owned the set of bases, which we kept in an old milk box from when we used to get our milk delivered. We had to go a little early to help set up the field. Normally, Greenbrier softball games had something of an informal feel to them, but the championship game was different. For us kids, it seemed like jumping to the big leagues. The foul lines were chalked, and an announcer read off the players' names on the line-up.

We were facing "The Yellows," sponsored by American Realty. They too had had a good season, taking the "National League" by storm, with a record of twelve wins and one loss. We were pretty confident going into the game, because we were the team that had handed them their loss. The Yellows started to arrive and warm up for the game. Each team watched the other as we warmed up, trying to size up the other players.

Coach Novosel and Dad got the team together to go over the line-up and positions. We were a couple players short, and they happened to be older players. For this reason, Pete Fahner (another eight-year-old) and I were placed in the outfield. Normally Pete played second base—that way, if a ball got through, the right fielder could cover. Outside of shortstop and first base, the outfielders played a bigger role than the infielders, because if a ball got past an outfielder, it could keep on going. Also, an older outfielder could throw the ball farther, thus keeping hits to the outfield to one or two bases. If we gave up some runs because our outfield was weaker than normal, we always had Scott and his home runs to keep us in the game.

Before the game started, we lined up on the foul line closest to our bench and recited the Pledge of Allegiance.

"...One nation, under God, indivisible, with liberty and justice for all. Play ball!"

The Yellows were up first, and we took the field. I was out in center field. Normally I'd have played short center. The first couple of innings were close, but The Yellows were winning the game, something like 7 to 3. They began to employ a special tactic to defeat Scott's home run hitting, as well. They flooded the outfield with players, except for the pitcher and short stop. The idea was to limit Scott's hitting to one or two bases, and then play the rest of the team normally. The chances of keeping a rally going were slim, because the two older players were absent from our team. Then came the sixth inning. A couple of dropped balls at first base gave The Yellows some important base runners.

The "Mighty Blacks" lining up for the Pledge of Allegiance (I'm third from the left with the orange hat, while Scott is third from the right). Standing behind the team on the left are Dad (in red) and Steve (in the green stripes). Coach Novosel is to the right of Steve.

Then it happened. A long fly ball shot out to center field. I felt good; it was just like the ball Dad had hit to me during practice. I aggressively went to the ball, but I misjudged it slightly. I jumped up, and I could feel it hit my hands. The ball slipped through my fingers, and bounced behind me. I spun around as fast as I could to get it. I threw it with all my might toward Scott, who was playing shortstop and who had

The 1975 Championship game drew kids from all over the neighborhood to watch the game. The crowd watches Scott at bat.

come out to be the cut-off man. I wasn't able to get it to him on a fly, but rather on a couple of bounces. By the time Scott got the ball into the infield, the Yellow player had crossed home plate. It was here the Mighty '75 Blacks fell apart. Flustered by the errors at first base, followed by my missed catch, many of the players began to break down. Scott attempted to rally the troops, but the team wasn't able to regain composure. We lost the championship game, 20 to 4.

The lesson Scott and I took from that game was never to go into a game overconfident, regardless of how good your team might be. As we pondered our newly found wisdom, we made our way down to the tennis courts behind the school to get a hot dog and some ice cream. We mingled with the kids in the neighborhood who had watched the game. I wasn't in much of a mood to talk, but I remained a good sport nonetheless. A little humility can be a good thing. After the hot dogs and ice cream, they handed out the trophies. Scott walked away with two trophies: one for the all-star game, and the other for The Blacks being the "American League" champs. I too walked away with a trophy, so the day wasn't a total bust. It was also the last season Dad ever coached, making it the last time he coached one of my teams.

The Fourth of July in Greenbrier

On the night of the 3rd of July, in addition to enjoying the summer festivals and fireworks, the kids in Greenbrier got their bikes ready to compete in the Greenbrier

Fourth of July Bike Parade, which started in 1963. At the time, only about one-third of the subdivision was completed, and it was the only time the route passed in front of our house. Later, parades began at Verde Park and wound their way up to Greenbrier School. Following the parade was the contest for best costume and best-decorated bike. As with every holiday, one Fourth of July in particular sticks out in my mind—the Fourth of July of 1973.

That year, Dad was working on the contest committee and had all the prizes set aside. I was pumped because I saw among the prizes the one for my age bracket. It was an outdoor adventure set that came with a trail belt, canteen, pup tent, backpack, axe, shovel, flashlight, and compass. The set was made of a colorful, soft but durable plastic material. It may not sound like much now, but to me it seemed like the greatest prize ever! I was determined to win it. The problem was, I had the worst bike possible, and my chances seemed slim.

The bike I had at the time was a giant tricycle, which of course by definition wasn't a bike at all, but it was what I had to work with. I did have one thing going for me, though—I was surrounded by earlier parade veterans and a crafty mom. The parade was always held in the morning of the Fourth of July, so the night before the parade my brothers and I decorated our bikes in the garage with red, white, and blue crepe paper and anything else we could get our hands on. Steve worked diligently on his bike, though many kids his age no longer competed. He still loved to decorate his bike, and didn't want to break with tradition, especially after having made the front page of the newspaper the previous year. Perhaps he was hoping that lightning would strike twice. Meanwhile, Scott was getting tired of working on his bike, and wanted to take a break to play some darts.

Playing darts in the garage was exciting. First of all, these were the days before plastic-tipped darts, so we used regular metal-tipped ones. Second, put a dart in any one of our hands, and you were asking for trouble. Just one fight, and look out! Scott stuck me a couple times over the years. If I remember correctly, I got him once in the lower leg after the dart deflected off the metal garbage can lid he was using as a shield. But that kind of thing didn't happen too often. What really made the games exciting were the various things you might hit if you missed the dartboard. The dartboard hung below shelves that

Steve and Scott the day of the 1972 Greenbrier bike parade.

contained cans of spray paint, paint thinner, spray-on adhesive, and various other toxic goodies. Everything seemed to come in an aerosol can at the time.

The dartboard we played with had a standard dartboard on one side and a baseball game on the other. We weren't the best dart players, and instead of even trying to play a regular game of darts, we flipped the board over and played base-ball. Scott started the game, and it wasn't long before a stray dart hit a can and a loud hissing sound filled the garage. We ducked for cover, hoping the can wouldn't explode. The can spun around as the air hissed, sputtering out red paint. When the hissing died down, it seemed safe to come out and check out the damage. The can lay in a pool of red paint, with the blue dart sticking out of it.

Looking down at the mess, Steve muttered, "I was going to use that paint!"

Scott threw the can away, and we went back to working on the task at hand—finishing our bikes—hoping Dad wouldn't come out and find yet another one of his spray paint cans destroyed.

While I worked on my bike, Mom was busy making my costume. I was going to be Uncle Sam, complete with top hat, white beard, blue vest, and a large red paper bow tie, all topped off with stylish 1970s plaid pants. If I wasn't a shoo-in for this contest, nobody was. (In truth, I looked more like a patriotic Cat in the Hat than I did Uncle Sam).

Scott and I woke up early and made our way downstairs for a quick break-fast before heading down to the park. Steve was already up and making some final touch-ups to his bike. Mom helped me get into my costume. It had rained the night before, so there were puddles on the ground. The worst possible thing would be if it rained during the parade, as crepe paper doesn't hold up well to water. The bike parade started early at 8:00 a.m., to allow everyone to make it to the local Fourth of July parade held by the village after the bike parade ended.

As I made my way toward the park, I noticed a group of kids already lining up with their bikes. I pedaled steadily up to the line to secure my position in the parade. Once situated, I waited with the others for the signal to start our journey toward the school. A crowd began to gather along Verde Drive. The more kids that came, the longer the odds against my winning the bike decoration contest. I sat nervously in place, hoping I'd even

Steve adds some final touches to his bike, July 4, 1973.

have a chance at obtaining the outdoor adventure set. Once everybody was in place, we got the go-ahead to start the parade. A swarm of bikes glided down Verde Drive toward the school in a display of patriotic splendor. I felt like a circus clown driving my gigantic tricycle. My costume didn't help, as the enormous paper bow tie and top hat doubled my wind resistance. Had the wind been blowing the other way, I probably could have caught the wind and sailed down the street to the school.

The judgment round.

At the school, we continued to the rear where the tennis courts stood for the judging of the bicycles. We were divided according to age and instructed to ride counterclockwise around the tennis courts. I was in the second-youngest category, which came before Scott's and Steve's groups. In Steve's category, no one else had really decorated their bike, so Steve was guaranteed to win. My age group wasn't so clear-cut. After we rode our bikes around for judging, we each got a little cup of ice cream with a wooden spoon, which I devoured while I waited anxiously for the judges' decision.

Dad's job as one of the organizers of the parade was to announce the results. As he came to my age group and read the winner's name, I assumed he misspoke. But he hadn't—I lost. The cool outdoor adventure set would go to some other lucky kid. Steve and Scott fared better than I did and won their respective categories (after which Dad reminded the audience that he played no role in the judging process). "Well, that's apparent," I thought! Just as I thought it was all over, Dad announced the winner of the costume contest—me! All these years later I couldn't tell you what I won that day, only what didn't win.

The Suburban Parents

From early on, my parents were active in the community. They helped the Greenbrier Civic Association with various small activities, like distributing directories or "no soliciting" stickers. Dad coached in the Greenbrier Softball League for a number of years, while Mom was active in the PTA. My parents befriended a number of couples in Greenbrier, with whom they played tennis and had cocktails. In the early 1970s they began a potluck group, where they met once a month and rotated hosting duties. When it was my parents' turn, they orchestrated a "Vegas night" and set up a roulette wheel, craps tables, and blackjack.

While my parents socialized downstairs, we "hid" upstairs. Dad set up the TV in their bedroom to keep us out of their way. If things became desperate, one of us ventured downstairs to find a bottle of Coca-Cola. This was thrilling to me, because I really didn't want to be seen or heard (mainly because I was already dressed in my pajamas). There were a number of times I drew the short straw and had to go. I think my brothers believed I was the least likely to get in trouble—but then, if someone did get in trouble, what better person than me? There was no time to dillydally. With my brothers' prompting, I had to get a move on.

I turned the handle all the way and held it, listening with my ear to the door for any sound of movement on the other side. When I was sure the coast was clear, I swung the door open and began my mission for the bottles of soda. As soon as I entered the hallway, I detected the "party" smell of scotch and wine, mixed with the scents of perfume the women wore. People got dressed up for these parties, which to me added an air of seriousness. Most of the games and people were in the downstairs family room or the living room/dining room. The upstairs hallway was dark as I had hoped, but there was a problem. Someone was in the upstairs bathroom. I had to think quickly. If the occupant had just entered, I might have time to get down the stairs, but I would have to be quick. If I was too hasty, I might make too much noise and be seen. I decided to duck into Steve's room, which was across the hall at an angle from the bathroom. That way, I would be able to see the bathroom light as soon as the door opened, but I would remain unseen.

I waited in darkness. Soon I heard the toilet flush and knew it wouldn't be much longer. The bathroom light slipped under Steve's door as I expected, and I heard the occupant exit the bathroom. I waited long enough for them to get down the steps and back to the party before left the safety of Steve's room. I crept to the top of the stairs, which was cast in a large shadow that provided some cover. I knew that when I reached the bottom of the stairs I would have to have a plan. I decided that a brisk but quiet walk to the hallway by the kitchen was my best bet. I hoped everyone was too absorbed in their Vegas game to look up.

Eyes straight ahead, I tiptoed down the stairs. As I reached the bottom, I made my break, moving at a quick pace across the floor. I rolled on my feet as I walked, heel to toe, to keep any sound to a minimum. As I reached the hallway, I heard voices in the kitchen and leaned into the closet slightly. It was Mom and another woman getting drinks. I waited quietly for them to leave, hoping no one else came for a refill. As they left, I made a beeline for the drinks. I nabbed the bottle opener and opened two bottles. I set the bottle caps on the counter, grabbed the bottles, and made for the hallway closet for cover until I could get back up the stairs undetected. Just then, a male guest went up the stairs to the bathroom. I could see the bathroom light reflected on the opposite wall, and it slowly disappeared as the door closed. It was now or never. Briskly, I walked to the stairs, made it past the bathroom, and darted into Mom and Dad's room. I did it! *Frankenstein Meets the Wolf Man* was on TV the WGN late-night feature. We were just divvying up the sodas when Mom peeked into the room.

"Do you boys need anything?"

We all shook our heads, "No," and returned to our movie.

Other times, families in Greenbrier got together for cookouts and other outdoor activities. I knew some families better than others because of activities like Indian Guides or softball. One of the Greenbrier couples my parents befriended was the Careys. The Careys moved into Greenbrier sometime in the late 1960s, and had three boys. Jackie Carey was Scott's age, Steve Carey was a year older than me, and Brian Carey was my age. Scott became good friends with Jackie Carey, while I was close friends with Brian. The Careys were very friendly, and the two families got along well.

As our family grew closer to the Careys, we saw a lot more of each other. My parents played tennis with Mr. and Mrs. Carey (the country was going through a tennis craze). Brian and I played together, and had sleepovers on a regular basis. The two families even spent spring break together at a resort in Rockton, Illinois, called Wagon Wheel, which even included an incident with drunken streakers. Those were the days. I didn't actually see the streakers, as they rambled down the resort corridor late at night, but I was awakened by the noise. Fortunately I was spared a face-to-face meeting, and as they say, it's never centerfolds who do the streaking, so perhaps I didn't miss much. In time, it was our close relationship with the Careys that landed me my first (and only) television appearance.

The Chicago TV Generation

Over the years, Chicago had a strong tradition of local children's television programming. For a kid like me, Chicagoland television had become part of everyday life. Every morning before school, most kids tuned into *Ray Rayner and His Friends* and *Garfield Goose and Friends*. After school, many kids watched Bill Jackson's *Gigglesnort Hotel* (or *BJ and the Dirty Dragon Show,* depending on the year.) Regardless if school was in session or not, at lunchtime almost everybody watched *Bozo's Circus*.

Bozo's Circus featured a ringmaster, clowns, and marching band, complete with a circus-style act in which the audience participated. The star of the show was

Bozo the Clown, portrayed by Bob Bell. Some people are wary of clowns, but that was hardly the case with Bozo. With a blue clown suit and white gloves, white frilly collar and buttons, and giant clown shoes, Bozo's defining feature was his hair, bald on top and sticking out like red cotton candy along the sides. His makeup was simple, with a large red mouth and black-lined highlights on his white face. It gave him a friendly appearance. Of course, he never appeared with the big red clown nose.

Bozo's disarming appearance and catchy name, not to mention Bob Bell's humorous performances, made *Bozo's Circus* a very popular show—so popular, in fact, that it was rumored to be almost impossible to get tickets. The waiting list was supposedly so long that the wait time extended several years. There were stories of expectant mothers signing up on waiting lists so that when their babies were old enough to enjoy the show, they might be eligible for tickets. By some fluke in the 1960s, Grandma Hinesley received tickets from a friend, and Steve and Scott saw the show live from the front row. By the time I was old enough to enjoy the show, I had very little hope of lightning striking twice, but it did. Again, due to a freak occurrence, the Careys ended up with eight tickets. Mom, Scott, and I joined Mrs. Carey, Jackie, Steve, and Brian Carey, as well as a friend of Steve's, to see Bozo's Circus live.

We drove to the studio in the Careys' station wagon. During the ride, we were all very excited about the prospect of being on TV and, most of all, the chance to be picked for the "Grand Prize Game." Sometime between leaving Greenbrier and arriving at the studio, Scott got so worked up he actually came down with hives. He was a good sport about it and toughed it out, but he looked like he had some exotic disease. Before too long we were in line to enter the studio. Mom and Mrs. Carey seemed to be having a good time, despite having to manage six hyperactive kids.

As they opened the studio doors, we filed slowly into the studio. I was surprised by how small it seemed in person. We marched past Mr. Ned, the ringmaster, who was decked out in his bright red jacket with tails and black top hat. The audience sat in bleachers. We sat in awe as the program got underway—it was surreal to actually be a part of *Bozo's Circus*! The big moment that every kid waited for was approaching—the Grand Prize Game.

If you've never watched *Bozo's Circus*, the Grand Prize Game was the focal point of the show. The game itself was called Bozo Buckets, which consisted of six buckets lined up in a row about six inches apart. The object of the game was to toss a ping-pong ball into each bucket. Before a player made his toss, Bozo or his pal, Cookie, displayed the great prizes the kid could win if he landed the ball in the bucket. The prizes grew progressively better until the sixth and final bucket, where they gave away a brand new Schwinn bicycle. In addition to the bicycle were silver dollars that were added each time the game was played. Like the lottery rolling over, the silver dollars would accumulate until someone won. Before the game began, Bozo picked a name from a bingo cage full of names of kids who had written into the show play from home. After a bucket was made, both the player in the studio and the lucky player at home won prizes.

The whole process of selecting the contestants was very exciting to a young kid. They picked two audience members—one boy and one girl—by using the "magic arrows." The magic arrows were two flashing white arrows superimposed in the center of the TV screen that pointed at each other, with enough space between them for an audience member. The arrows alternated flashing back and forth, while the cameraman quickly panned randomly over the audience. The selection was usually pretty quick; if not, you were wishing you'd taken some Dramamine. When the camera stopped, normally the head of an audience member was between the two arrows. Sometimes they'd land on an adult and have to restart the process.

The night before we went to the *Bozo Show*, I dreamed of being picked by the magic arrows. The crowd was cheering as I made my way down to make my tosses. Soon I was lined up for the sixth bucket. The pressure was intense as the drum roll began, with millions of kids watching me. Then I woke up. What a gyp! For me, the Grand Prize Game would remain a dream, because the magic arrows didn't fall on me. When I saw them carry out the Bozo Buckets, I realized for the first time that the buckets were attached to a board, and they looked a lot closer in person than on TV. I think I would have stood a decent chance, had I been selected.

The show went faster than I expected, and the next thing I knew, we were doing the "Grand March" out of the studio. I did walk away with a souvenir that day. They gave each of us a Bozo button, which I promptly lost somewhere in the abyss that was my room.

Indian Guides

When the Iron Curtain fell in early '90s, American cultural life began to take an unexpected turn. In a time when most Americans viewed Marxism and socialism as failed political systems, they let their guard down to extreme leftist political beliefs. It was then that something began to happen that wouldn't have been possible during the Cold War: political correctness and multiculturalism. Under the guise of multiculturalism, various interest groups began to gain political leverage, primarily through self-segregation. Such interest groups began to represent every race, nationality, gender, religion or sect, lifestyle, and sexual orientation. Suddenly, the

American people had to worry about the words they used when speaking or writing. Saying the "wrong" thing, telling the "wrong" joke, and possibly looking at someone in the "wrong" way could lose you your job. But who decided what was "wrong"? Companies began to fear litigation if an employee was offended. Christmas parties became "holiday parties" overnight. The great irony is that for years, America feared the "Godless communists," and suddenly, our country was becoming "Godless." Politically correct behavior and policies began to creep into everyday life and change American cultural institutions, for the sake of not running the risk of offending another culture, either current or past. One casualty of this cultural change was the YMCA's Indian Guides.

The Indian Guides began in the 1920s as a program designed to promote the bond between father and son, signified by the motto "Pals Forever". In Greenbrier there were other programs similar to Indian Guides, such as Cub Scouts, but Indian Guides provided the exotic factor of an Indian tribe, which added to a kid's imagination and made it more appealing. I later joined Cub Scouts when Dad became too busy to participate in Indian Guides, but it wasn't as enjoyable.

Because of the age difference between my older brothers and me, they were already in the program when I was born. This meant I was surrounded by Indian Guides for the first seven years of my life. First I observed my brothers going through the program, and, when I was old enough, I too joined the fun.

Our Indian Guide tribe was the Eagle tribe. The Eagle tribe belonged to the group of tribes in the northwest suburbs called the Michigan Nation. Typically, the Indian Guides program used established tribes and tribe names. The Eagle tribe name came from its original members. I'm not sure if the Eagle tribe was formed because Greenbrier didn't have an established tribe or because there wasn't room in existing tribes in the area. Regardless, Dad and my brothers were involved from the start. Our tribe met regularly once a month, but bigger events like campouts were held by the Michigan Nation.

Indian Guides didn't have a uniform per se, but rather a tribal Indian vest and headband. I remember that before I was old enough to be involved in Indian Guides, I would sneak down to Dad's home studio and try on the chief's headdress. We each had our own Indian Guides name, too—we were the Bears. Dad's Indian name was Walking Bear, Steve's name was Running Bear, Scott was Climbing Bear, and I was Little Bear.

There were various awards that little "braves" could earn, which added to your Indian appearance. One such item was a feather you could add to your headband.

Dad and me—"Pals Forever"

The feathers signified the number of years you were in the program. So, even though Scott and I were in the same tribe together, he had more feathers than I did because he was in the program longer. When a brave participated in an event, he received a patch commemorating that event. Each brave also had a necklace with beads and eagle claws. Eagle claws were earned in addition to patches for Nation events.

The Bear Family, posing for a picture in 1969.

Indian Guides held a number of events throughout the year, such as parades, popcorn sales, and Christmas tree sales. One popular event for the Eagle tribe was the Michigan Nation Kite Flying Contest. During my family's time with the tribe, the Eagle tribe built the biggest kite imaginable, which stood fifteen feet high and ten feet across at its widest point. The kite was the size of a car. It was made with long bamboo poles and a heavy black plastic tarp. It was amazing to watch this gigantic kite go up in the sky. The kite required rope instead of kite string to hold it up. It was truly something to behold. Although the kite contest was always a great deal of fun, the most popular events were the campouts.

We got ready for the spring campout as we always did, by packing our sleeping bags and pillows, along with some extra clothes. In the spring of 1973, Scott was still in Indian Guides, and he packed his things along with me. This was going to be a good campout. We always looked forward to the spring campout, for the campfire and the various games we would play. The nice thing about Camp Duncan was the fact that we slept in cabins. The cabins resembled army barracks, and sleeping in bunk beds was always an adventure.

As we arrived at Camp Duncan, the weather grew overcast. The campgrounds were muddy from the previous day's rain, and it looked like it might start to rain again at any moment. We unloaded our gear into our cabin as quickly as we could. Many of the other members of our tribe had also arrived.

"Hey, Brian, when did you guys get here?" I yelled over to Brian Carey as I entered the cabin.

"A little while ago."

"Is that top bunk taken?" I asked, pointing to the bunk where he'd placed his stuff.

"No, it's free. You can take it if you want," he replied, as Jackie and Scott entered.

"Come on, they're about to start the tug-of-war competition!" Jackie yelled out.

I tossed my stuff on the top bunk, and we all headed for the area where they held the tug-of-war contest—one of the highlights of our spring campouts. We had a good number of kids in our tribe, which gave us a bit of an advantage. That, and the fact that the boys in our tribe were all extremely competitive. This year's competition

Now that's a kite!

was going to be a bit of a challenge, however, as the previous day's rain had made the ground slightly muddy and soft. There before us was the long rope with loops tied at each end for the anchor man. Tied to the center of the rope was a white handkerchief. The tribes lined up to begin the competition. Soon we were battling against the other tribes. With each competition, I dug my feet into the muddy ground. After a short while I was covered in mud from slipping and falling. I never gave up, though. Scott, our anchor man, was also covered in mud. When all was said and done, the Eagle tribe won the day, but the celebration was short-lived, as we were all filthy and caked in mud. We went to get ourselves cleaned up.

After dinner and the bonfire, all of the braves were completely exhausted from the activities and games of the day. As we made our way back to our barracks, it began to rain. The cabin was cold and damp as I climbed up to my sleeping bag on top of the bunk. Soon it was lights out, and I snuggled down into my sleeping bag, trying to keep warm in the chilly night air. Shortly the steady sound of the rain hitting the roof of the cabin put me to sleep.

As the morning came I lay quietly in my bunk, still sleepy from the restless night of trying to keep warm. Other kids were gathering their things together and packing up before breakfast and the closing ceremony. I looked down to see Brian rolling up his sleeping bag, and decided I'd better do the same. Soon Scott came walking up to Brian and me.

"Hurry up! Dad wants you to get your stuff in the car!" he barked, like a drill sergeant.

"Grrrrr!" I growled back.

With my sleeping bag and dirty clothes in tow, I made my way across the half-mud, half-gravel grounds to our car. There stood our blue Catalina, covered in mud, with the trunk gaping open and Dad sorting the contents inside. I handed my stuff to Dad, who continued his methodical way of packing the trunk. I ran back to find Brian to join him on the way up to the main lodge for the big breakfast.

We entered the main lodge and were greeted with a hearty breakfast of scrambled eggs and sausage. Each of the tribes had a long table to itself. There was a lot of commotion in the large hall as breakfast went on. As we finished up our meals, one of the chiefs called out and thanked various people for their support and time. Then, much to our surprise, it was decided that as part of the closing ceremony, each tribe would sing their tribe song as loudly and proudly as they could. The chief said he wanted to see which tribe could sing the loudest. I figured we should have little trouble with Scott on our team, since he was loud all the time. However, Dad found himself under a little pressure because the Eagle tribe didn't have a tribe song, as our tribe wasn't a traditional YMCA tribe. Thinking fast on his

In addition to campouts, Indian Guides sponsored a number of activities.
Above is the Michigan Nation 1974 Christmas Party flyer, drawn by Dad

feet, Dad came up with an idea on the fly. While one of the tribes was struggling through their song, trying to remember the words, Dad got the Eagle braves together to tell us his idea. We would sing a tribe song to the tune of "Bingo" but instead of spelling BINGO we'd spell EAGLE. When our turn came, Dad stood up and began to lead us in song:

"The Michigan Nation has a tribe, and EAGLE is our name-o!"

After several verses of song, our tribe had nearly sung itself hoarse. We easily out-sang the other tribes, because we all knew the tune. I don't think the other tribes appreciated our efforts all that much, as it must have seemed to them like we took a shortcut, but you couldn't knock our enthusiasm.

Although the campouts were a lot of fun, most of the Indian Guides experience was going to the meetings, where we did crafts, listened to stories, ate treats, and spent time with our dads. It was a good experience. At the end of each meeting, the tribe recited our tribal prayer. I'm not sure if ours was an official YMCA prayer or not. It doesn't matter either way. The fathers stood behind their sons. Everyone outstretched their arms, which we slowly lowered as we came to the end of the prayer. Our prayer was recited to the tune of "Taps," and I believe it was originally a lullaby:

Day is done,

Gone the sun,

From the lake,

From the hills,

From the sky,

All is well, safely rest, God is nigh.

It's a prayer that is no longer heard in Greenbrier, except in the memories of those who sang it while there still were Indian Guides to sing it.

Last Days of Summer

Growing up in Greenbrier during the late 1960s and early 70s was best enjoyed during the summer months. The freedom we exercised as kids allowed us to experience the full range of childhood that Greenbrier could offer. As each summer came to a close, most of the kids of Greenbrier had enjoyed their fill of wandering the neighborhood, swimming at Frontier Pool, playing softball, hanging out with friends, playing games, exploring the nursery, and going to the White Hen.

When August reached its midpoint, a sense of dread began to fill every kid's mind. School was just around the corner, and the first verification of this inevitable truth was the classroom assignments we received in the mail. Depending on the year and on which teachers were teaching your grade, that letter could be a life-changing event. This was especially true at Greenbrier during the 1970s, when you could land in a multi-age class of two grades. At Greenbrier, there were first- and second-grade multi-age classes and fourth- and fifth-grade multi-age classes. If you were one of the lucky souls to be sent into a multi-age class, you were stuck with the same teacher for two consecutive years. I waited with bated breath in August of 1976 to find out if I was going to get off easy with a one-year sentence or have to do real hard time with a two-year stretch. I was caught off guard during our Sunday dinner. While engrossed in *Wild Kingdom*, as Marlin Perkins narrated from a safe distance while Jim Fowler wrangled an alligator in the Everglades, Mom said:

"Tom, your new class assignment came in the mail yesterday, it's over on the counter."

"Great, may I be excused?" I asked nervously.

"After you put your dishes in the sink, you may," she responded.

I picked up my dishes and brought them to the sink and then made a bee-line for the mail. There it was, underneath the Polk Brothers bill. I slowly opened the letter.

"Oh, no!" I thought, "I need to conference with someone about this."

"Mom, I'm going over to Doug's!" I yelled, as I bolted out the door.

Cutting through my neighbor's backyard, I ran as fast as I could to get to Doug's house. A moment later I rang his doorbell. Doug's mom answered the door. With one look at me, she turned and called for Doug. He came downstairs from his room and appeared at the door.

"Hey, do you feel like going to the park?" I asked.

"Sure," he said, as he turned to yell to his mom, "Mom! I'm going to the park!"

"Be back before dark!" was her response.

We made our way through a couple of backyards and were soon swinging at Verde Park.

"No way, you got him? I heard he's tough," said Doug, sympathetically.

"Tough isn't the word, I heard he's hit kids before with a yardstick."

"Well, at least I don't have him."

"What's worse is that I'm stuck with him for two years!" I said, resigned to the fate of my two-year sentence. "Let's go to my house."

We started walking down Champlain Street when I saw my brother Scott running around in front of my house. Scott and some of his friends, along with Steve and Bentley from across the street, were playing Kick the Can.

"Hey, can we play?" Doug and I asked.

"Yeah, go ahead and hide, Scott's it!" said Steve, a little out of breath from running.

Doug and I took off to find a hiding spot as Scott counted.

"All ye, all ye, all ye, all ye, all come free!" Scott yelled.

I waited quietly behind one of the evergreen bushes in our front yard until Scott was out of sight. I would have to make a quick break for it if I was going to be able to kick the can before he tagged me. It was getting dark, and I could tell the streetlight by our house had just turned on. Scott was nowhere to be seen, so I went for it. I ran as fast as I could to the can, which was some fifteen yards away in the circle of light from the streetlight. Out of the corner of my eye, I saw Scott barreling toward me. The can was a mere five feet away when Scott lunged to tag me. As I stretched my leg to kick the can, I lost my footing and slid with my right knee along the asphalt street. Although I was able to avoid the tag and kick the can, I ripped a hole in the knee of my pants.

"This is not my day," I said to myself.

Doug came running up.

"Tom, I've got to go, the street light is on. My family is going to my uncle's for the last week before school. Want to meet the morning of the first day of school and walk together?" he asked.

"Yeah, sure. I can't wait."

CHAPTER 5

Greenbrier School Days

My First Day

On September 5th, 1972, halfway across the world in Munich, Germany, members of the Israeli Olympic Team were taken hostage and ultimately killed by the Palestinian terrorist group Black September. While this was happening, I was getting ready for my first day of school. Blissfully ignorant of the sad events in Munich, I finished my breakfast and watched the beginning of *Romper Room*. As the clock ticked away, my days of freedom were coming to an end. As with the situation in Munich, I was equally ignorant of what the next twelve years would have in store for me. I was very excited at the prospect of starting school. Finally, I got to do what Steve and Scott were doing each day.

Mom came into the kitchen and helped me tie my shoes. Scott, who was sitting at the table with me, asked Mom if she would tie his shoes too. Mom looked at Scott with disappointment and tied his shoes. He

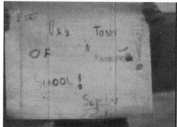

Scott holds up a sign indicating my first day of school.

could tie his own shoes, and she knew it. Ironically, I think it was this attitude that got Scott more dates in later years than Steve or I. Sometimes you just had to have the gall to ask, and Scott had it in spades.

I had a feeling this day was going to be a spectacle, because Mom broke out the 8-mm camera. She filmed Scott and me holding up a sign for my first day of school. It was a sunny but brisk day, so I put on my Cubs jacket, and then made my way to school with Scott and Mom. The first day of school was usually the only time that parents walked their kids to school. I met up with Doug and his mom and little sister along Verde Drive, which was littered with kids of all ages. The first day of school seemed different from any other day of the school year. All the kids were dressed in their new clothes, carrying their required materials: a pack of "number 2" pencils, a pink eraser, three-hole-punched loose-leaf lined paper, folders, a smock, and the ever-important box of tissues. We wouldn't use the smock or tissues for the first six months, but we had to have it the first day, without exception. Welcome to the world of conformity!

As we arrived on school grounds, Scott ran to the fourth-and fifth-grade entrance on the other side of the building. Meanwhile, Doug and I played for a short time on the cast-iron playground equipment. Teachers and parents stood around amid the chaos of that first day. Soon the first bell rang, and we were gathered together and lined up, single file, to enter the school at our assigned entrance. As I was marched into the school, it dawned on me that I was on my own.

After a couple hours of what seemed more like playtime than work, I emerged from the school as excited as when I first went in. Everyone had early dismissal, so Scott joined Mom and me as we walked home. I ran ahead and joined Doug.

"That wasn't too bad. I think school is going to be fun!" I chirped enthusiastically.

"Yeah!" said Doug, grinning from ear to ear.

It was all just wishful thinking.

Doug (right in white jacket) and I (left in Cubs jacket), along with many other Greenbrier kids, walking home after our first day of school.

Mr. Thomas Price, I Hereby Sentence You to a Term of Two Years

Every kid goes into the first day of kindergarten with the excitement and mystery inherent in starting school. It is a moment of achievement and feeling like you're growing up. I had that feeling. My parents built up my expectations, and my brothers seemed to enjoy school. In 1972, Steve was starting junior high school at the same time I went to kindergarten. It was an exciting time. For many students, the excitement of going to school wanes as time goes by. For me, I lost it in the fall of 1976, when I entered fourth grade and began my two-year sentence in the multi-age classroom of James Modec at Greenbrier Elementary School.

Awaiting my sentence.

The School

In the early days of the Greenbrier subdivision, the kids of Greenbrier went to Wilson School, which could be as far as a mile and a half away from some residents. To get to Wilson School, Greenbrier kids had to cross busy Palatine Road, and there weren't sidewalks to walk on. It was not an ideal location. The Greenbrier Civic Association requested that the district provide bus service for the kids because of the safety issue of crossing Palatine Road. They were denied. After all, these were still the days of rugged individualism, when "a little hardship built character."

More than two years after the first houses were built in the Greenbrier subdivision; Greenbrier Elementary School opened its doors for the 1964-65 school year. Due to budgetary concerns, the school was built in two stages. The first part of the school, built in 1964, consisted of two stories with twelve classrooms. The second part was to be added at a later date, as the community grew. It became apparent during the first months of the 1965-66 school year that enrollment was going to exceed expectations. That was the same year Steve entered kindergarten. Arlington Heights School District 25 was feeling the pressure of the growing number of new students. Some classes at Greenbrier that year were doing double shifts, causing many Greenbrier parents to complain. In December of 1965, the school board approved the second single-level, six-classroom addition. The final layout for Greenbrier School was completed in 1966, and it was this building that I entered for the first time as a student in September 1972.

Greenbrier School wasn't the only area of expansion in our school district. Between 1960 and 1972, the population of Arlington Heights ballooned by more than 43,000 additional residents. District 25 built ten new schools and additions to five existing schools to meet the need of the growing student population. In the 1969-70 school year, the school district peaked at about 10,000 students. It wasn't unusual for a classroom to have more than thirty kids, and the district was struggling to meet the needs of its students.

Principle Alan Swanson, with a mixture of students sitting at the front entrance of Greenbrier school during the 1977-78 school year (this photo was taken from the first ever Greenbrier school year-

A Hard Act to Follow

When I first attended school, I was excited and happy to be there. There were other kids in my kindergarten class I already knew: Doug Brooks and Brian Carey. I got to know one friend of mine, Tom Berg, because Scott was friends with his older brother, Bob. Sometimes it was good to have older brothers. For one thing, I was less intimidated by older kids because odds were I had a brother who was older than they were. A "family reputation" with the school staff was often a mixed bag of blessing and curse.

When following in the footsteps of my brothers, there were times I had to deal with their reputations (sometimes positive, sometimes negative). As the oldest, Steve was a hard act to follow. He was a very conscientious student. He was smart, and he stayed out of trouble. If trouble came to him, he would disappear like he did at home. Because he was born in November, Steve entered kindergarten at the age of four. This meant he was young for his grade. Because most of his friends were in the year behind him, Mom and Dad decided to hold him back in fifth grade, meaning he got to enjoy an extra year of school at Greenbrier. Lucky him! He always received good grades and was well behaved. To teachers he must have seemed like an angel. His reputation might have helped me in school if it weren't for two things: the six years between our ages, and Scott.

Scott's reputation in school was a little different from Steve's. Scott had the benefit of following Steve, and teachers had high expectations. Like Steve, Scott was smart. He was also a fairly conscientious student. What made Scott really different was his mouth. He was a firm believer in the First Amendment and never let an opportunity to share his opinion go by, whether someone wanted it or not. As I entered school, most of Steve's teachers had

Steve's kindergarten class photo from the 1965-66 school year (Steve is the first child on the top row, next to the teacher).

moved on, but Scott's hadn't. I'm sure I was a marked man before the first words ever left my mouth. Although I had nothing on Scott's ability to smart off, it didn't help matters that I too didn't know when to keep quiet.

The Multi-Age Classroom

When Steve and Scott attended Greenbrier School, it was overflowing with kids. The classes were overcrowded, so the school district was always looking for new and creative ways to make the best use of their classrooms and cut back on staff. As the 1970s began, new teaching concepts were being tested. One such concept was the multi-age classroom. Steve and Scott escaped the multi-age classroom experiment, whereas my elementary school experience was dominated by it. Four of my six years in elementary school were spent in a multi-age classroom. Only in kindergarten and third grade was I able to enjoy a normal classroom setting.

The multi-age classroom, as the name implied, combined students of more than one age and grade. Typically there were only two grades in one classroom, although there could be more. The idea was to let students progress at their own paces and not be limited by the restraints of a traditional single-grade classroom. Students moved freely around the multi-age classroom and were responsible for doing their own tasks. Another supposed advantage was that older students could assist younger ones, while reviewing material themselves. The program was implemented with the best of intentions.

My first experience with a multi-age class came during first and second grade. Luckily, ours wasn't always handled as such, because our classroom was joined with the one next door by a retracting divider. The other class was first and second graders, as well. When it came time for an age-specific subject, the class-room could be split, with first graders on one side and second graders on the other.

Even so, it was never structured like a traditional class. The result was that at times, there was no organization or structure. Students might believe that they were doing things correctly, only to realize later that they weren't. The teacher might go for some time before recognizing that a student was having a problem with a subject—I mean, how can you tell the difference between a student working at his own pace and a student struggling with a subject? Also, instead of keeping an eye on how the class was doing as a whole, the teacher had to track thirty students at various levels. Since students moved at their own pace through their book or sub-ject packets, it was easy for students to fall behind or not know where they should be because there were no set benchmarks against which to measure themselves. It was almost like a self-study course with a babysitter.

Basically, the teacher would hand us a book and instruct us to work at our own pace. As she moved on to the next student, I would turn to Tom Berg and ask, "Hey, what are you doing after school?"

The Buddy System

Tom Berg and I were great friends while growing up in Greenbrier. We had many things in common. We shared the same first name. We both had an older brother who was four years older, which meant we knew many of the same people. We were both in the Eagle Tribe in Indian Guides. We both loved sports and we played against each other in the 1975 Greenbrier Boys' Softball League Championship. We were both also born and raised in Greenbrier. We also shared a different bond of brothers—that enduring four years of multi-age classes together at Greenbrier School.

Tom and I were always in the same classroom, with the exception of kin-dergarten and third grade. Many times we'd meet up on the way to school. Things were different during the 1970s—parents didn't congregate around the school, and there wasn't a major traffic jam of vans and SUVs at the beginning and end of each school day. Everyone walked to and from school, with the exception of students outside Greenbrier who lived over a mile away. Our first two years together began in first and second grade with Mrs. Nicholson. Each morning after walking to school, we played on the cast-iron jungle gym or played tetherball, or just ran around the open area. Once the first bell rang, we lined up in front of our assigned doors.

During the wintertime, the entrance hall was lined with racks of green snow brushes. We had to brush all of the snow off our clothes with the green plastic bristles. Although still relatively new at the time, Greenbrier School was simple and plain. Many of the interior features, such as tile floors, red brick walls in the hallways, plain birch cabinets, and long heat registers (which constantly blew air, regardless of what time of year it was) were common to the schools in the district at that time. Of course, there wasn't any air conditioning, so at the beginning and end of the school year, it felt like you were doing time in a hot box at some prisoner-of-war camp (complete with camp guard, checking to see if your homework was done).

Every morning we followed our daily routine. Once I hung my jacket its hook next to the hand-cranked pencil sharpener, I went to my desk and got ready to recite the Pledge of Allegiance. When Tom and I were in Mrs. Nicholson's class in first and second grade, we always sat next to one another. Part of our morning recitations in first and second grade included a rendition of "My Country, 'Tis of Thee," in which Tom and I changed the lyrics to "My Country, 'Tis of Feet" to get a laugh out of the other kids.

It's a Jungle Out There

As in most schools at the time, the Greenbrier School social hierarchy was usually hashed out on the playground during recess. The attitude that "boys will be boys" was still prevalent during the 1970s. This was also true when it came to fighting. Girls and boys handled their social pecking order in different ways. Whereas girls had a tendency toward the manipulative and mean, with the end goal of socially isolating the target of their bullying, boys were more upfront and physical. If a boy was being taunted by his peers, he was really being called out to defend himself and his pride. Many times the confrontation got physical, and then it was over as fast as it began. It was even possible for two boys to fight until one had a bloody nose or lip, and then make up and be friends the very same day without holding a grudge.

Nobody called CNN or Fox News every time there was a fight on the playground. Nevertheless, no one wanted to be sent to the principal's office and have their parents called. I certainly didn't want that. If two boys wanted to settle a dispute, they set a different place and time for the fight. The most popular location for such an event was Verde Park.

If you look on a map of Greenbrier today, you won't find Verde Park. Years later, Verde Park was renamed Happiness Park. (What kind of name is that?) I always wondered if the park district discovered that kids would fight there. A name like Happiness Park undercuts the drama of the confrontation.

"After school, I'm going to kick your ass at Happiness Park! You know the place with rainbows, fairies, and sugar plums." It just doesn't quite have the same ring to it.

In any event, in the days before Happiness Park, there was Verde Park, and if you were looking for a playground fight, that's where you'd find it. Recess was a time of elementary school diplomacy. You might organize plans to play after school or see who wanted to trade Wacky Packs or baseball cards. If a conflict ensued, it was also the time you laid down your challenge or were challenged by someone else.

If there was going to be a fight after school, the news spread like wildfire on the playground. At the end of the school day, a parade of kids marched down Verde Drive to the park, like Romans filing into to the Colosseum. The crowd formed a circle around the two contestants, and the battle ensued. Usually the kids wouldn't attack each other right away, choosing to build up excitement in the crowd by taunting each other. If one fighter had more friends at the fight than the other, it could get pretty intimidating. In some cases, one of the combatants would cave in and back down. The bloodthirsty crowd dispersed in disappointment. If there was a fight, the mob was treated to a kid version of no-rules fighting. Most fights were brief. Typically, the fight lasted until one kid's nose or lip started bleeding. Another way a fight might end was if one kid got into a headlock and had to give up. Either way, no one was ever seriously hurt in any of the fights I witnessed.

On the playground, you had to make the choice of defending yourself or becoming the brunt of some brutal teasing. I chose to defend myself. I dealt with enough teasing at home with Scott. The nice thing was that when you defended yourself, it was like getting a free pass from the taunting for a couple of years. That's just how boys were.

Hot Dog Day

As the noon hour approached, my stomach began rumbling. At the time, students were discouraged from eating lunch at school, and we all went home instead. Only students who had no other option, due to living too far away or having no other means to get home for lunch, ate at the school. Those students who did stay at school had to bring a sack lunch, because the school only provided 1/3-pint milk cartons (for the low price of four cents).

Most of the kids at Greenbrier would have wanted to go home anyway, because who in his right mind wanted to stay at the school? When it came time for lunch, the teacher lined us up, and soon we were running down the sidewalks toward home, for a little lunch and some TV. Mom always greeted me at the door when I arrived, and then she'd make me a sandwich.

Later, in the fall of 1977, I became a latchkey kid when Mom reentered the work force. Each day I came home for lunch and made my own peanut butter and mayonnaise sandwich, with corn chips and a Twinkie. I watched *Bozo's Circus* or *Popeye* while I ate. Afterward, I rushed back to school with Doug and/or Tom before the bell rang. We talked about the day's events as we went—it became our daily routine.

Once in a while, something special happened at Greenbrier, which kept all the kids at school for lunch. That day was Hot Dog Day. The concept for Hot Dog Day seems laughable now, but in 1974 it was a big deal. The PTA organized a day when kids could place an order for a special hot dog (either plain or with ketchup), a can of soda, and potato chips. A true Chicagoan would never order a hot dog with ketchup, so, for a lack of other options, I always ordered mine plain.

The funny thing about Hot Dog Day was the elaborate procedure involved in ordering a simple hot dog. We received permission slips and order forms two to three weeks in advance. On the long-awaited day, a metal vending box was produced, just like the ones the vendors at Wrigley Field used. The hot dogs were distributed, and any time an order was messed up, I got to enjoy some lunch time entertainment by watching the PTA ladies run around, trying to fix it. Nowadays, it's hard to comprehend the sheer joy a simple thing like Hot Dog Day could bring to a kid in elementary school.

School Mom

Mom helped with Hot Dog Day. She began volunteering when my brothers entered school. She was active in the PTA, she helped our teachers at school, and she helped make costumes and props, as well as painted backgrounds, for school plays. She also served as a chaperone during field trips. The nice thing about going to school close to a large city like Chicago was the number of cool places to go on a field trip. We took a number of field trips in school, and it was nice to have Mom along when we went to places like the Field Museum, the Museum of Science and Industry, or Brookfield Zoo. Besides, it probably kept me out of trouble. Over the years, she volunteered quite a bit of time to the school. The last year that Mom was really active was when I was in third grade, with Miss Marines.

The Spirit of 1976

Third grade was easily the best school year I experienced. The stars aligned for me that year, and everything seemed perfect. First off, I wasn't in a multi-age classroom that year, so I always knew where I stood. There is something to be said for "normalcy." It was the year of the Bicentennial, and the positive patriotism seemed to lift my spirit. 1976 was also the year for the Olympic Games. The Olympics may not seem all that special now, but during the Cold War, everyone watched on the edge of their seats, hoping we'd beat down the communist hordes that emerged to compete from behind the Iron Curtain. As if that wasn't enough to make third grade special, Miss Marines was my teacher.

Miss Marines was a voluptuous new teacher, straight out of college. I can't imagine there was any boy in my class who didn't have a crush on her. She was quite striking, with brown shoulder-length hair, big brown eyes looking out from large-rimmed glasses, and a figure one usually doesn't see teaching third graders. Best of all, she liked me.

Throughout 1976, Bicentennial mania was ever present. I was swept up by the excitement of it. I became fascinated with our country's creation, and developed, for the first time, a deep interest in history (perhaps with a little help from Miss Marines). Although the presence of the Cold War surrounded all of us, it was during the Bicentennial that the differences between our freedoms as Americans and the lack of them in communist countries, mostly represented by the Soviet Union, appeared most distinct.

As I became more aware of geography—I collected maps of all kinds—it began to sink in that there was a whole half of the world that was cut off from us. We were told that people who lived there couldn't freely choose where to live, what kind of house they could have, where they could study, where they could work, what kind of car they could purchase, or where they could travel. Their world was dominated by their government, from cradle to grave. These people were watched, listened to, and many times manipulated without their knowledge. This wasn't a *Twilight Zone* episode, it was the real thing. As kids, we'd hear these stories in school and periodically on TV, but you never were one hundred percent certain that everything you heard was true. However, after finding out what the Nazis had done during the Second World War, anything seemed possible. It was. In 1976, most people assumed the world would stay split between east and west, or that civilization would end instantly in a nuclear flash.

Nuclear war was a real concern of the kids growing up in the postwar period, and 1976 was no exception. After the fall of the Iron Curtain and the rise of terrorism, there is talk in the media today that gives the impression that the world is a more dangerous place now than it was then. I think it's easy to downplay the danger the Soviet Union presented, now that the immediate danger of a Soviet attack has passed. At the time, people built bomb shelters, schools ran emergency drills, and radiuses of potential damage were calculated to give an estimation of how bad an attack might be. Living near Chicago, you assumed that in the event of a nuclear launch, you had about half an hour to say your prayers. As a whole, we weren't worried about a building getting bombed or even a whole city; we were concerned about complete world annihilation. Just as with the uncertainty of today's terrorism, no one knew if the Soviets might just try to take over Western Europe or launch a "first strike" attack. When one considers that the Soviet Union was the same country that killed millions of its own people during the 1930s, it didn't seem so far fetched that they might risk a nuclear war. Thank God we had a place like the Olympics to compete internationally without killing each other. As usual, the United States fell short of the Soviet Union and East Germany in the 1976 Olympics. We'd have to wait until the winter of 1980 for our next chance.

Picture Day

There was one day in the school year that you could see me with neatly combed hair, and that day was Picture Day. When I first entered school, Mom made sure I was dressed well for Picture Day. By the time I reached third grade, Mom's persistence began to wear down, and I started wearing any T-shirt I thought was cool at the time. In retrospect, I had a topsy-turvy understanding of what was cool. On picture day in Miss Marines's class, I wore my Muhammad Ali T-shirt. In 1976, everyone loved Muhammad Ali. Today, I don't think I could name three heavyweight boxers, but in the 1970s, heavyweight boxing was on network TV, and as a kid I saw almost every major bout. With someone like Howard Cosell announcing and Muhammad Ali in the ring, it made for real entertainment. Normally a Muhammad Ali shirt would have been the ultimate in cool in 1976, except my T-shirt depicted Muhammad Ali fighting tooth decay. At least it was a positive image. Picture Day would at least offer some time away from class while we went to have our pictures taken. Each year was the same: Stand in line, hand over your order envelope, then wait a couple of months until the pictures arrived. The only difference in 1976 was that I actually smiled.

I Can See Clearly Now

Everyone has heard the story of the ugly duckling, which resonates with kids as they go through awkward development stages, grow up, and blossom. I must not have read the story correctly, because sometime after third grade, I began operating in reverse, going from a cute kid to an ugly one. The root of the problem began as third grade came to an end. Miss Marines noticed what other teachers didn't see, that I was squinting in class. Having glasses herself, she must have recognized the signs of poor eyesight, and she dutifully informed Mom of her suspicions. Not long after school ended and summer vacation began, Mom took me to an eye doctor to get my eyes examined. The exam seemed harmless, until the doctor gave me eye drops to dilate my pupils. When he turned the lights back on in the examining room, I thought I was going to go blind. I was informed that day that I needed glasses, and that I would officially belong to the group of kids called "four eyes."

What a difference glasses can make—(top) my Bicentennial third grade picture, (bottom) my fourth grade picture. Notice that I'm not smiling.

I'm not sure if Mom was using her Hinesley sense of frugality or if she wanted to ensure that her youngest son wouldn't get a date any time in the next seven years, but she fulfilled both ends when she picked out the frames for my glasses. I didn't fully grasp how ugly they would be as we drove home that day with my eyes still half blinded from the eye drops. My world changed two weeks later when Mom drove me back to the eye doctor to pick up the glasses. As soon as I put them on, I couldn't believe the difference. I was amazed at the clarity and definition of the world around me. I was excited by my newly found gift, until I looked in the mirror. I guess life has its trade-offs.

Doing Time

As we agreed that August night in 1976, Doug and I walked to school together the first day of fourth grade. It was that fall that I began my two-year sentence for fourth and fifth grade in Mr. Modec's class. I dreaded it. He had a reputation for being tough. He was a real "throwback" to the days of unlimited teacher power. By the time I entered his class, he had been teaching for close to twenty years. Before coming to Greenbrier School the year it opened, he had worked at Wilson School on Palatine Road. This meant that even before Greenbrier School was built, some poor Greenbrier kids still had the misfortune of landing in his class.

Overall, James Modec had a good reputation at Greenbrier. He was one of the most senior teachers on staff, and he became team leader for the school. I believe he was also looked at by the other teachers as a resource for keeping rowdy students in line at assemblies and recess. His classroom approach wasn't very subtle. He had a thick wooden yardstick with one end broken off. He even gave the yardstick a name: "Charlie." As the story goes, he broke Charlie while hitting a student who misbehaved. I don't know if there was any truth to that story, but Mr. Modec certainly didn't shy away from the tough teacher image.

Although very rare, corporal punishment was a possible disciplinary measure in schools during the 1970s. Unknown to any of the students in our class, a junior high school teacher in our district named John Fender was fired for hitting students in 1972. This incident concerned the school board, who didn't support teachers abusing students but were also reluctant to drop corporal punishment altogether. The disciplinary rules were vague when the incident happened, and the case went to court. Fender initially won the case and was to be reinstated. Instead, the district appealed the ruling, and five years after the incident occurred, won the appeal. In the meantime, the district rewrote the rules for "unusual disciplinary matters" to state specific guidelines as to when or if corporal punishment could be used. The new rules made corporal punishment for disciplinary purposes next to impossible. But, all we knew was that corporal punishment was an open option.

Mr. Modec used this confusion to maintain a threatening presence. Monitoring our classroom as we worked, he walked around the room tapping Charlie on his leg while whistling or humming a tune. Mr. Modec never hit anyone during my time in his class, but if kids were talking when they weren't supposed to, he hurled a chalkboard eraser at them. Actually, the most intimidating aspect of Mr. Modec wasn't Charlie or the flying erasers, but his appearance as a whole.

To me, he looked like an ogre. He stood five foot ten, which made him seem like a giant to a ten- or eleven-year-old. He was husky, but not obese. He had short, shaggy, matted brown hair. He wore short-sleeved dress shirts and a tie that came down to his belly button, making the tie five or six inches too short. Accompanying his somewhat disheveled appearance was the smell of cigars and aftershave. Normally, with other teachers, I wouldn't be intimidated or bothered by such an appearance, as I was no poster boy for fashion or neatness myself. However, Mr. Modec had a glass eye. To a ten- or eleven-year-old, you can imagine the effect. Couple that with his gruff personality, and you understood Odysseus's motivation to escape the Cyclops's cave. Worse still, I could never tell which was the real eye and which was the glass one. It was unnerving. If he started yelling without addressing the object of his anger by name, you didn't know whether he was talking to you or someone else. If an eye was "staring" at me I would freeze in place, only to realize moments later that he was yelling at someone else.

Your Reputation Precedes You

Long before entering his class, I knew of Mr. Modec's reputation. Steve and Scott both escaped having Modec as a teacher, but that didn't mean they didn't have to deal with him. Mr. Modec earned some extra money as a recess monitor, so was dictator of the playground—even during Steve and Scott's time. He refereed games such as kickball and soccer, and reportedly had had a tendency to play favorites. When it came to sports—regardless of the sport—Scott played with passion (maybe sometimes with a little too much passion). When Scott felt something was unfair or that a bad call had been made, he shared his point of view. Not many students would take such liberties with a teacher. Scott, of course, had to be exceptional.

So, for a couple of years, the name Price must have had a familiar ring to Modec's ears. Mr. Modec loved me from the start, the way one would love a bad cold. I'm not one hundred percent certain why I started off on the wrong foot, but I can say it never improved. I think he felt he had to ride me hard to break me of some of my bad habits. For instance, apart from Picture Day, I almost never brushed my hair. That drove him crazy. My desk was almost always disorderly, which also bothered him to no end. Clearly, I was not one of his favorites.

However, like many teachers, Modec did have favorites—mostly girls. There were several boys who managed to attain favoritism status. The family of one of my fellow students, the Zettlmeiers, owned a German delicatessen that Modec frequented, and they made sure he had an ample supply of gummi bears in his desk drawer. This gave Bill Zettlmeier a little extra wiggle room in our class. In other words, he didn't have to dodge any flying erasers. I didn't have that luxury. So, I had to endure the two years of misery on my own.

The Popcorn Party

There was a miserable day in November of 1976 that I will never forget, although it had nothing to do with Modec. Like any other morning, Scott's alarm clock woke us up. Mornings were hectic that fall. Mom was working part time as a secretary. Steve was in his sophomore year of high school, and Scott was in eighth grade. Both of them had to catch their buses before I had to leave for school. I got dressed and went downstairs for a bowl of cereal. My brothers were rushing around the house, and soon, Steve left to catch his bus. I sat at the kitchen table watching *the Ray Rayner Show* over a bowl of Lucky Charms. Ray Rayner, dressed in an orange jumpsuit, was chasing Chalveston the Duck around, trying to feed him some lettuce. This was great entertainment. Scott ran through the kitchen, grabbed his sack lunch, and darted out the door. I didn't have a sack lunch, because I still walked home for lunch.

I put my cereal bowl in the sink as Mom bid me farewell and went to work. I returned to watching TV. Frasier Thomas's *Garfield Goose and Friends* came on. I watched as Frasier Thomas introduced an episode of *Clutch Cargo*. I loved the show, although it was a little weird. The main character, Clutch Cargo, was an adventurer who also traveled around the world with a little boy named Spinner and his dog, Paddlefoot. I don't know what his relationship was to the little boy, but as a kid you didn't think much about that. Basically someone would have some mysterious problem that Clutch Cargo and friends would solve. The cartoon was presented in a cliffhanger format of short two-minute episodes. It wasn't the exotic adventures or Clutch's weird relationship with Spinner and Paddlefoot that made *Clutch Cargo* unique, but rather the use of "Syncro-Vox Technology." Syncro-Vox Technology involved live-action mouths that were superimposed onto the cartoon faces of the characters. It was strange yet hilarious at the same time.

As 8:30 came around, *Garfield Goose and Friends* came to an end, and I gathered my things together to leave for school. I always looked forward to Fridays, as two days of mental peace followed, but this Friday promised to be extra special. Periodically, Mr. Modec scheduled a popcorn party for the kids in the class, and this was the day. As long as you weren't behind in your work, you could participate. I was doing fine in class, so I was eligible and looking forward to a fairly carefree afternoon. Modec's popcorn parties were a spectacle. Modec himself took the lion's share of the popcorn. These were the days before microwave popcorn, so he had three popcorn poppers going at once. After the popcorn was popped, it was dumped into large paper grocery bags. As if popping the corn with a large amount of oil didn't make the popcorn greasy enough, Modec melted sticks of butter and doused it, then shook the bags, leaving them stained with grease. Periodically he grabbed a big handful of popcorn and stuffed his face with it. The sight alone could put you off popcorn for quite some time, but the party-like atmosphere was so enticing that you tried to put those images out of your mind. Besides, it had been a while since the last party, and I was pumped up for popcorn. Unfortunately, I had to wait much longer than I'd planned.

All I Want for Christmas

I met up with Tom Berg and his little brother Timmy on my way to school. Along with my books and folders, I carried a jar of Orville Redenbacher's popcorn. Tom brought the butter.

When we arrived at school, Timmy took off toward the second-grade entrance while Tom and I continued to the back of the school and the tennis courts. The bell rang, and we filed into the school. We made our way upstairs to Modec's classroom, the stairwell filled with the noise of kids marching up the steps. It wasn't long before we entered the classroom and headed over to the coat hooks to hang up our jackets. I placed my jar of popcorn on the counter next to the sink with the long curved faucet that never seemed to shut off completely. This popcorn party looked promising, judging by the amount of popcorn ready for popping.

The morning went slowly, as the anticipation for the popcorn party drove me to distraction. The only thing left between me and popcorn was gym and lunch.

"Line up for gym!" Modec bellowed.

Soon everyone was scrabbling to get in line. I jammed my papers into my desk and joined the other students.

Gym was held in what was called the Multi-Purpose Room, which doubled as a theater for school plays and assemblies. It had a small basketball court, and the floor was made of green clay tiles with white lines for basketball. Off to the left was a wooden stage.

A glimpse at the Multi Purpose Room in action (note the use of the gun in the school play).

We marched down the hallway in single file like a group of convicts on their way to chain gang duty. Modec marching along side us to make sure no one escaped. Once we reached the Multi-Purpose Room, we were released into the gym teacher's custody.

I always enjoyed gym. There was nothing better than some physical activity to get your daily frustrations out of your system. There were some activities that we did on a regular basis—dodgeball was the best for releasing that built-up tension. If we weren't playing dodgeball, however, we could always hope for the parachute or the giant canvass-covered cage ball, which we kicked while riding little square scooters. If the cage ball wasn't there, we still might get lucky and get to do scooter races.

On this day, the gym teacher wasn't in the creative spirit, so we ran around the white circle in the center of the basketball court on the tiled floor. We were packed together as we ran around the circle. Tom Berg and I were playing around, and Tom pushed me and I tripped. Normally I would have been OK, because the fall didn't hurt me. It was the next couple of kids who fell on my head that did it. As I hit the ground I screamed at Tom, and that's when another student fell on me, forcing my open mouth onto the tile floor. The impact broke my two front teeth. I cried and started to panic. I was rushed to the nurse's office, where they called my mom. She left work and headed for the school, while I waited in the office. My teeth broke in an odd way—in the shape of an upside-down letter U. When Mom saw me, she was furious at the school's negligence, but these were the days before people litigated at the drop of a hat, and we didn't take any action against the school. As a result, I missed the popcorn party. There would be other chances for popcorn parties even as fourth grade came to an end, because I still had one more year left of my two-year term in Modec's class.

The Benefits of Being Older

I had mixed feelings when I entered the fifth grade. On one hand, I had to deal with Mr. Modec for another full school year. But, while that wasn't a pleasant prospect, fifth grade still had its perks. Some of the advantages to being a fifth grader included serving as a crossing guard—which meant you were top dog and no longer one of the downtrodden. You could also participate in the school's newly formed drama club and the special fifth grade field trip to the state capital of Springfield.

Of the three benefits of being a fifth grader, the only one that truly turned out to be something special was the field trip. Doing "patrol duty" had its down side. Whenever it was my turn to serve in the spring or fall, it rained, and in the wintertime it was below freezing. Even if the weather was good, you were still the last kid to get home. As for the drama club, I didn't get the lead and was bumped to understudy. What that really meant was a spot on the choir, if you wanted to participate at all. Which I did, and I wound up singing "Come Sail Away," by Styx, with Jim Kluka. We practiced that song over and over again. Before it was all over, I can't say I was a fan of the song anymore. Plus, singing it as a choir didn't do the song any favors. To liven it up a bit, I changed a word here or there to see if I could mess up Jim Kluka, who stood close to me. On the night of the performance, Jim asked me not to make him laugh. He was sweating bullets as the key part of the song approached. "...We live happily forever, so the story goes. But somehow we missed out on that pot of mold..." Fortunately, Jim's laughter was drowned out by the rest of the singers, and he was able to recover his composure before the end of the song. Although choir may not have been the best experience, the field trip to Springfield had real promise.

There were two field trips specific to fifth graders. One was to the Deerfield forest preserve, where we were supposed to pack a year's worth of learning nature and the environment in one day. The highlight was putting on wading boots and going into a pond to hunt crawfish. It was messy, smelly, and mildly disgusting—in other words, perfect for ten- and eleven-year-olds. But the trip to the forest preserve wasn't anything new for any of us who had been in Indian Guides or Cub Scouts. During elementary school, we took a number of field trips to see museums, plays, and places of work, such as the Arlington Heights Fire Department, but the mother of all field trips was the Springfield trip.

The appeal of the Springfield field trip had more to do with its distance from home than the interesting subject matter found at the state capital. We had to leave at the crack of dawn and return late at night, and we took charter buses with reclining seats—this was the big time! We also had to bring extra money for our road trip dinner. Each time my friends and I discussed the trip, the anticipation built up that much more. By the time the trip was upon us, the excitement was at fever pitch.

The day before the trip, Modec delivered instructions for the following morning. In my mind, I pictured a bomber squadron briefing, where I sat with the other fifth graders to hear about our next mission. All of us, veterans of numerous field trips, were reminded that "this was the big one." Squadron Leader Modec barked the orders.

"Stay in tight formation, follow your leader, keep your noses clean, and we just might make it home safely! We'll rendezvous at 04:30 hours, and if all goes to plan, we should return by 22:30 hours at the latest. That is all, carry on."

"Four-thirty in the morning?" I turned to Tom Berg, who looked equally troubled by the time.

"Just a reminder: Don't forget your sack lunch because we won't be able to stop if you forget it. Also remember to bring money for dinner and souvenirs. We are not responsible if you lose your money, so make sure you know where your money is at all times."

As I sat at home the night before the trip, I had only a vague understanding of just how long the bus ride was going to be. As fate would have it, the journey would be less miserable for me than for students of previous years. Steve and Scott each received a Mattel electronic football game for their birthdays, which happened to fall right before the trip. Luckily for me, I was able to borrow one for the long ride downstate.

Although primitive by today's standards, the electronic football game became an instant hit among all the kids I knew. You could play by yourself or with a friend. The game used little red LEDs for football players. Your player's LED shined brighter than those of the defense. You pressed the arrow keys to move your player on the field, in an attempt to dodge the defensive LEDs chasing your player. I owe much of my incredible thumb dexterity to that game. If you didn't make a first down or if you kicked the ball, the game made two quick cricket-like chirping sounds to indicate that the ball had been turned over, and it was the other player's turn. This meant if Scott and I were playing the game in the darkness of our bedroom when we should have been sleeping, we knew when the other person lost possession. That was when you "accidentally" hit the kick button, forcing the other player's team to kick the ball.

Mom woke me up the morning of the field trip, and I headed downstairs for breakfast. I was half asleep as I entered the kitchen, and dimly noticed it was still dark out. Mom reminded me that I had to hurry and finish breakfast and get dressed. There was nothing on TV at four o'clock in the morning, so I scarfed down my breakfast and hurriedly got dressed. Because I had to be at school so early, Mom was going to drive me there before going to work. Equipped with the electronic game, a small camera, a sack lunch, and my small wad of money jammed in the front pocket of my jeans, Mom dropped me off at the school. The charter buses were already lined up outside, waiting to be boarded. I said a quick goodbye to Mom before turning around and searching for Modec's class. I spotted a sleepy Tom Berg standing around in our group.

A couple of parents volunteered to be chaperones, so I was spared the misery of having to stay with Modec the entire trip. As our groups entered the bus, I paired up with Tom. This was the first time any of us had ridden on a chartered bus,

Lincoln statue in New Salem, Illinois.

so it was an exciting moment for us all as we settled into our reclining seats. I took the window seat, which afforded me a view out the window, but unfortunately the Illinois countryside offers little of interest besides cornfields. Soon I had the hot morning sun in my face, and I found myself envying Tom, who had fallen back asleep. Soon I broke out the electronic football game. The chirping sounds from the game joined the roar of the bus's engine as we sped toward Springfield.

Four and a half hours and a thousand football games later, we arrived. You could almost smell the corruption of state government when you stepped off the bus, but as a little kid I didn't recognize it. Illinois is the Land of Lincoln, and much of the focus of the field trip was on Honest Abe. Over the course of the day we saw just about everything Springfield had to offer. We toured the old capital building, the new capital building, Lincoln's home, and his tomb. After we ate our sack lunches, we drove to New Salem, which is a historic recreation of the small village where Lincoln grew up. Up until this point I had hoarded my money and hadn't yet bought a souvenir. The money was slowly burning a hole in my pocket as I spotted the souvenir shop next to the visitor center.

A Plate for Grandma

I stepped into the souvenir shop and tried not to look too desperate to buy something.

"May I help you find something?" called the woman behind the counter.

"Just browsing, thanks," I replied, with an equally nice smile.

Having spent a great deal of time shopping with Grandpa Hinesley, I had a raised level of awareness of people all too willing to help me part with my money. I hated to go home empty-handed, though, as it wasn't everyday I traveled to Springfield, but there wasn't much to my liking. Finally, I spotted a small plate with a picture of Lincoln and his childhood home. I had no need for a plate, but when I saw it I knew it would be perfect for Grandma Hinesley.

She had a small plate collection from the various places she and my grandfather had visited over the years, and I thought of her the instant I saw the plate. I was always very close with Grandma Hinesley. She was soft-spoken, friendly, never judgmental, and always pleasant. I

Opening Christmas presents with Grandma Hinesley in 1972.

enjoyed spending time with her and Grandpa Hinesley, and would beg to sleep over whenever I could. The one down-side of sleeping over was that Grandma Hinesley wasn't the best cook. In the mornings, however, she made good poached eggs, which I loved to eat with toast. Poached eggs may not seem worthy of praise, but this is the same woman who made macaroni and cheese taste terrible, and that came in a box! Sometimes you have to look for the silver lining.

When I slept over at Grandma's, there were many times I got to talk with her alone. She moved slowly around the kitchen because of her stiff muscles, and she had large glasses and dyed short red hair. She always beamed at me when she brought me my plate of eggs and toast. I must have annoyed her, because I loved to ask her everything about her past. I'd ask about her childhood and her parents and relatives. I got frustrated when she couldn't remember things or if she simply didn't know the answers to my questions. It was during these moments that I realized just how lucky I was. Unlike me, Grandma Hinesley never knew her grandparents. She didn't know what they did or how they died. At the age of sixty-six, she reflected back on the various questions I asked her and told me she had just never considered them before or bothered to ask. Even at the age of ten, I found that sad. When I saw the Lincoln plate behind the counter, it reminded me that I was lucky enough to know she had a plate collection.

"Excuse me, how much is that small plate over there?" I asked the woman behind the counter. I gestured to the plate.

"It's seven dollars."

In a move inspired by Grandpa Hinesley himself, I asked, "Will you take five fifty for it?"

For the rest of the Springfield trip, my only concern was getting that plate home in one piece. It wasn't long before we boarded the buses once again to head home. I showed Tom the plate and stored it in the overhead bin as safely as I could. Then I turned back to Tom to see if he wanted to play some electronic football. An eternity later, we arrived back at school. Dad was waiting there to pick me up. He was on time, as always. Much to my own astonishment, the plate made it home safe and sound, and just as I knew she would be, Grandma Hinesley was delighted with the purchase.

Up Against the Wall

The multi-age classroom produced an unintended yet interesting type of competition in Modec's class. Even though students generally worked on their own, Modec tried to maintain the illusion of order by having a time slot for each subject. This meant that when it was time for math, all of the students worked on their math units, regardless of what level they had reached. Some students excelled, while others struggled. It was pretty frustrating because your progress was measured by the quantity of the work you did, more than the quality. Even if you did your work perfectly, you could still be way behind the leader.

There were typically four types of students in our class. The first loved school, had smarts, and worked hard. Then there was the student who wasn't really smart but worked hard. Third was the student who was smart but didn't put forth the effort to do his best because he was bored or hated school. Last, there was the student who wasn't cut out for school at all. My impression was that Rob was one such student.

Rob was a good kid. He loved to play pick-up football and kickball and fish in the reservoir, but school was not for him. That's why we were all surprised that Rob was leading our class in math. He was ahead of all of Modec's pet students, which got everyone's attention, even Modec's. When a student like Rob excels in a subject, it's a great morale builder for the rest of the students, because if he could do it, so could you. It's important to praise that student in front of the class to demonstrate what students can really do when they apply themselves. Mr. Modec decided the time was right to showcase Rob's achievement.

It was always a big deal in Modec's class when he addressed us all at once. This was because in the multi-age class, teachers didn't "teach" (in the traditional sense), because all of the students were at different levels. Most of the time Modec sat behind his desk, eating candy and humming to himself. He answered questions if you approached his desk, but he never had to do any correcting because students corrected their own work by using an answer key. When you completed a unit, you turned in your work for him to note in his grade book. He then gave the papers back to the student to put in their work folder. When it came time for parent conferences or our quarterly report card, he called the students up for a teacher-student conference. At the conference you would cross-check your work with his grade book, and he would tell you where you stood in class and what you had to do to improve. So when he called Rob up to the front of the class, it was a special occasion.

"Everyone, I want your attention," Modec bellowed as he beckoned Rob up to the front of the class.

Rob made his way up and stood proudly next to Mr. Modec. He seemed slightly embarrassed but nonetheless proud.

Modec continued, "Last year at this time Rob was having a lot of trouble in math. This year he has worked harder than anyone and is now several math units ahead of the next best student. Because he's done so well, I'd like him to demonstrate to everyone how to do some of the long division problems he's been working on."

At this point Mr. Modec wrote a couple of long division problems on the chalk board and asked Rob to do them for us. I have to admit I was curious to see Rob do the problems because I was several math units behind him. So I stared intently along with the other students. Rob stood there for a while, staring shrewdly at the chalk board, contemplating how best to tackle the problem. After several moments, it became apparent that Rob was having some difficulty.

"What's the matter, Rob?" Modec asked. "What are you waiting for?"

Rob continued to stare at the chalk board. Modec already knew what the problem was. He hadn't called Rob up to praise him for his hard work, but rather to expose him for cheating in front of the whole class.

"You don't how to do the problems, do you, Rob?" Modec asked, sternly. "You've been copying the answers from the answer key, haven't you?"

"Yes," Rob mumbled, looking down at his feet.

"I didn't hear you," Mr. Modec replied.

"Yes," Rob responded, a little louder.

"You know what that's called, Rob? Cheating. Go back to your seat."

Rob made his way back to his seat, looking proud no longer. I had never thought that I could feel bad for someone who cheated, but I did that day. Rob was completely humiliated in front of the whole class. I'm sure before the day was over just about everyone who knew Rob knew the story. He missed several recesses as punishment. One might think that Modec's up-front approach would have deterred Rob from ever repeating his mistake, but I heard stories to the contrary. I too would suffer some public humiliation from Mr. Modec, although it had nothing to do with academics.

Inspection

As fifth grade came to an end and springtime arrived, Mr. Modec decided that it would be a good time to do a surprise desk inspection. Our desks were both a place to write and a place to store our folders and supplies. The teal steel desks had a hinged top and a bin underneath for storage. Periodically, Mr. Modec inspected students' desks to make sure they were clean and orderly. The great irony was that his own desk never appeared orderly. Many times he would give notice that he was going to inspect our desks. This would give students time to straighten up and make sure things were in order. I can't say for certain, but I have a suspicion I was the target of the surprise desk inspection. In a few short weeks, I would be walking out of Greenbrier School and moving on to Rand Junior High School.

After he announced the surprise desk inspection, I broke out in a cold sweat. My desk was almost always a mess. I was always in a rush when putting things away to get lined up for recess, lunch, or gym. As Modec made his way around the room, I opened my desk to see how bad it was going to be. There were papers everywhere and other folders with papers falling out. Everything had been sandwiched in there in a hectic manner, and I only had a few moments before Modec arrived at my desk. I was trying my best to straighten things up when Modec stood beside me. I decided to take a page out of Scott's book and take a more brazen approach.

"My desk isn't really ready for inspection yet. It'll just take a moment," I said, without any shame.

Modec didn't even reply, but instead picked up my desk and walked toward the door of the room. I sat there dumbfounded for a second before following him. He was going to make me straighten up my desk in the hallway so everyone could see me working on it. I followed him out into the hallway. Then he did something I didn't expect. He dumped everything from my desk all over the floor. The contents flew everywhere. Pencils rolled away as folders spilled papers out onto the ground. I guess it was type of a going-away present. I spent the rest of the afternoon cleaning up the mess.

Sentence Served

As the last day of school approached, I can't say I was sorry to leave Greenbrier School. The last couple of years had been a wonderful experience, but in the end, I was as happy and excited to leave after fifth grade as I had been when I entered Greenbrier as a kindergartner.

When I left Greenbrier School for the last time, I left the multi-age classroom experience behind me, as well. Tom Berg and I went on to junior high school and then high school together. Being a lab rat for the whole multi-age classroom experience was enough experimentation to last me my entire school career, as far as I was concerned. Unfortunately, the experimentation was just starting. Rand Junior High School was one big testing site for educational theory of "meeting the individual needs of the student" and mainstreaming. To this day, I'm still waiting for the paycheck for participating in their study.

CHAPTER 6

A Break From the Action

Breaks and Freedom

When I was younger, holidays represented a magical time for me. As the seasons changed, my hopes wrapped around Halloween candy and Christmas presents. With each holiday came its own mystique. Some meant more to our family than others—to me, Halloween was always special. Thanksgiving was a time of home and family, while Christmas had all of the best features a holiday can possess, with sweets, family, and the exchanging of gifts with those you care about. While these holidays may be celebrated in other countries, there is something unique about how Americans observe them. That may have changed a little over the years, as the holidays have become more commercialized, and personal time more restricted. In some ways the personal touch has been lost, as people rush to simply keep up with the next approaching holiday, which has almost become just another turn of the business cycle. I remember a time when the holidays seemed more personal and less forced. If anything, they represented a break from the action.

A Holiday for My Sweet Tooth

Halloween was a big event in our house, but it was the Halloween of 1973, while I was in first grade in Mrs. Nicholson's class, that stands out in my mind as the best one. From the beginning, Halloween of that year promised to be a great one. Both Steve and Scott were still of trick-or-treating age, and I would be able to go around the neighborhood with them and feel cool about being with older kids. Additionally, Dad and I were going to enter a costume contest with the Indian Guides, with some really special costumes.

Mom (with a little help from Dad) had spent a fair amount of time working on special handmade costumes for Dad and me. Normally, the Halloween costumes I wore were Price kid standards, like a savage pirate one year and a bloody vampire the next. This year was different. Because we were the "bear" family in our Indian Guide tribe, we were making bear costumes. Although none of my costumes over the years had been the prepackaged ones you'd buy at a store, this year was going to be something of a chal-

Mom poses in front of her bear costumes.

lenge for Mom's costume-making skills. Mom rose to this challenge like no other. After many days of hard work, sewing, papier-mâché, and some painting, Mom created the greatest Halloween costume I've had the honor to wear. The body of the bear costume was brown corduroy, to which Mom added a white furry belly. It was a one-piece costume, similar to a jumpsuit with a zipper in the back. Mom also sewed brown mittens for the hands. The coolest part of the costume was the giant papier-mâché heads. The mouth of the bear acted as the viewing window. The two costumes matched each other nicely, and were ideal for Walking Bear and Little Bear.

My excitement increased as Halloween approached. Preparing for Halloween added to the fun of the holiday. The main decorative event was carving pump-

kins. Normally we picked out our pumpkins at Goebert's Farm, which bordered Greenbrier. In later years, the Goebert family sold off parcels of their land to developers, but in 1973 they had a pumpkin patch just north of Techny drive. Wandering through the pumpkin patch as a kid I felt just like Charlie Brown's friend Linus, except I didn't wait overnight for the Great Pumpkin. In addition to the pumpkins themselves, we bought gourds to use for the pumpkin's nose or ears. Usually we waited until Halloween was only a day or two away before we carved our

Mom and Scott work on their pumpkins in October 1973.

pumpkins and set them outside. For one thing, we didn't want the pumpkins to rot, and we also didn't want to give any of the neighborhood kids the opportunity to smash them.

Judgment Day

Dad and I got ready for the Indian Guides Halloween party, where we were entering the costume contest. We packed the giant bear heads in the backseat of the car. I also carried a Tupperware container full of homemade Halloween cookies—pumpkin-shaped sugar cookies with iced jack-o'-lanterns on them. The jack-o'-lanterns smiled up at me as I held the cookies in my lap on the way to the party. When we arrived, I had to put on my bear head in order to carry the cookie container.

I walked slowly up to the school, where the party took place, hoping I wouldn't fall over because of the giant head. It felt like having a big bubble around your head, like the metal helmets deep sea divers wore. I was probably able to see about the same amount as deep sea divers, too, because my vision was limited to what I could see out of the little bear's mouth. By the grace of God I made it into the school and placed the cookies on the treats table without falling over or crashing into something.

Once I deposited the cookies, I was able to move more freely. Everybody was looking in the bear's mouth to try to see who I was. Some kids tried to stick their fingers in the mouth, which irritated me to no end. They had to try to look inside because when they asked me who I was, they couldn't understand my muffled response. I felt like I was in my own soundproof chamber, because when I spoke, the sound didn't seem to leave the giant head, and I felt like I was talking to myself.

Shortly, they announced that the costume contest was about to begin. I managed to find Dad despite the lack of vision and the sweat now stinging my eyes. We lined up with the other father-and-son teams to be judged. Mom's long hours of hard work paid off that night, as our costumes definitely stood out. The judges marched up and down the line—each one peeking into my bear's mouth to see my sweating, smiling face. Then the judges gathered together and said they'd announce the winners later in the party. We stepped away, and I quickly

Dad and I getting ready for the Indian Guides Halloween costume contest.

discarded the huge bear head to play some Halloween games, like bobbing for apples.

After running around and playing games for a while, I approached the treats table and tasted one of Mom's cookies. They ran out of punch, so one of the moms took out another large can of fruit punch-flavored Hi C from underneath the table and punched two holes in the top to make some more. As I took one of the newly poured cups, one of the judges began to announce the winners of the costume contest. Then they did the unexpected and called our name. We had won! Dad and I made our way up to the front of the crowd to get our ribbon. As the party began to wind down, I was full of punch and cookies. I said goodbye to my friends and helped Dad put the giant heads in the backseat of the car. On the way home, one solitary jack-o'-lantern grinned at me from the Tupperware container in my left hand, while my right clutched our winning ribbon.

While Dad had only one occasion to wear his costume, I was carted off to a costume contest at Randhurst Mall, where I won a disappointing second place. The last chance I'd have to show off Mom's work of art was at Greenbrier School's traditional Halloween parade.

The Halloween Parade

In 1973, the school parade was something to see. It wasn't simply a quick walk around the perimeter of the school; instead we marched right down the middle of the neighborhood on one side of Verde Drive to Verde Park, then back again on the opposite side. These were the days before the costume police made sure we didn't show any blood and gore. Marching alongside me that day were kids dressed in a wide variety of costumes. There were football players, cheerleaders, vampires, angels, pirates, Indians, executioners, and every monster imaginable. There were even cowboys and soldiers with toy guns, if you can believe it.

The challenge for me was going to be making it all the way down to the park without tripping or running into a street sign. Mrs. Nicholson lined us up, and everyone started going crazy. I heaved the giant head onto my shoulders and waited in line. Of course a second grader started sticking his fingers in the mouth while I stood there helplessly in line. Mrs. Nicholson ushered us out of the classroom and out the first- and second-grade doors to line up with the other students on the sidewalk.

It was a beautiful fall day, and the trees that lined the parkways of Verde Drive showed off their fall colors. A light breeze blew as we began to walk down Verde Drive toward the park. I had to be careful not to run into the Raggedy Ann in front of me or stop abruptly and be slammed in the back by the Indian warrior behind me. I looked out the best I could to see if I could spot Mom in the crowd of onlookers who'd gathered to watch the parade. Unfortunately, I couldn't take my eyes off the person in front of me for too long, so I waved at everyone like Richard Nixon on the previous year's campaign trail. We reached Verde Park without incident, and crossed the street to head back toward the school. By the time we got back, I think I had sweated a gallon inside the bear head, and was relieved to take it off. Nobody could concentrate for the remainder of the day, in anticipation of the night of trick-or-treating that was in store for us. When the bell rang, a whole school full of monsters and other creatures were let loose on the community.

An Extra Hand

The night of the year's great candy grab had finally arrived. Every kid loved Halloween for this very moment. When I was six years old, I enjoyed tagging along with my brothers as they trick-or-treated. My brothers usually brought a few friends with them, as well. Hanging around with the older kids always made me feel like I was little cooler than the average six-year-old. In other years, I usually had one or two friends with me, like Tom Berg or Brian Carey, because their older brothers were the same age as Scott. This year I wanted to stick close to Steve and his friends. Scott did too, mainly because of Steve's Halloween creation.

At the age of twelve, with his thirteenth birthday just nine days away, Steve's days of trick-or-treating were coming to an end. This Halloween, he intended to make his last days of trick-or-treating pay off. Steve came up with an idea to make a dummy trick-or-treater to take along with us to get extra candy. I think Steve was less concerned about the candy and more interested in seeing if he could trick people into believing that his dummy was real. When Steve set his mind to something creative, you knew it was going to be good.

I watched Steve work his magic. He dubbed his masterpiece "Lance." Lance consisted of a styrofoam head that Mom used to store one of her wigs, a bright red cloak, an evil skeleton mask, and a broomstick that fit inside a hole in the bottom of the head and acted as the body. Through an opening in the back of the cloak, Steve was able to hold the broom handle from

Steve and Lance.

behind. He also made a fake arm, complete with skeleton glove, that he could extend out to receive candy. I watched as he pinned the rubber mask to the styrofoam head so it wouldn't move around, using sewing pins that he took from Mom's pincushion by the sewing machine. He then colored in the eyes using Dad's markers. His final touch was to affix a padded hanger to give Lance shoulders. Then he turned it toward me to test it out.

"What do you think?" he asked, adjusting the cloak a little in the back.

"It's pretty good. I wonder if it'll work?" I said in awe and admiration, thinking he just might be able to pull it off.

"We'll find out."

The real test would unfold after the sun went down.

Trick-or-Treat

Right after school, before I watched Steve add his finishing touches to Lance, I did some quick trick-or-treating with Mom. I was having a great deal of trouble with the bear costume, so I switched to dressing up as a pirate for the second wave of trick-or-treating with Steve, Scott, and their friends after dark. Scott wore the standard Price vampire costume, and Steve dressed up as a hooded ghoul. Mom put a red bandana on my head, and I asked Scott to grab me a pillowcase.

A pillowcase was the way to go when it came trick-or-treating, as opposed to a plastic bag, which could rip, or a plastic pumpkin head, which was too small. A pillowcase was lightweight, durable, and, most of all, could carry a ton of candy in the event you hit the mother lode. Because Steve was going to have his hands full with Lance, Mom sewed two huge zippered pockets into the lining of his hooded cloak. That way, when he collected his and Lance's candy, he could just drop it into one of the pockets and move on without missing a beat.

Steve's and Scott's friends had gathered at the house and were forming a small group on our driveway. I grabbed my things and went outside to join them. Mom yelled something to Steve and Scott about keeping an eye out for me, which I'm sure fell on deaf ears as we made our way down to the sidewalk and headed for the first house. I had to run to keep up with my brother's group, but I managed, while holding my plain white pillowcase and orange UNICEF box. (I did my part in solving the world hunger problem in 1973 by collecting change in my UNICEF box, which resembled a box of Arm & Hammer baking soda with a slot on top. It was the least I could do for the starving children halfway across the world while I was out wandering the neighborhood, collecting as much candy as my little arms could carry.) The box jingled as I ran to keep up with the rest of the group.

As we approached each house, our level of excitement doubled, not only from seeing what kind of candy was being handed out, but also from wondering whether or not Lance would be able to get candy. It was all in the presentation. When we approached a new house, we formed a tight group, and Steve positioned himself (and Lance) in the middle toward the back, while I stood more in front, obscuring a clean view of Lance's body. Most people did a head count before distributing the candy to our outstretched hands. Lance worked like a charm. Only a few people realized as we rushed off to the next house that they'd been had, but most people never noticed Steve's extra hand.

The Art of Trick-or-Treating

During our years of trick-or-treating, my brothers and I got to know which houses had the best candy, and which houses to avoid if possible. This is where having older brothers paid off, because they had several years of weeding out those bad houses before I ever even donned a Halloween mask. There were three categories of houses you approached on Halloween: the big givers, the conventional givers, and the garbage givers.

The big givers, of course, were those houses you planned your night of trick-or-treating around. These wonderful people gave out full-size Hershey bars, Snickers, Three Musketeers, or Nestle Crunch bars. There were a number of big givers in Greenbrier, and it wasn't uncommon to get a full-size candy bar while trick-or-treating during the 1970s. While so-called "fun-size" candy bars originated in the late 1960s, they were still a few years off from becoming popular in Greenbrier, and we benefited from that delay.

Although there weren't fun-size candy bars, Hershey Miniatures and a similar Nestle product were typically handed out by the next group, the conventional givers. The conventional givers were the houses you targeted between the big givers wherever possible. The conventional givers gave out the Halloween standards: Smarties, Tootsie Rolls or Tootsie Pops, Lifesavers, candy corn, little boxes of Milk Duds or packets of Sweet Tarts, and, later, fun-size candy bars. At these houses you went away happy, and it was these houses that provided the bulk of the Halloween booty. The conventional givers got into the spirit of Halloween very much in the same way the big givers did.

But not everyone in the neighborhood joined in the joy of Halloween. There were people in Greenbrier who felt obligated to have something to hand out, and their choice of candy reflected it. Because almost everything I received from them went straight in the garbage, I called them the garbage-givers. I'm not one hundred percent sure if it was a conscious effort on their part to get the most awful candy to discourage kids from returning the following year, but it sure seemed like it, and it was a strategy that worked just the same. The funny thing is that there are companies out there that must believe their candy is awesome when it sells well during Halloween, never dawning on them that nobody would even feed it to a dog any other time of year. I believe the garbage-givers bought candy for much the same reason that a camper buys insect repellent. One candy that fit into that category for my brothers and me was the Mary Jane Peanut Kisses by Necco, which came in black and orange wrappers. There must have been kids who enjoyed the Peanut Kisses; but I certainly wasn't one of them.

It wasn't only store-bought, bad-tasting candy that was a problem, but homemade items and fruit, as well. Accepting homemade food like cookies, Rice Krispies treats, or brownies from a stranger was a definite no-no. Those foods were tempting, but popcorn balls doused with corn syrup were not. The food may not have been tainted, but you'd be crazy to risk it. The same went for fruit. All the urban legends about razor blades in apples and needles in bananas guaranteed that fruit went straight into the garbage. What were they thinking, handing out health food on Halloween anyway? It was an invitation to have their windows soaped or house toilet-papered.

Such miscreants were out there, too, roaming the streets in search of a pumpkin to smash or a vacant house's windows to soap. When Steve and Scott were still fairly young, they both had their pumpkins smashed. Mom always told the sad story of how Steve just couldn't understand how someone could do that to the pumpkin he'd worked so hard on. Innocence lost. It's the little things that harden you to later life. In a way, I'm surprised Steve never came up with a clever way to booby trap his pumpkins after that.

Tricks weren't always limited to youngsters, however. Besides candy, there were sometimes other things to consider as you went trick-or-treating, because there were people who'd go the extra mile to give you a good scare. We approached one such house, with a darkened driveway and a three-foot row of bushes lining it on the house side. A single light illuminated the porch. As we shuffled up the driveway and got close enough to see the porch, two or three kids who were several steps ahead of Scott and me spotted some coins on the porch, perhaps from someone's UNICEF box. There was a slight rustling sound, and Scott froze and stuck out his arm to hold me back, as if he saw something I couldn't. One of the boys bent down to pick up the coins, but was unable to lift them off the porch. As he was distracted by the coins (which were glued to the porch), a man in a white sheet jumped out from behind the hedges and screamed out, scaring the bejesus out of everyone. Luckily Scott had spotted some movement behind the bushes and prevented me from suffering a heart attack on the spot. Everyone had a good laugh, got their Peanut Kisses, and got the hell out of there, vowing not to go back the following year. After covering the four corners of Greenbrier, everyone was pretty well spent, so we made our way home to see how well we did.

When we arrived home, it was almost ten o'clock. My pillowcase had served me well, and I dumped its contents on my bed to be examined. I had a good offering of gum: Double Bubble, little Wrigley gum packs, and little wienie-shaped gum. I also had plenty of hard candies and suckers. I was a little disappointed at my chocolate haul, but that's because anything short of one hundred percent was somewhat disheartening. I was most happy about the fact that I didn't have too much garbage that I needed to throw out. There were some bad candies, but, as a whole, the trick-or-treating was a success. I changed out of my pirate costume and got ready for bed. We had school the following day, and it was getting late. Scott turned on the radio to WLS, and we listened to "Monster Mash" as we chatted about Lance's success. Soon I drifted off to sleep. It was a truly happy Halloween.

The Meaning of Thanksgiving

It was an unusually warm late November day in 1999. The sky was gray and the streets and houses of the German town of Oranienburg had a thin layer of dirt, giving the town a dreary appearance. I drove through the narrow streets in my rented VW Passat, along with my wife, step-daughter, and small son. As I drove, I was looking for a sign that read "Gedenkstätte" or "KZ Museum". I spotted the sign and followed it. I had a little trouble finding the museum, since it was off the beaten path, but at last we made it, and went inside.

Oranienburg is a small town just northwest of Berlin. On a business trip to Germany, I decided to take a few extra days of vacation and bring my family with me. We were had left Berlin on the way to Hamburg to meet a friend of mine. It was November 25th, and Thanksgiving. I felt that Oranienburg would be a good place to stop and reflect on why we should give thanks—because it was the home of the former concentration camp Sachsenhausen. As we walked through the museum and camp grounds, it was easy to find reasons to be thankful. While the meaning of Thanksgiving was easy to understand as we walked through the memorial to human suffering, it still wasn't Thanksgiving without enjoying an American-cooked turkey and all the trimmings at home. So, in November 1999, we didn't have a Thanksgiving, even though we gave thanks that day.

Thanksgiving can mean something different to each person. What I discovered while overlooking a mass grave in Sachsenhausen was that Thanksgiving was about home and the feeling of comfort that went along with it. Maybe I felt that way because Mom's preparation for Thanksgiving was so deliberately consistent that if I were blindfolded and seated at the dinner table, I'd already know where everything was, from turkey to mashed potatoes, whether it was 1972 or 1982.

Thanksgiving, Price Style

Thanksgiving was always the same, year in and year out. While Christmas had its traditions, there was always the spontaneity of gifts that you gave or the hope that Santa would bring you something special that made each year stand out. It was the uniformity of Thanksgiving that made it unique. It gave it the feeling of home and comfort, like a Norman Rockwell painting. Mom was the one who made it happen. Although Mom never said so, Grandpa Hinesley may have caused Mom a little undue stress each time he and Grandma visited. It never seemed that way to my brothers and me, but I think Mom believed that the appearance of the house and the taste of the food reflected solely on her, as if she stood alone in the spotlight. If that was the case, then there was no spotlight bigger than the one cast by Thanksgiving.

In addition to the uniformity of dinner and the Thanksgiving atmosphere, we had consistent patterns of behavior. Football blared on the TV while Dad napped on the living room couch. My brothers and I would sneak off at some point for a quick round of the quarterback game before anyone arrived, and the game went on until the banging came from below. When Grandma and Grandpa Hinesley showed up in the late afternoon, we'd all greet them as they came in the door. Although Grandma wasn't known for her great cooking, she did make a mean pumpkin pie, and she always brought a pair of them. Frisky darted around the house when they arrived, and Steve even came out of his cave to say "Hi" after having worked on his latest Super Fuzzy comic. Then came the obligatory moment when my brothers and I had to show we had good manners by staying downstairs to keep our guests company. Mom would be busy in the kitchen, trying to show that she was under no stress whatsoever, when she would ask my brothers and me,

Mom, the master of Thanksgiving, even while pregnant with me.

ever so sweetly, to help her set the table. Her pleasant manner, while somewhat artificial, was nonetheless an effective way to get our participation. It was hard to turn down such a polite request.

While the turkey cooked in the oven, Grandma and Grandpa Hinesley waited in the living room. Grandma could always be found drinking a glass of wine and smoking a cigarette, while listening to one of my brothers or me provide her with an update on school or sports. Once Mom started transferring food to the table, she'd ask everyone to sit down. Dad carved the turkey, as each person sat down at his or her traditional spot at the table. Once everyone was seated, someone would ask Mom about the Hawaiian rolls, which she always forgot to take out of the oven. As a result, the rolls had an unintentional crispy bottom. Once she had the rolls sorted out, she'd ask if anyone wanted to say grace. One of my brothers or I would blurt out, "Good bread, good meat, good Lord, let's eat!"

Dad put an end to the snickering and fulfilled his annual obligation by praying very seriously,

"Bless us, O Lord, for these Thy gifts, which we are about to receive from Thy bounty. Through Christ our Lord, Amen."

"Amen."

Then began the passing of the seemingly endless stream of food. The selection of food, the china, and the silverware remained consistent from year to year; only the people at the table were a year older. Most of the food Mom prepared was long-standing traditional Thanksgiving food, like turkey, stuffing, mashed potatoes, and gravy. Yams and cranberry sauce were Thanksgiving favorites as well, although I wouldn't touch them with a ten-foot pole. Other staples like corn, green beans, Waldorf salad, and a few sticks of carrots and celery found a place on my plate. Mom also made a Jell-O of which hardly anyone ate more than a bite, yet it made the cut each year. It was a lemon Jell-O with shavings of carrot in it. It wasn't bad, but I wouldn't call it good, either. But, it was unique and always there. It was the Jell-O, in a way, that was a signature of Mom's Thanksgiving dinner, and no matter where in the world I was for Thanksgiving, I would never run across that Jell-O again. The Jell-O that I barely ate became a nostalgic memory of home.

After dinner, we'd help clear off the kitchen and dining room tables so we could play pinochle. When our stomachs could handle it, we'd take a brief break in the games of cards to enjoy a piece of Grandma's pumpkin pie. I enjoyed those moments of peace during those precious days away from school. Going back after Thanksgiving wasn't as bad as it might seem, because the first day back opened the official race toward Christmas, and things seemed that much more cheery.

'Tis the Season

Christmas was by far the most important holiday for our family, because it brought the family together on so many different levels—from decorating the house or buying a Christmas tree to going Christmas shopping and trying to find the right present for someone. As December of 1974 approached, there was a feeling of Christmas in the air—stores began setting up Christmas displays, and TV Christmas specials filled the airwaves. More importantly, Mom cast a "Christmas spell" over our house. She decorated the entire house in a special way, using Christmas candles, figurines, red ribbons and garlands, Christmas stockings, and mistletoe. She also set out candy dishes and peanut and walnut trays. She prepared the entire house from top to bottom, as if we were going to have a big Christmas party, but we were the only guests.

Mom cleaning up in preparation for the holiday festivities.

Although Mom was the queen of decorating, she enlisted my brothers and me to help clean the house. Usually we'd get different assignments. This year I got the family room, which wasn't too hard to clean. I vacuumed a little with the old Hoover, sprayed all the wooden furniture with Pledge, whipped off the dust and the nicotine residue left from hours of heavy smoking. I was happy to do it, because I had high hopes for Santa. As Christmas grew near, I figured I might need to do some make-up work to stay on the "good" list.

Dad and Christmas

Some people say there is no Santa Claus. In my world, Dad was Father Christmas. As long as he was around, there was a Santa in my house. In later years, he looked the part, too (minus the beard, of course). Christmas had to be his favorite holiday. He seemed to get as excited as we did about some of the gifts we received. There were a number of years we got an AFX race car set. AFX made HO-scale slot cars and race tracks that Dad assembled late on Christmas Eve while we were asleep. Of course, in the morning Dad played with them right along with us.

Mom made the house feel like Christmas, but most of the activities and traditions of Christmas outside the home revolved around Dad, such as stringing Christmas lights outside the house, Christmas shopping, and bringing home a Christmas tree. Affixing the Christmas lights to the house was always an interesting adventure. Each year Dad untangled the lights we had stored away, and tested them.

We used the common Christmas lights of the time, which were about the size of an egg and came in all colors. If you kept the lights on for a long time, they got super hot. These were the days before anyone thought of plastic clips attached to the house that could be used to clamp down the wires and hold the lights. Instead, Dad climbed on the roof and used a staple gun to attach the lights to the house. It could be a little tricky: If you accidentally hit the wire while it was plugged in, it could give you quite a shock. It just added to the holiday entertainment. Our family didn't go overboard when putting lights

Dad, Scott, and me at Christmas in 1989.

on our house, although for several years, we did have a full-size plastic Santa that lit up! Once he was damaged, our days of big outdoor displays were over. When the Christmas lights were up, the next thing we needed to get was the Christmas tree.

For about seven years in a row, my brothers and I joined Dad for the annual Indian Guides Christmas tree sale. Although we sold Christmas trees all that time, I don't remember buying a tree from Indian Guides. It may have been because the trees we sold weren't all that good, or it could have been that Dad enjoyed the hunt for a great Christmas tree so much more. In December 1974, as with most years, about three weeks before Christmas, the great hunter took his three sons out to hunt for the perfect Christmas tree. Our traditional hunting ground was Route 12 (Rand Road) north of Dundee Road. Today the area along Route 12 is mostly developed, but back in the 1970s, the area north of Dundee Road was very much like a rural highway. There were some homes, farmland, gas stations, and even a motel or two that resembled the Bates Motel from Psycho. Our hunting expedition began in the afternoon on that cold gray Sunday.

As American as Apple Pie

We all piled into the blue '72 Catalina, the workhorse of the Price family, and began our quest. I looked out the window as we traveled north on Route 12. Once we passed Dundee Road, the scenery began to change. I kept my eyes peeled for a lot of Christmas trees. We passed one lot that had Christmas trees on the corner of Lake Cook and Rand roads, because their offerings didn't look too promising from the road. A short time later, as we approached Route 22, off to the left I saw something that made me smile: a tower with a giant apple on top. It was the first recognizable feature of Bell's Apple Orchard. It was customary on the great hunt to stop at Bell's Apple Orchard for some refreshments.

Bell's Apple Orchard had been a family-owned business since 1939. It was a place you could go to pick your own bushels of apples. After Grandpa Hinesley's apple orchard stories from his days in Iowa, I wasn't inclined to run out into the orchard to bust my keister picking apples. What attracted us every year to Bell's was their store of apple goodies, which included everything from apple juice to iced apple pastries. We parked the car and went inside. The interior was a cross between a bakery and a general store, except all the products were apple related. The sweet smell of apples and sugar filled the air. We approached the glass display counter to look at all of the apple treats. I was partial to the doughnuts and the caramel-covered apples, but everything there was good.

The apple orchard was about as close as I got to health food during the 1970s. I don't think you could really say the apple sweets were all that healthy, but when you consider that these were the days when fast-food places were on the rise, then it wasn't so bad. Anyway, the only one I remember preaching about health food was body builder/juice enthusiast Jack LaLanne. Besides, if an apple a day keeps the doctor away, then a pie with about a dozen apples in it ought to keep you covered for at least a week or two. Throw in a dozen or so apple-cinnamon sugar doughnuts, a dozen caramel apples, and a box of iced apple pastries, and you could skip your annual check-up. At least I think that's how Dad saw it, as he placed his order with his Viceroy cigarette dangling from his lips.

"Can you throw in a gallon of apple cider with that?" Dad asked, squinting from the cloud of smoke drifting toward his eyes.

We never left empty handed. Dad grabbed a handful of napkins and put them in the bag with the sugared doughnuts, then handed the bag to me. Steve carried a box of caramel-covered apples and a gallon of cider, while Scott carried a box of caramel-covered apples with nuts. Dad carried a box of iced apple pastries, which he handed to Steve once we were in the car. Because the doughnuts were the easiest to eat in the car, I distributed a doughnut to everyone as Dad headed for our next stop, the Christmas tree lot.

The Tree

Each year when Dad led our hunt for a Christmas tree, he had one primary concern: size. He wanted a giant tree. Each year we performed the same vaudeville act of trying to get the tree to fit in our house. As we pulled into a lot with a number of promising trees, we knew what was in store for us. I licked the remaining sugar off my fingers, wiped my hands quickly with a napkin, then put on my gloves and braced myself for the cold weather as I opened the car door. My brothers and I looked at the various trees, testing them to see how dry they were and how well they maintained their needles. We were happy to see that Dad had found a tree to his liking; because the quicker he chose a tree the sooner we could get out of the cold. Soon Dad and a worker from the tree lot were tying the gigantic tree to the top of our car. The windows had to be open a little for the rope to wrap around the tree and the car, making for

a brisk drive home. On the way, we held onto the strands of rope that held the tree in place, praying that the tree didn't slide off the car between the tree lot and home. Once we got home, the real comedy began.

Because we had double-entry doors, getting the large tree inside the house was the easiest problem to overcome. Scott and I brought in the apple goodies and placed them on the kitchen counter while Dad and Steve untied the tree from the car. I opened the double doors. From that point on, every year was pretty much the same. Dad negotiated the tree into the foyer and realized it was too tall to stand upright in the house. He leaned the tree against the staircase, found a hand saw, and began to "modify" the tree to be able to fit it in the living room. After a few feet had been hacked off the top and bottom of the tree, it was finally able to clear the ceiling.

With a satisfied look, Dad mumbled, "Just like downtown."

After Dad made the final adjustments to the tree stand to get the tree to stand more or less straight, we stood back to admire it. Although it wasn't quite as nice as it looked on the lot before pruning, it was ready for decorating. Satisfied with our hunting efforts, we made our way to the kitchen for a celebratory caramel apple.

Mom's Touch

Mom led the effort to decorate the tree. Once we had the tree indoors, we waited two or three days for the branches to drop to their natural positions before we started decorating. Mom knew just how to get us into the spirit of Christmas by coordinating the tree decoration with a new holiday TV special airing that Tuesday night. When the time was right, Mom planned for us to begin decorating the tree right after dinner, have some hot cocoa, and watch the show. We looked forward to it with anticipation.

When I came home from school that day, Mom asked me to go into the crawl space to get the Christmas ornaments. I braved the dust and spider webs and brought out the ornaments and silver tinsel garland. After dinner, we decorated the tree as planned. Dad's role in the tree decorating process was the lights. Steve put some Christmas music on the VM stereo console downstairs and turned it up so we could hear it in the living room. Dad tested the lights, only to find that about half of them worked. He mumbled a few un-Christmas-like words as he fiddled with replacing bad bulbs. The rest of us started sorting through the various boxes for our favorite ornaments. Scott gave Dad a hand stringing the lights on the tree while Steve and I located the silver tinsel garland. As with everything, there was an order to decorating the tree-well, at least as far as the lights and the garland were concerned. After we hanged the garland ever so carefully, we moved on to the ornaments.

Mom loved Christmas ornaments. Each year she'd get us each our own special ornament to commemorate that year's Christmas. She also enjoyed crafting handmade ones. It seemed like there was a time when we were making ornaments at every Christmas function. We made them at school, at Indian Guides, at Cub Scouts, and even at home. We used all kinds of materials—pine cones, clothing pins, felt cutouts, and styrofoam balls with cloth, ribbon, or little aluminum stars pinned to them. And of course, there was always plenty of Elmer's Glue.

Luckily, we also had a wide assortment of standard ornaments to balance out the craft ornaments. We also hung candy canes on the tree but were strictly forbidden to eat them until Christmas morning. I guess it was just something else to look forward to. Hanging the ornaments was a free-for-all. By the time we were, done it looked like a tornado had hit our living room. There were empty boxes and unused hooks everywhere. We did make record time decorating the tree, which was good for us, because we had a mess to clean up before the show. Working as a team, my brothers and I hurried to straighten up. When we finished, Dad turned on the Christmas tree lights and turned off the room lights so we could all marvel at our sparkling tree. That beautiful family moment lasted all of five seconds as my brothers and I darted into the kitchen to watch our Christmas special.

We all sat in the kitchen and waited for the holiday special to begin. The show we were about to watch was called *The Year Without a Santa Claus*, and it instantly became one of my all-time favorites. We enjoyed a hot cocoa while watching it. After the special I went upstairs to get ready for bed, humming the "Heat Miser" song. I had to get some sleep; after all, it was a school night.

Christmas Break

I put on the clothes Mom had laid out for me the night before and skipped downstairs for breakfast. It was ten days after we decorated the tree, and my last day of school in Mrs. Nicholson's class before Christmas break. I poured Honeycomb cereal into my brightly colored plastic bowl as I watched *Ray Rayner and Friends* on TV. Steve and Scott were rushing around getting ready to leave. Mom made sure each of them had his sack lunch as they left to catch the bus, then went back to preparing the Christmas cookies for our class Christmas party.

A short time into *Garfield Goose and Friends*, Frazier Thomas introduced one of my favorite holiday short films: *Hardrock, Coco and Joe: the Three Little Dwarfs*. You can probably find a version of the short film on the internet. The black-and-white short film features a catchy song and Claymation to tell the story of three of Santa's helpers, who are helping Santa deliver toys on Christmas Eve. I used to identify with the three mischievous dwarfs because of my brothers. Once you've heard the song, it's difficult to get out of your head.

"I'm Hardrock, I'm Coco, and I'm Joe."

The other black-and-white short film WGN showed during Christmastime was *Suzy Snowflake*. *Suzy Snowflake* was about ringing in the snowy season. I was just happy it wasn't *Suzy Snowflake* that was playing this morning—even worse than the three little dwarfs' song was the song from *Suzy Snowflake*. You didn't want that annoying song stuck in your head. I finished my cereal and got ready to leave for school. I bundled up in my L.A. Rams winter coat and knit hat, pulled on my green rubber boots, and headed out the door to school when Mom called out,

"Don't forget your teacher's present!"

I almost forgot. If a teacher's gift was supposed to be a bribe, I failed miserably. I never knew what to get a teacher: a scented candle, some gourmet popcorn, or perhaps a mood ring? For some reason I thought it would be a good idea to give a small bottle of perfume from Wieboldt's. Thinking back on it, a pet rock would have been funnier, except they didn't come out until the following year.

I navigated the partially shoveled sidewalks, with my perfume gift in hand. Any time I spotted a stretch of sidewalk with packed-down snow, I ran up to it, then slid across the slick snow as if I were riding a snowboard. I was running a little late, and most of the kids were a short distance ahead of me. As I reached the crosswalk by the school, the first school bell rang, which meant the students could begin to enter the school. I hurried to the second-grade entrance. There was a crowd of students all dressed in their bulky winter coats, slowly filing into the double-door entrance like a herd of sheep guided into their holding pen. I, too, joined the group while a teacher barked orders to brush the snow off our clothes and boots. The tiled entrance floor was covered with a black rubber mat that was drenched from all of the melting snow from the boots and clothes. I obediently grabbed a green brush from the wooden rack and began to brush off my boots. Then I removed them and set them alongside the other boots that lined the hallway just outside our classroom. I deposited my perfume offering at the teacher's desk, and made my way to my seat.

School seemed to ease up in the early days of December. This day was mercifully quick. Not long after Mom dropped off the cookies, we enjoyed a brief holiday party, with cookies and fruit punch-flavored Hi-C served in small paper cups. After helping clean up, Mom left, and the class finished up the remaining activities of the day. The excitement increased with each minute that brought us closer to 3:30. Soon I was buttoning my coat, pulling on my boots, and lining up to leave. As the bell rang, you'd have thought they had just liberated the Bastille. Kids burst out of the school, screaming with delight and reveling in the euphoria associated with Christmas break.

The List

Tom Berg and I met up with Doug on our way home. We wound our way down the wintry streets of Greenbrier when the topic of Christmas presents came up.

"Hey, Tom, did you write your Christmas list yet?" Tom asked, as I slid along a snowy patch of sidewalk.

Frowning slightly at the thought, I replied, "No, not yet. I started it but never finished it. Do you already know what you want?"

"Yeah. Have you seen the new Planet of the Apes toys?" he asked.

"You mean the ones like the G.I. Joes?"

"Yeah."

"I've seen them on TV—they look pretty cool!" Doug added his two cents.

"I guess they're cool," I said. "Have you guys seen the new G.I. Joe with Kung Fu Grip?"

"Yeah, it looks awesome, I've got one on my list," said Doug. Tom nodded in agreement.

"I've got to finish my list," I said thoughtfully.

Doug disappeared through the Leopold's backyard to get to his house, while Tom and I continued up Champlain Street to my house. As we came up to the edge of our driveway, I turned to ask Tom if he wanted to stay for a while, when I was hit square in the chest with a heavy snowball.

Tom and I had just walked into a snowball fight between Steve, teamed with his close friend Bentley Patterson from across the street, and Scott, who had joined forces with Bentley's older brother Bruce.

Out of the corner of my eye, I spotted another large snowball sailing toward my head. I ducked just in time. I turned to Tom and yelled, "Take cover!"

Tom didn't need to be told twice. He took shelter behind the blue Catalina, with me close at his heels.

Thud! A snowball hit the Catalina hard, spraying snow everywhere. I couldn't see where it had come from, so I tried to stay low while I packed a snowball in my wet knit gloves.

I should mention here that Steve and Bentley used to make the biggest snowballs imaginable for a pair of fourteen-year-olds. They had to be fourteen inches in diameter, which seemed like a cannonball to a second grader. Getting hit with one could practically knock you over. Tom and I joined the fight the best we could, and an hour later we were covered with snow. It was getting close to dinnertime, and Tom needed to go home.

"See ya, Tom!" I called out. Then I remembered there was something else I wanted to ask him. "Are you going to the Indian Guides Christmas party tonight?"

"Yeah, we'll be there," he said, as he ran off toward home.

The Wish Book

As I entered the house, Frisky ran around excitedly, as if he hadn't seen me in ages. I took off my boots and jacket, and set my wet gloves next to the heating vent to dry. Mom was in the kitchen making hot dogs and macaroni and cheese, one of my favorite meals. Then it dawned on me what I had planned to do before the snowball pelted me: finish my list! I had a little time before dinner. I located the sheet of drawing paper on the fridge where I had jotted down a few things, and decided to start from scratch. I grabbed a pencil and a drawing pad from the kitchen drawer, and began my search for what I needed to complete my list, the Wish Book.

Every year around September, Sears, Roebuck and Company sent out their "Wish Book for the Christmas Season." This was in addition to the standard catalogs they sent out twice a year and was the greatest source for Christmas list inspiration. Inside the precious Wish Book were all sorts of items for everyone's Christmas list, such as clothes, tools, jewelry, furniture, and, most importantly, toys and games.

As far as Christmas lists go, Steve's was by far the most detailed, listing even the stores where he'd seen the items. Scott would wait until the last minute to make his list. Several years, he didn't make a list at all. When Scott was older he made the mistake of going Christmas shopping with Dad by himself when he hadn't made a list.

"Do you want a new basketball?" Dad asked.

"Yeah, that'd be cool."

"Merry Christmas, grab that one," Dad would say, and proceed to buy Scott's Christmas present in front of him. So much for surprises.

I preferred to be surprised when it came to Christmas presents, so I always made a list. I looked around for the Wish Book but couldn't find it anywhere. So, I went to the person who seemed to always know where things were—Mom. She had the unusual ability of knowing the location of almost every item in the house. It was kind of frightening, actually. I usually made an attempt to look for things, but after the second round of searching each room, I lost patience like every other male in the Price family and went to the great detector of lost objects.

"Hey, Mom! Do you know where the Sears Catalog is?" I shouted.

"Did you check under the stack of newspapers on the chair, in the dining room, next to the server?" Mom shouted back.

I ran into the dining room—the chair had a pile of about a week's worth of newspapers I began to sift through, when I spotted it. Maybe Mom should have worked for the police helping to find missing persons, because when it came to finding things, she had a gift.

I briefly marveled at Mom's talent as I began to thumb through the Sears Wish Book. I had to hurry, because dinner would be ready soon. There was great deal to choose from. I was almost guaranteed to get some clothing items for Christmas. My brothers and I felt that getting clothes for Christmas was kind of a gyp, but Mom, in true Hinesley form, saw Christmas as a time to give practical and useful things. I could respect Grandpa Hinesley giving me a package of socks: I mean, in his time you'd be damn grateful have a package of new socks, so I knew it meant something to him. Mom cleverly figured if she was going to spend the money on new clothes anyway, Christmas was the best time to do it. Not that she never gave good gifts—she did. She often personalized some gifts by finding that special something you might not ask for but that she thought you would love. But on the whole, she was practically minded. If you were going to be thrown in the pool, you might as well be ready to get wet. With that philosophy in mind, I added certain clothing items to the list so I'd at least get something I wanted. I started with an L.A. Rams sweatshirt and a slick jean jacket.

When making the Christmas list, there were always items you knew you'd never get in a million years, but you still had to take the chance that Santa would bless you with some super-cool gift. Things like a pool table or drum set would make the list. Sometimes you just had to shoot for the stars. After jotting down the small number of clothing items, I went straight for the back portion of the catalog, where the toys were. As I looked through the pages, I noticed something new that caught my eye. It was girder-and-panel set, where you could build your own skyscrapers. The picture in the catalog showed a kid standing next to the Sears Tower, and the building was taller than the kid! Awesome! I had to write that down. Then came a number of pages with educational toys. Boring! I didn't need a View-Master—I'm sure there was one in the old toy box. I skimmed through the pages of hobby kits—I got my fill of crafts in Indian Guides and Cub Scouts. They had a nice selection of games, I thought, as I added Stratego and Rock 'Em Sock 'Em Robots. I was writing so much down, it's a wonder I didn't develop carpal tunnel syndrome. Finally I found what I was looking for: action figures. This was time to go for the gold and ask for everything possible. What did I have to lose? First, I added the Planet of the Apes figures to my list, but my heart was set on the G.I. Joes.

If you like action figures, G.I. Joe was the cream of the crop in 1974. It's true that there were other action figures that had gained some popularity, like Big Jim, but he was nothing compared with G.I. Joe. G.I. Joe was bigger, had better accessories, was durable, and was still like a military figure—well, maybe more like a mercenary. The anti-war movement began to have an influence on toy manufacturers in the late 1960s and early 70s. By 1974, G.I. Joe wasn't the clean-cut soldier Steve had when he was seven; he was a bearded adventurer. Stripped of his military uniform, G.I. Joe was now part of the "Adventure Team." The unintentional consequence of this change was to make G.I. Joe a non-affiliated mercenary that would kill anything that moved. I just had to add him to the list! Another great thing about G.I. Joe was his new hands, which had "Kung Fu Grip"—it was brand new in 1974. This was a huge improvement and took away the frustration of trying to have a G.I. Joe hold accessories. I'd received G.I. Joes in the past, but this G.I. Joe was definitely a must-have item.

I was finishing up my list, and decided I should do a quick once-over to make sure I had everything covered. When making your Christmas list, it was important to consider what your friends had, so that when you got together you had the same kinds of toys. Not all friends shared the same taste in toys. Tom Berg, for example liked G.I. Joes. Doug Brooks and I made a Lego city that Doug kept at his place. Brian Carey liked the Fisher Price Adventure People. The Adventure People were different from other action figures in that they were based around themes that involved recreational activities, like motocross, water skiing, and scuba diving. They were designed to allow kids to play at being adults who were out having fun. In the end, it didn't matter if we played with G.I. Joes or with Adventure People, because life requires conflict, and inevitably, somebody would fight over one of the bikini-clad girls, or there would be a dispute over who owned the boat. The action figures didn't have guns, so one guy would grab a boat oar and the other a chainsaw to settle their differences. I guess mankind is doomed—so much for social engineering!

I finished my list just in time for dinner. I placed my newly completed list on the refrigerator in plain view of all gift buyers. "I should be covered," I thought, as I sat down at spot at the kitchen table. The evening news blared in the background as we ate dinner. I had to hurry somewhat because I had to get ready for the Indian Guides Christmas party. It meant an evening with friends, Christmas cookies, a grab-bag gift, and singing Christmas carols with Dad.

Shopping for Mom

The next day brought our annual shopping trip for Mom. Christmas shopping for Mom was always a team effort. Dad had a method to his gift shopping—each year we'd get Mom a big-ticket item, then each of us was entrusted with a set of regular gifts. For example, my role on the team was to give Mom slippers each year. I became an expert, of sorts, as to the exact kind she wanted. I believe it became such a standard gift that she began to depend on my getting slippers for her each Christmas. Even if I wanted to give her a different, more special gift, I still had to buy her slippers; otherwise, I felt I had let the team down. The first stop on the Christmas shopping spree was always Woodfield Mall.

Christmas shopping at the mall with Dad was always an adventure. We sped down Route 53 in our green 1973 AMC Hornet Hatchback. For a smaller car, the Hornet packed some power. Steve rode shotgun, while Scott and I were crammed into the back. We exited at Woodfield Road, which was always exciting because you had to immediately cut across two lanes of traffic to get to the shopping center. The way Dad drove, I held on for dear life and hoped I'd survive the trip to celebrate Christmas one more year.

The parking lot was jam-packed. We settled for a parking spot on the outer rim of the mall's parking lot, just outside Sears, Roebuck and Company. As with almost everything Dad did, this was by design. It was our holiday tradition to enter the mall through Sears. Climbing out of the car, I could just make out the building on the horizon. Now the great hike began. We made our way to Sears across the snow- and slush-covered parking lot, like Robert Peary's team trekking to the North Pole. The wind blew hard, but I was bundled up pretty well in my official NFL Los Angeles Rams team jacket and knit hat (complete with a little ball on top).

As we entered the store, we were greeted with the familiar smells of chocolate and sweets from the candy counter just inside the entrance. This was the true reason we always entered through Sears. We circled around the counter, admiring the wide array of confections displayed before us. There were chocolate stars with white sprinkles, caramel squares, peanut brittle, chocolate-covered toffee, and other confectionery delights, but we came for the peanut clusters. It was a tease, though, because Dick Price's method dictated that we could only purchase items from the candy counter after we completed our shopping task.

One item on our shopping list for Mom was a pewter plate or cup. Really, anything made of pewter would fulfill Mom's "pewter requirement." The place to find pewter was the upscale store, Marshall Fields. Every year we stopped there for an item Mom wanted, and the previous year's visit had been a memorable one.

At that time, we went to Marshall Fields to buy Mom some perfume. As the youngest, I became the guinea pig for the various scents Dad wanted to test. The result was that I was sprayed with about ten different perfumes before a choice was made. There we were in Marshall Fields' Perfume Department, with me smelling like a woman's magazine, and Dad still had another fragrance he wanted to test. I reluctantly raised my arm to be sprayed. At the same time, Dad bent down to smell the fragrance. The result was that I accidentally hit Dad in his large nose with my perfumed hand. I realized instantly I had made a mistake. Instinctively Dad took a swat at my head. I incorporated my speedy, catlike reflexes that would later suite me well as a goalie, and ducked out of the way. As luck would have it, Scott was standing directly behind me, holding a purple bottle of perfume. Dad's hand smacked the bottle out of Scott's grasp, and we all watched the bottle drop to the floor as if in slow motion. As the bottle hit the ground, it made an explosive popping sound, and completely disappeared from sight. A split second later, a swarm of Marshall Fields employees surrounded me, asking me if I was all right. Besides being very embarrassed and smelling like a perfume factory, I was fine. We decided not to buy any perfume that day.

As we entered Marshall Fields this time around, I was thankful no one recognized us from the previous year. We made our way to the basement level, where they kept the fine china and pewter items. The store bustled with holiday shoppers. We looked over the pewter items, and my brothers and I were astonished at the prices of the seemingly small objects, as we always were. Dad finally settled on a pewter cup that had an ornate handle with a little swirl at the end. Satisfied with his choice, he worked his way over to the counter. Dad was typically a man of good spirits—one might even say he was jovial at times. This was not one of those times. He had to deal with the holiday traffic and crowds at Woodfield, which during the Christmas season was packed with people like a market in Calcutta. On top of all that, of course, he had to deal with the three of us, and we weren't exactly the best-behaved boys in Cook County. The strain began to show.

Dad found a spot at the counter and waited to be served. Behind the counter were two women pleasantly chit-chatting away. Dad waited patiently for them to finish their conversation. While he stood waiting, more and more people began to gather around the counter, also waiting for service. It was at this point that I first sensed danger. I glanced at the women who were still chatting, then back to Dad, who was now a deep shade of red.

"ARE YOU GOING TO SELL ME ANY OF THIS SHIT, OR WHAT!?" Dad bellowed, in a loud booming voice that I swear people in the parking lot could hear.

He slammed the item on the glass counter. It seemed as if the Christmas music stopped and everyone looked our way. The two women behind the counter froze like deer caught in the headlights, mouths open, gawking at Dad, who had had enough and gave up trying to buy the pewter cup. Steve, Scott, and I all scattered in different directions to avoid being seen. We converged with Dad as he stormed out of the store. We all had a good laugh about the incident while eating peanut clusters in the Hornet on our way back home.

Christmas Eve in Greenbrier

Christmas Eve was a day packed with activities. Last-minute shopping was traditionally one of them. After our failed attempt to obtain a pewter item at Woodfield, we tried Randhurst Shopping Center next. Once again, we packed into the Hornet. When we arrived, we rushed through the stores, making sure we had all of our gifts covered. Finally, in Wieboldt's, we hit pay dirt when we found pewter candle holders—mission accomplished! Meanwhile, Mom was getting things ready for the night's festivities. Christmas Eve dinner was almost a rerun of Thanksgiving dinner, minus the lemon-carrot Jell-O. I wasn't as concerned about what we were going to eat as much as I was about what was under the tree.

Everyone celebrates Christmas in his or her own way. Our Christmas tradition was pretty simple. After a large dinner, we exchanged presents. The next morning, we woke up to find what Santa had brought us. So really, it was a two-phase process. I'm not sure if there was any logic behind how this was done, but the result was that we got to enjoy and thank everyone for the presents we received from each other. Also, those gifts didn't compete directly with the presents my brothers and I received from Santa. Another benefit with the two-phase process was that if you missed out on getting what was on your list in phase one, there was always hope Santa would come through for phase two. I was somewhat luckier than my brothers because I had a birthday in early January, which served as my emergency present back-up day.

Scott and I proudly display our G.I. Joes on Christmas day, 1970. The one downside with my 1970 G.I. Joe was that the hands never seemed to hold things well. That was solved in 1974 with the Kung Fu Grip.

When we returned home from Randhurst, I ran into the kitchen to occupy Mom so the others could sneak in the gifts and wrap them in the living room. There were several plates of Christmas cookies sitting out that Mom had made the night before. Mom had a way with cookies, and Christmas cookies were her specialty. When Dad told me the coast was clear and the presents were wrapped, I snatched a few mint meringue cookies and ran upstairs to change my clothes.

Grandma and Grandpa Hinesley arrived around the standard time of 4:00 pm, and Frisky charged around the house, coming dangerously close to the Christmas tree and the presents underneath. My brothers and I welcomed them and added their presents to the ones already under the tree, all the while trying to figure out what might be inside each one. Grandma and Grandpa went into the kitchen to join Mom. In the confusion, I sneaked a handful of dinner mints from a mint tray in the living room. Steve went downstairs and put on *Holiday Sing Along With Mitch Miller* on the VM stereo console, and soon my brothers and I were running around, acting silly, singing "Must Be Santa," energized by the sugar from the mints and Christmas cookies.

Once the turkey was ready, we settled down for dinner. Dad said his normal prayer to signal the start of the feast. My brothers and I bolted down our meals and asked to be excused. We waited expectantly for the opening of presents to begin. Steve was the master of the ceremony and handed out each gift and announced who it was from. He kneeled patiently in front of the tree as everyone gathered around. I sat down next to Grandpa Hinesley on the couch, anxiously awaiting my first gift. Dad set up the 8-mm movie camera to capture the magic of the moment. With a loud click, the room was flooded in hot, white light from Dad's Sun Gun II movie light. "Sun Gun" said it all—just a glance in its direction could blind you temporarily. Our movie camera didn't have sound, so we were saved from having any stupid utterance saved for posterity. Sometimes limited technology can be a good thing. The steady clicking of the camera began, and Steve was given the go-ahead to begin handing out gifts.

While I hoped for some interesting toy, Dad seemed to only get practical gifts, like tools of some kind. One year he received a toilet seat. Merry Christmas! Mom made out a little better because she celebrated her birthday at Christmas. She was thrilled when she opened her pewter candle holders—if she only knew what trouble we went through to get them! I secretly think her favorite gift was the pair of slippers I got for her. Steve brought me a large box from Grandma and Grandpa Hinesley. We were all briefed before Christmas to show the utmost appreciation for whatever we received from them, so I was prepared to display my well-rehearsed reaction when Steve handed me the gift. I kept telling myself to act surprised when I saw a bag of socks. I began to unwrap the box, which seemed a little large for a bag of socks, but I figured Grandpa was just making use of whatever old box he had around the house. I tore away the wrapping paper and opened the box to discover not a bag of socks, but a stuffed "Hubert" the Harris lion, mascot of Harris Bank, where Grandpa Hinesley banked. I was so happy not to get socks that my reaction may have seemed like I had waited my whole life for one. I'm sure Grandpa Hinesley was pleased.

Under the burning light of the Sun Gun II, everyone seemed happy with their gifts as the number of presents under the tree dwindled down. I was desperately hoping for a G. I. Joe with Kung-Fu Grip, but I was run-

Steve, under the blaring light of the Sun Gun II movie light.

ning out of gifts to open. When Steve handed out the last gift, it became apparent I would have to place my hopes on Santa for phase two.

The Mystery of Santa Claus

Each year as Christmas comes around, the mystery of Santa lurks in the minds of many a young child. Is Santa real? Will I sneak a peek at him this year? Will I hear him? How will he know what I want? As I looked out the window into the dark night sky, I wondered where he was. Steve explained away some of the mystery that surrounded Santa Claus when he chatted with me about him. Steve recognized my confusion as to why there were different store Santas, when there was supposed to be only one Santa. Steve took out the letter S book from our *World Book Encyclopedia* set and

Steve, me, and Scott pose for a photo opportunity with a Mall Santa.

explained to me that Santa couldn't be everywhere at once, so he sent out his helpers to gather information for him. Then he opened the encyclopedia to the entry about Santa Claus.

He showed me the picture and said, "Here's the real Santa."

Relieved my Christmas wishes were in good hands, I was able to relax a little. I also wanted to be sure that I was on my best behavior so I didn't mess something up at the last minute and wind up with nothing.

After Grandma and Grandpa left, we went upstairs to go to bed. It was always hard to get to sleep on Christmas Eve. Excitement from the new toys and gifts we'd just received, along with the anticipation and uncertainty of what we'd find in the morning, was enough to keep anyone from dropping right off to sleep. Scott and I whispered back and forth as to what we might find in the morning. We shared our deepest hopes and our biggest fears. Secretly, I hoped to catch a glimpse of Santa. I tossed and turned a great deal that night, before my eyelids grew too heavy keep open. I decided to rest them while listening carefully for any sounds of reindeer or a sleigh.

Rise and Shine, Sleepy Head

I awoke with a start and realized I had fallen asleep. Sunlight peeked through our heavy drapes. I looked over at Scott and saw he was still asleep, or at least too comfortable to get up. On Christmas morning I was always an early riser, as was Steve. Scott was not. I crept out of bed, trying not to make too much noise. I made my way down the hallway. Steve was just getting up, too, and we went downstairs together. From the top of the steps, the first sign that Santa had visited was the bulging stockings that hung on the double entry doors. My stocking was the closest to the stairs, and I took it down and carried it into the living room. Under the tree were three separate groups of toys. Unlike us amateur gift givers, Santa worked more efficiently, because none of the gifts under the tree were wrapped. There was simply a card with a name on it in front of each pile.

I located my pile of toys, and scanned it for a G.I. Joe with Kung-Fu Grip. I didn't see one. While I was a little disappointed, I knew I had my birthday as my back-up; besides, I'd done pretty well. I noticed that Santa must have a Sears Wish Book, because I saw many of the toys I had written down, as well as others in my brothers' piles. I'd received a few the Planet of the Apes figures, and an Evel Knievel figure and motorcycle. As I looked through the toys, it was a little overwhelming. I was looking at the Evel Knievel and motorcycle when Steve asked if he could look at the World Famous Building Set. I agreed, and joined him in building the Sears Tower. I worked with him long enough to know I would rather play with the Evel Knievel action figure and left the building to him. Scott soon made his way downstairs to see what he had in the way of gifts. After a short while, Mom and Dad came down and enjoyed the pleasure we received from our toys. Each of us wanted to show them something neat about what we'd received.

We continued to play with our toys the remainder of the morning. Then I was struck by the odd feeling that the anticipation and mystery connected with Christmas was over until next year. I went over to the Christmas tree and removed a candy cane, and played with my new toys some more. While much of the excitement was over for the Christmas of 1974, we still had Christmas dinner over at Grandma and Grandpa Hinesley's house ahead of us. But really, Christmas dinner was just another excuse to play cards.

Last Chance for Big Prizes

As my eighth birthday came around, I really had only one wish, and that was the G.I. Joe with Kung-Fu Grip.

As the youngest, I was also slightly disadvantaged by the fact that I didn't have as many birthday parties as my predecessors, probably because my parents no longer had the energy to put up with the drain of such parties in later years. Whereas Steve would go on having parties until he was thirteen or fourteen, mine ended when I was nine or ten years old. Even if we didn't have big parties with a large group of friends, we still had family parties, for which Grandma and Grandpa Hinesley came over for dinner, cake, and a game of cards (any excuse for a game).

That may not seem like much, but during the 1970s in Greenbrier, kids my age didn't have big birthdays. I never invited twenty kids to a laser-tag party or to an amusement park or anything crazy. My birthday parties were always kept simple. The gifts were simple, too, but I didn't expect otherwise. When I did have a birthday party, and I didn't always have one, it was at our house, with cake and some party favors with matching paper plates and fruit punch. We'd play a game or two, make a lot of noise, open presents, and say goodbye. My lack of a big birthday party wasn't unusual; as a matter of fact, I don't remember anyone having a big birthday party, and I don't remember anyone having a party after they were ten years old. When I turned eight, I didn't have a birthday party. That's not to say we didn't celebrate.

My birthday celebration started at school. At Greenbrier, students were allowed to bring treats to share with the other students. Mom always made cupcakes with chocolate frosting. When you distributed cupcakes among your peers, it increased your popularity significantly. This was especially true if your Mom made good cupcakes. Then you received special treatment for the rest of the day.

At home, I received special treatment, as well. Grandma and Grandpa Hinesley showed up around dinnertime. I was able to choose what dinner I wanted. I always felt funny making the request, though, because I was otherwise never consulted about what dinner was going to be. After dinner we'd have a homemade yellow cake with chocolate frosting. I made a wish and blew out the candles. On my eighth birthday my wish came true, and I was presented with the gift I had waited the whole winter for—a G.I. Joe with Kung-Fu Grip.

CHAPTER 7

Seeing America

The Great Forty-Eight States

I took a fishing trip to northern Wisconsin with my son recently. We'd taken trips before to various locations around the country, but almost always by airplane. As we packed up the car and he loaded his Gameboy and a portable DVD player, I realized there was a lot he had missed during our travels between destinations. While he crossed many states by air, he didn't experience them. Even during our trip to northern Wisconsin, his attention was glued to his Gameboy. It's funny how things have changed from the time when my brothers and I traveled with Mom and Dad. Back then, it was all about seeing America.

During summer break when I was seven years old, I scrambled to get my things together as the double fan roared away from my bedroom window. I gathered some toys, my pillow, and my blanket. I knew Mom had packed all of my clothes and other things. I made my way down the hallway toward the stairs and looked out the window. Dad was busy packing the trunk of the blue '72 Catalina with our assorted suitcases. It was a bright, sunny July morning, and it looked like Dad was getting hot. Mom was standing at the front door as I came downstairs.

"Do you need any help?" she called out to Dad.

"Nah, I think I've got it," Dad said, with his head still in the trunk.

"Hey Mom, can I put these in the back seat?"

"Go ahead, but don't bother your dad."

The rear passenger door was open, and Scott put something inside the car. I stood next to him to wait my turn, then threw my pillow and blanket up in the back windowsill. I deposited the few plastic army men I had with me in the middle of the back seat. That's where I'd be stuck for most of the trip, anyway. It was mid-July, 1974. Watergate was getting as hot as the July weather, and undoubtedly Nixon was sweating almost as much as Dad was as he loaded the trunk of the car. While the president tried to figure out how to convince the American public he wasn't a crook, we packed for our 1974 summer road trip.

During the early 1970s, summer break usually meant Greenbrier softball, swim lessons at Frontier Park, Fourth of July Bike Parade, and an all-American-style road trip. Because Mom hadn't reentered the workforce yet and Dad was self-employed, they were able to schedule three weeks for vacation almost every

Our family in a glass-bottom boat at Silver Springs in Florida (note that Dad has the 8-mm movie camera). Mom is sporting shades, while the three of us lean into the picture. Thats me, Steve and Scott (along with a ramdom vacationer).

summer. Although I didn't realize it at the time, I was quite lucky to get to take these trips. I didn't know friends who flew places for their vacations, because it was typically too expensive to travel by air with a family of five. It was much more common to travel by car.

Coming from Chicago, which is located pretty much in the middle of the country, our long road trips were broken down into two categories: the East Coast, and the western mountain region. We never made it all the way to the West Coast as a family, but it wasn't for the lack of hours on the road. The nice thing about road trips, in contrast with flying somewhere, was that you saw more of America between each destination. Dad loved America, and, geographically speaking, there isn't really anything that the United States doesn't offer if you want to see it. From beaches and oceans to open plains and mountain ranges, from deserts and great lakes to forests and corn fields, you name it, America has it.

Years later I'd tell Dad how interesting Europe was, Germany in particular. His response was, "I still haven't seen everything in the United States, and here, I don't have to learn a new language."

Well, he may have had a point, and it was because of this attitude that my brothers and I were treated to tours of the United States from an early age.

In the summer of 1974, we were taking a trip out west. The previous two years, we took back-to-back trips down the East Coast to Florida and Walt Disney World. On those trips, I don't think we missed a tourist stop or activity along the way. That was another benefit of driving, because we could spontaneously do various things along the way, like stop at Six Flags in Georgia or Disney World in Florida. One day we'd be at a historic location like Gettysburg or St. Augustine; the next we'd be watching alligator wrestling or taking a ride in the glass-bottom boats in Silver Springs. I don't know how we did it all, but we did. This year, our vacation theme was the Wild West.

This trip would be slightly different from previous road trips in a number of ways. In January of 1974, the national maximum speed limit of fifty-five miles per hour was enacted as a result of the Emergency Highway Energy Conservation Act. The goal of the new law was to reduce fuel consumption during the so-called energy crisis. On a trip out west, where there can be long stretches of road between any places of interest, the new speed limit was going to add to the strain of three restless boys in the car. Another difference was that we were going to be joined by Grandma and Grandpa Hinesley, who would drive their own car. They joined us on the trips out West because Uncle Herb and his family lived in Cheyenne, and we would all go and visit at one time. Traveling great distances by car requires a team effort for the trip to go well. I was lucky to be the youngest because I was able to learn lessons from past trips where things didn't go so smoothly.

The Four Travel Lessons

Lesson one—car discipline. Driving on a long trip can be stressful enough. Add to the mix a co-pilot who can barely read a map and two or three screaming kids in the backseat, and you have all the ingredients for a potential catastrophe. Although Dad was typically in good spirits while traveling, he had his limits. Just like U.S. Homeland Security uses threat-level alerts to indicate increasing degrees of danger, Dad sent signals of his own to alert you of the increased chances of getting smacked if your behavior didn't improve.

The first warning level was, "Guys, give it a rest." If you reached this warning level, you knew you should quit screwing around, but you also knew it was still a casual enough warning that you weren't in trouble at this point.

The second warning level was, "Do I have to get your attention?" When you heard this warning, you were definitely in the danger zone. You were walking a tight rope at this point, and it was the last verbal warning you were going to get.

After receiving two warnings, we were fair game. Dad had an amazing reach for a man his size. Usually a man's arm span matches his height. In Dad's case, his arm span was several inches longer than he was tall. It's possible that smoking stunted his growth. I'll never know, but I do know this: If you reached the third stage, you'd better be ready to duck out of the way of those gorilla arms. There was no better example of that lesson than the one from the family's trip out West in 1966, before I was born.

On that occasion, Grandpa Hinesley couldn't leave work, so Grandma Hinesley joined my parents and brothers in the car for the road trip. After several hours on the road, Steve and Scott were beginning to get on Dad's nerves.

"Guys, give it a rest."

The short attention span of my brothers, who were five-and-a-half and three-and-a-half, caused Steve and Scott not to heed the first warning, and soon they were screaming and roughhousing again.

"Hey! Do I have to get your attention?"

After a brief pause, Steve and Scott continued fooling around. In a flash Dad, swung back to correct the problem, and there was a loud smack! Besides the hum of the road, there was total silence in the car.

Then Dad turned to Mom and said, "I think I just smacked your mother."

From the backseat of the car came the small voice of Grandma Hinesley as she squeaked, "You did."

Lesson two—keep a head count. On the road, the various rest stops, souvenir shops, and tourist destinations can be packed with people. Keeping track of kids as they run in the crowd can be a challenge. Communication is always important. If we went somewhere big, we usually agreed upon a highly visible meeting place so that if one of us got separated from the rest, we knew where to look. Just as it's wise to double-check your hotel room before leaving to make sure you didn't leave anything behind, it's important to keep a head count before getting on the road again after making a stop. Again, this lesson comes from the 1966 trip out West.

When traveling with kids, sometimes the simplest things take a little more time, such as going to the bathroom, eating a meal, shopping, or walking on a trail. Dad wasn't known for his patience. He had a tendency to walk fast and keep everyone moving at an up-tempo pace. During one stop, Mom and Grandma Hinesley intended to switch seats for a little while so that Grandma could take a break from the kids and sit up front. Dad waited patiently for Grandma Hinesley to slowly climb into the front seat and close the door. Then he drove away. Mom, however, hadn't yet opened her door, and Steve and Scott waved goodbye to her out the back window as she disappeared from sight. A few miles down the road, Dad realized Mom was missing. Lesson learned.

Lesson three—learn to share. Sometimes you have to make do with what you have. Having two brothers sometimes means you have to share candy or toys. It was always good to be grateful for what you did have, because it could always be worse. I learned that lesson from another event that took place on the 1966 trip. When driving west from Chicago, there are long stretches of road where there is little to see or do. If you travel along I-90 in South Dakota, you'll begin to see large billboard signs or painted barns advertising Wall Drug. The billboards kill the monotony of the road as well, because every minute or so a new sign appears to advertise free ice water, five-cent coffee, or any number of various items sold or displayed at Wall Drug.

Along the way, one of the signs my brothers saw advertised ice cream. It wasn't long before my brothers began begging for ice cream. Dad peered into the rearview mirror and said, "We'll see, maybe if you guys behave." Dad had a weakness for sweets. I think he often enjoyed offering them to us as much as eating them himself. Every mile brought them closer to the exit for Wall Drug, and the excitement at the possibility of getting ice cream grew. Finally they reached the exit and turned off toward Wall Drug, which included a number of shops in addition to the drugstore itself. The store was designed with the average tourist in mind. Everything someone on the road could want or need could be found at Wall Drug. Dad parked the car on the street in front, and my brothers and Grandma Hinesley waited in the car while Mom and Dad went inside.

The place was packed that day, and Dad got in line to buy five chocolate ice cream cones and a bag of ice. He waited and waited and finally got to the front of the line. Soon Dad walked away from the counter with a paper tray that held the five ice cream cones and a ten-pound bag of ice hooked on his right pinky. The bag of ice was starting to strain his finger, so he was glad to spot Mom in the crowd.

Dad held out the tray of cones and said, "Can you grab this?"

Mom thought he meant the bag of ice and took that instead. The unexpected change in weight from the bag of ice caused the tray of ice cream cones to fly up to his chest, smashing all but one ice cream cone all over the front of his shirt. The hot day, the long drive, the long wait, the screaming kids, and now a shirt full of chocolate ice cream was too much for Dad to handle, and he stood there shaking, growling like a grizzly bear, and trying not to explode. At a loss for words, all he could get out was, "Clean it up!" Mom and an available employee helped him clean up the best they could. When Mom and Dad got back to the car, Steve and Scott yelled, "Where's the ice cream?" Dad approached them at the car window, with the huge chocolate stain on the front of his shirt, shoved the surviving chocolate ice cream cone at them, and barked, "Share it!"

Lesson four—always follow directions. One thing that was for certain was Dad always kept his word. If he gave directions, he meant it word for word. If he said be home by dark, he meant be home by dark, not ten minutes later. Just as whenever he promised to be somewhere it was like money in the bank, he expected the same of us. Dad didn't like excuses. There was no better example of this than on our 1969 trip out to the East Coast.

We had made a stop somewhere in Pennsylvania at a souvenir shop that Mom wanted to visit called Strawberry Fields. I was only two-and-a-half years old, and Mom brought me along in the store. Steve and Scott didn't want to go, and asked if they could wait in the car. They sat with Dad in the car and waited. After a short while, Steve and Scott grew restless and begged to go into the store instead of waiting in the car. Irritated, and knowing they could be a handful for my mom, especially when she already had to deal with me, he gave them a warning:

"If your mom has to send you back to the car because you're not behaving, you're going to get a spanking. Do you understand?"

Both Steve and Scott nodded and headed into the store, as happy as could be. When we went on our family vacations, Mom and Dad gave us some spending money—usually about five dollars—to buy a souvenir or small toy. It so happened that Steve and Scott each found something they wanted, and asked Mom for some of their vacation money. Having bought their toys, and not wanting to wait in the store, they asked Mom if they could return to the car. She said it was fine with her, so they skipped off to the car. Seeing his two boys return to the car without Mom and me didn't make Dad happy, and he was always good to his word.

When Mom and I returned to the car, we wondered why Steve and Scott were crying. After hearing of his mistake, Dad later commented that although they may not have deserved it just then, he was just making up for all the times they were bad and got away with it.

On the Road Again

As Dad finished packing our trunk for our 1974 trip, Grandpa Hinesley's bronze 1968 Buick Electra 225 slowly pulled into our driveway. Grandma and Grandpa Hinesley decided to come inside for a cup of coffee before we hit the road. Frisky welcomed Grandpa Hinesley by doing laps around the living room.

"How are you doing, there, Frisky?" Grandpa said in a funny high voice, as he reached down to pet the dog. Grandpa loved to spoil him. He went over to a jar of dog biscuits that we kept on the counter and pulled a few out to feed the dog as he sat down for his cup of coffee. Grandma, too, made her way into the kitchen to sit down. Mom filled up the coffee Thermos that she kept with her at all times in the front seat on long road trips, then poured the remaining coffee into four cups. It wasn't long before the kitchen was filled with cigarette smoke as Mom, Dad, and Grandma Hinesley puffed away at Mom's pack of Viceroys. Mom made sure she had a full carton of cigarettes with her before we left. When they'd finished their coffee, Mom rounded up my brothers and me, and soon we were zooming away in the Catalina for our three-week stint. We began our great trek westward by heading south on Route 53 to the Northwest Tollway, I-90.

The interstate highway changed the American road trip by bypassing many smaller towns between destinations and by avoiding the slower traffic in those towns. It also made some of the smaller tourist attractions seem off the beaten path. Anytime we saw a sign for a tourist attraction, needed gas, or just wanted to eat, we'd pull off the interstate for a while and drive through the closest town. We drove along the bumpy Illinois interstate, paying tolls every few miles. After paying the final Illinois toll, the roads became smooth, and there wasn't a toll in sight as we crossed the boarder into Wisconsin.

Finding the Right Hotel

When traveling on the road, getting a nice room for the night is of chief importance. If you're traveling to a new place where you've never been, it could be something of a gamble. In the late 1960s and early 70s, brand awareness was becoming embedded in many Americans' minds. One thing you looked for in a brand was consistency. Some brands had become national icons. If we were on the road, we knew what we were going to get when we saw the McDonald's Golden Arches or the orange roof of a Howard Johnson's. The brand that best represented consistency in hotels during that time was Holiday Inn. Wherever we went, we always felt confident in the quality of Holiday Inn. They had the coolest, most recognizable sign, which you could easily spot from the road. When I spotted the Holiday Inn sign from the road, it was like finding my home away from home. That feeling provided a certain comfort when we were so far away.

Although comfort was important, my brothers and I always focused on the extras, like the swimming pool or game room. Each time we checked into a new place I developed a feeling of ownership about my hotel. My brothers and I had a routine we typically followed when we arrived at a new hotel. First, we checked out the room, got some ice from the ice machine, and then darted out to the pool or game room to play around until Mom and Dad were ready to go do something. Once we were actually in the room, Steve and Scott each claimed their respective beds, while I was always stuck with a rollaway bed that Dad had arranged for at check-in.

The first hotel we stayed in during our 1974 trip wasn't a Holiday Inn, but a knock-off called the Star Motel in the Wisconsin Dells. (The Wisconsin Dells didn't have a Holiday Inn at the time.) Shortly after we arrived, I was excitedly looking for the ice bucket so I could run and get some ice, even though we didn't need any at the moment, when I came to the bathroom. I checked the bathroom for cleanliness, and was pleased to see the paper band wrapped around the toilet seat. It was common at the time for toilet seats at hotels to have a paper band around them, which gave me the feeling the seat was brand new, because you had to unwrap it to use it. Of course the seat wasn't brand new, but at least in my mind, the paper band always fulfilled its psychological purpose. In addition to providing the security that the bathroom was clean, this paper band also served as an advertisement for the Tommy Bartlett Water Ski Show. Nothing was sacred from advertising in the Wisconsin Dells.

American Kitsch

If you traveled the United States and saw all of its wonderful landscapes, great cities, and historical sights, your trip wouldn't be complete without the all-important spectacle of the roadside oddities found across this great country. I'm talking about the carnival-like tourist attractions like the Corn Palace in South Dakota, the Cathedral of Junk in Texas, and the alligator wrestling in Florida. It's what I'd like to call American Kitsch. There is one city I know of that's entirely devoted to it; and that's the Wisconsin Dells. During the 1970s, it had a carnival atmosphere. The city has changed slightly over the years to become more like an amusement park than a carnival, but it's retained some of its carnival feel. The town itself isn't very big, and most of the attractions are limited to two main roads—Broadway Road and Wisconsin Dells Parkway, also known as U.S. Route 12, which is the same Route 12 bordering Greenbrier on the northeast side (Rand Road).

The excitement filled the car as we exited at Route 12 and began to snake our way through the town. It was easy to experience sensory overload when driving through the Wisconsin Dells. Each attraction and hotel or motel was trying to outdo the others with their sensational advertising signs. It was almost too much to take. To a kid, it was like looking at candy through a store window. I wanted to try everything. I was such a sucker for an enticing billboard. There were signs for go-carts, the wax museum, the Wonder Spot, helicopter rides, the Tommy Bartlett Watershow, the Original Ducks, and Fort Dells. All of them visually screamed for your attention as we drove onward toward our hotel.

Along Route 12, we searched among the many signs and attractions for the Star Motel, and it wasn't long until the familiar sign came into view across the street from Storybook Gardens. Dad parked the car near the lobby and went inside with Grandpa Hinesley to check in, while Mom and Grandma stayed outside with Steve, Scott, and me. My brothers and I took in the wonders of the attractions surrounding us. Although I was probably already too old to really enjoy it, I looked longingly over at Storybook Gardens. There was something that intrigued me about the fairy-tale figures brought to life in that fantasy world across the street. If I wasn't too old to enjoy Storybook Gardens, Steve and Scott were definitely too old for it, so there was no chance I would get to go. That was one disadvantage to being the youngest of three boys: You were rushed through your childhood in order to keep up with your older siblings. The Tommy Bartlett Show was one of those attractions automatically associated with the Wisconsin Dells. The same can be said about several other Dells attractions: the duck rides through the Lower Dells, and breakfast at Paul Bunyan's restaurant, as well as the showdown with Black Bart at Fort Dells and the oddities of the Wonder Spot-not to mention, of course, watching the German shepherd jump onto Stand Rock. They were all part of the Wisconsin Dells experience. In addition to the main attractions, there was a never-ending parade of other vacation activities, like go-carts, mini bikes, and helicopter rides. We could have easily have spent our entire vacation there, and there were several years we did just that, but we had a packed schedule for this trip, and one day was all we got this time around.

After playing around in the playground for a while, my brothers and I decided to go upstairs to the room to try to

The three of us playing at the Star Motel in 1970.

influence Mom and Dad as to where we'd go first. Steve and Scott wanted to try a new place that hadn't been at the Dells the last time we visited: Riverview Park. Riverview Park looked pretty cool from the road and the signs we saw. They had mini bikes, go-carts, and other rides and games you might find at a carnival. While I too wanted to go to Riverview, I also wanted to go on the duck rides again. The cool thing about the ducks was that they

Dad and I in pursuit of Scott's go-cart at Kartland.

were real World War II amphibious vehicles, like those that took part in battles such as D-Day. However compelling my argument for the ducks may have been, my idea was shot down in favor of Riverview Park. The rest of the afternoon was swallowed up by a series of activities we commonly did at the Wisconsin Dells.

As the day came to a close, we all went out and got a quick bite to eat, after which we made our way back to the motel room. At that point, Steve, Scott, and I started going crazy. The three of us made up a game with rolled-up socks, and all the stomping around and jumping on the beds probably drove everyone in the motel crazy. Fortunately, this time no one got seriously hurt. After a while, Dad popped in from the adjoining room and told us to keep it down and turn the lights off. With the lights out, we cracked jokes in the darkness and started a giggling spree. After Dad's second warning, we piped down, but we still had smiles on our faces as we went to sleep.

All-You-Can-Eat

If gluttony is an American sport, then its stadium is the all-you-can-eat restaurant. What better way to feed a family of five on the road? Sometimes we had no idea where we were going to stop for a meal, but when we were in the Wisconsin Dells, I always knew where we were going to eat breakfast. There are a number of restaurants in the area, but nothing said breakfast to me like Paul Bunyan's restaurant. A legendary giant lumberjack, Paul Bunyan's name adorned the best all-you-can-eat restaurants I've ever been to. We all waited for morning to come just to be able to go to Paul Bunyan's for pancakes and buttermilk doughnuts. The waiting area was a gift shop, with all sorts of knickknacks and tourist souvenirs. They also had a fine selection of toys I liked to browse through. Mom and Dad wanted us to finish packing before we went to breakfast, because we were checking out and getting ready for the next stretch of the trip. That was all the motivation we needed, and soon our stuff was packed away (maybe not neatly, but packed nonetheless).

Dad loaded the car as we brought out our suitcases to throw in trunk. My stomach was growling by the time Mom said it was time to go. We checked out of the Star Motel and drove down Route 12 to Paul Bunyan's. The parking lot was crowded when we arrived. The restaurant looked like a log cabin straight out of the north woods. Although they were busy, it appeared we were still early enough to beat the morning rush, because the line wasn't that long. Once we got inside, my brothers and I made a beeline for the toys. My vacation money was beginning to burn a hole in my pocket, when we spotted some toy guns. We each grabbed a gun and started "shooting" at each other when Mom called for us to come sit down.

Paul Bunyan's had a rustic look on the inside, as well. The walls were made of logs stripped of their bark and coated with lacquer. Antique tools, animal traps, stuffed animals, and trophy fish covered the walls. We were seated at a long wooden table covered with a red-and-white-checkered tablecloth, and given metal plates and cups. Then came the endless supply of food: scrambled eggs, pancakes, bacon, sausages, and, best of all, buttermilk doughnuts covered with sugar. No one left hungry. On a full stomach and a full tank of gas, we started out for our next destination—Dead Lake.

A Lifelong Passion

Dad truly loved fishing. Whenever the Price family visited relatives when he was a boy, he always escaped to go fishing nearby. His love for the sport stayed with him his entire life. His first fishing buddy was his brother Milt. In the 1950s, Dad went fishing with Milt, Aunt Nancy's husband (Uncle Bill), and Grandpa George. On one such occasion, Milt and Dad shared one boat, while Uncle Bill and Grandpa George shared another. They came up on a nice cove that allowed the occupants of the two boats to cast to the shoreline in opposite directions. As they worked the shoreline, the boats began to drift toward each other. Dad saw a spot where a tree reached out over the water. Hoping he might catch a bass in that spot, he pulled back to cast— but his lure had snagged on something. Not to be deterred, he jerked yet again, this time a little harder. Then he heard a groan—and, turning around, discovered that he had hooked Uncle Bill through the nose.

I used to enjoy Dad's fishing stories. Before we were old enough to go with him, Dad went fishing with a couple of his friends. One trip led them to the Chippewa Flowage in northwest Wisconsin to go musky fishing, a popular location in the late 1950s. Muskies are an aggressive predatory fish that can grow as heavy as sixty-five pounds, and as long as fifty-five inches. When Dad and his friends first arrived, they hired a guide to get a feel for the best fishing spots on the lake. They agreed to meet the guide early the next day.

The next morning, they assembled their fishing gear and met up with the guide. He greeted them in a baseball cap, sunglasses, and a gun holster. It struck Dad as odd that the guide was carrying a pistol.

Dad asked, "Why do you carry a pistol? Are there bears around here?"

"No," the guide replied, "It's in case we get a big musky—we don't want him flopping around in the boat."

Dad whispered to his friends, "Surely he's not serious—he's going to shoot a hole in the boat!"

Soon enough, one of Dad's friends had a large musky on the line, and it leapt out of the water. Afraid the fish was going to escape; the guide took over the reel. The musky continued to jump. Holding the fishing pole high in one hand and yanking out his revolver with the other, the guide aimed the pistol and began shooting the musky repeatedly, to the horror of Dad and his buddies. They landed the musky, all right, but more importantly, Dad was just relieved that no one was shot! They decided right then and there that they could do without a guide for the rest of the trip.

Finally we were all old enough to sit somewhat quietly in a boat and we now were taking our first fishing trip as a family. Dad's excitement was contagious, and we all got pumped up before the trip.

What Swims in Dead Lake?

We traveled north along I-94, past the twin cities of Minneapolis and St. Paul, across much of Minnesota. As we entered the western part of the state, we approached our next destination, Dead Lake. Even at the age of seven, it was a mystery to me why we would book a cabin for a fishing trip at a place called Dead Lake. For the last fifty miles or so, we all took turns joking about how the lake got its name. It didn't exactly inspire thoughts of great fishing, but, always optimistic, the family was up to the challenge.

Once we exited to get to the resort, the real entertainment began as Mom and Dad tried to figure out how to get there. I looked out the back window at Grandma and Grandpa's car as they followed blindly along. I chuckled to myself as I could almost hear Dad utter a Dickism—"the blind leading the blind." I looked over at Steve, who was also reveling in the humor of the situation and smirking. Then Mom said, "I think we were supposed to turn back there." The three of us burst out laughing from the backseat, and were quickly silenced by, "Guys, give it a rest!"

The car crept along the backwoods road. It was beginning to feel like Mom and Dad were leading us deeper and deeper into the woods like Hansel and Gretel, when a clearing broke through the trees and we could see the cabins. It may have been late in the day, but we made it. The cabins had a rustic appearance and were painted white with green trim. As Dad looked for the owner/operator, my brothers and I got out of the car and headed for the lake.

We were all curious about what a lake called "Dead Lake" would look like. As we came to a clearing, we could see it. There was a slight drop-off that made a little beach of sorts. Off to the left was the pier stretching out into the lake. On the other side of the pier were a number of aluminum boats. A couple of them had motors; the others, which were not being used, were turned upside down.

"I wonder if there are fish in there?" I thought to myself, as I looked out over the lake.

"Hey, look at this!" Steve said, as he bent down to pick something up.

"Let me see!" Scott began to crowd Steve.

I, too, wanted to see what was so interesting. I moved closer to get a better look for myself. Steve had found a garden snake, and was holding it in his hands while Scott grabbed at it to get a closer look. As a tussle was about to begin for control of the snake, Dad called us over to the car to help unload it. It was late in the day, so we'd go out on the lake early the next morning. Mom held open the wooden-framed screened door to the cabin as I schlepped my suitcase, pillow, and blanket inside. I quickly looked for the best place to stay. Once everyone was settled, Mom made sandwiches.

Dead Lake would be our home for the next week, before we made our way westward across North Dakota and part of Montana toward Yellowstone National Park. There would be other stops along the way, but none as long as the stay at Dead Lake. I was in for a real treat on this trip—this was going to be my first time actually fishing with Dad. I had heard all the stories about the hook in the nose and the shooting of the fish, as well as a few others. Now, I was ready for my turn.

When we weren't fishing, we'd grab lunch, then go hunt for snakes, which were surprisingly easy to find, or go for a swim in the lake. Steve spent his time hunting for snakes or trying to strike up a vacation romance with a slightly older girl who was also from the Chicago suburbs. She seemed interested in Steve, but as the little brother, I found the girl's presence annoying. Scott and I ribbed Steve about his newfound love every opportunity we got. When we weren't irritating Steve, Scott and I were swimming in the lake. Most of the time we took turns trying to stand up and balance on a large inner tube while the other tried to knock the balancing one off.

It was getting late. I ran over to Grandma and Grandpa Hinesley's cabin to see how they were doing. I joined them in a game of three-handed pinochle while Steve and Scott played four-handed pinochle against Mom and Dad. I was still learning the finer points of the game, so a great percentage of the time was filled with helpful tips and reminders on how to play out my hand. Leaving wiser than when I went in, I headed back to our cabin and went to bed with the anticipation of the first day of fishing.

Fishing with Dad

It seemed like I had just closed my eyes when I heard Dad's voice in the distance, speaking in an even and low tone, "Rise and shine, sleepy head." I opened my eyes to see if my ears were playing tricks on me and saw Dad standing in the doorway of the dimly lit room. The sun hadn't quite come up yet, and the light from the kitchen crept into the room from behind where Dad was standing. As I sat up, I noticed that Steve was already up, while Scott turned over one more time with the hope of getting a few more winks before heading out. I got up and got dressed. Mom sat at the kitchen table with a cup of coffee and a cigarette. I poured a bowl of cereal as Steve was finishing his. Dad grabbed several fishing rods, seat cushions, and his tackle box and went out to set them in the boat. Soon Steve left the cabin to join him. As Scott finally stumbled out of the bedroom to get some breakfast, I finished up, and headed down to the boats to go fishing.

My thoughts about fishing before I stepped on the boat were numerous. It was mysterious to me, and as I looked out over the lake I wondered, "Are there a lot of fish in the lake?" "Will I catch a fish?" "Are there any monster-sized fish in the lake, like the Loch Ness monster?" and "Is it called Dead Lake for a reason?" I would be in Dad's boat, so I was in the capable hands of a fishing veteran.

While Dad was passionate about fishing, he didn't approach fishing the way professional fishermen do today, with special gear like trolling motors, special boats, fish finders, and holders for multiple rods. Dad kept it simple, with rods, lures, and a net. Before any fishing trip, Dad always got a good map that had depths and other geographic features of the lake. He studied it for what looked to be the best spots to fish long before we ever hit the water. Because Dad didn't have any fish-finding device, he made up for it by trying to cover as much of the lake as possible, casting every single spot he thought had potential. This was somewhat in contrast to my fishing experience up to that time, which consisted of still-fishing with a bobber and a worm. Still, fishing is more of a test of patience, while you wait and pray for a fish to decide to strike your bait. It makes me yawn just thinking about it. By introducing me to a casting approach with jerkbaits, Dad took me out of the world of static reactionary fishing, which seemed boring and tedious, and turned me on to an active way of pursuing the fish. No strikes meant we moved on until we began to have luck. It wasn't long after fishing with Dad that I too shared his passion.

Dad gave me an orange life jacket to wear, while Steve and Scott carried their life jackets and set them in the boat with their other things. Everyone climbed in. Dad used an oar to push us away from the shore into deep enough water to start the motor. He primed the motor, pulled on the cord, and a number of pulls and a few God-damn-its later, the motor started. We were off with a roar of the engine as the propeller churned the water behind us.

The first morning of fishing was more about learning how to behave in the boat and how to cast than it was about catching any fish. Sound carries tremendously when fishing in an aluminum boat. Every bump, dropped lure, or movement of any kind seems magnified ten times when you're on a quiet lake. Steve and I were normally quiet and soft spoken, but every time Scott talked it was like he was using a megaphone (then again, that could just be a little brother's perception). When we settled on a spot to cast, Dad tied a swivel leader to my line and attached a medium-sized lure. After half a dozen practice casts, I was casting like a pro. After several hours on the lake, I still hadn't caught a fish, but I enjoyed casting just the same.

On the second afternoon, I carried my trusty Zebco rod and reel, along with my small tackle box, down to the boat. This time I got to sit in the very front. Dad got the motor started, and before you knew it, we were zooming away to the steady drone of the motor. Sitting up front was a new experience. I enjoyed the way the boat bounced on the small waves, splashing a mist of lake water in my face as we ventured to our next casting spot.

Dad spotted a shore line that looked good and slowed the boat down. The motor made a low growling sound. Then he killed the motor, and the momentum of the boat carried us slowly into position. We all tried to be as quiet as possible. Dad wanted to put the anchor in the water. As luck would have it, the anchor was right by me. It was hardly what I'd call an anchor, it was just a paint can filled with cement with a large metal eyelet in the middle tied to a thick yellow nylon rope. I tried to lift the anchor up but had difficulty, and it bounced on the side of the alumi-

Here I am—the proud fisherman, displaying dinner.

num boat, a making loud banging noise. Steve leaned over to help me, and two or three loud bangs later we managed to get the anchor in the water.

"Well, so much for not scaring the fish," said Dad.

We all chuckled quietly, not that noise was a great concern right then. Soon we were casting away. As I was daydreaming about how I could have lifted the anchor without making any noise, I suddenly felt my line jerk. In a panic, I pulled hard on the line.

"I think I got something!" I called out.

"Keep your rod up!" was Dad's response.

It's a funny thing when fishing with a group of people—everyone shares the excitement when a fish is on the line. Everyone looks to see how big it is, what kind of fish it is, and whether you're able to bring it in. Steve grabbed the net, and I did my best to steer the fish inside it. Soon the fish was in the boat, and Dad took the hook out for me. It was a medium-sized bass, and the first fish I caught while casting. After you catch your first fish, it's like having a weight taken off you because you don't have the pressure of being the only person not to catch one. It seemed like we had found a lucky spot.

The Minnesota Wiz

When fishing, it can sometimes take a long time before you find a spot where the fish are biting. You can boat around a lake for hours looking for a good location, so once you find one you're very reluctant to leave. It was at this point that I had a problem.

"We need to go back," I said, squirming in my seat. The three of them looked at me like I was crazy.

"Why, what's wrong?" said Dad.

"I need to use the bathroom."

"Number one, or number two?"

"Number one."

"Well, go over the side of the boat."

"What?"

"Go over the side of the boat."

My brothers found my predicament amusing, and snickered as I looked at Dad as if I'd misheard what he just said.

"There's no one out here. Don't worry about it."

That's easy for him to say. How was I going to live this down? The choice between going in my pants and going over the side of the boat was an easy one, although both options were humiliating. So, I did what I had to do. I stood up and did my business. My brothers laughed hysterically. They even came up with

I'm taking a nap on the road in the back windowsill of the car (don't do this at home)!

a clever name, dubbing me the Minnesota Wiz. They would chant it periodically, just to bother me. But, between the misery of not using the bathroom and enduring their witty joke, I'd take the joke. Well what comes around goes around, because my brother's bladders humbled them as well, while we were in the boat. However, somehow I retained the title. As the sun started to go down, we decided to call it a day and head back to the cabin. When we arrived, I told Mom all about the fish I caught.

It was on this trip that I first ate some of the fish we caught. After Dad cleaned them, Mom fried them with butter or oil. It was actually pretty tasty. I was a little worried about eating the fish, due to the paranoia that the fish were contaminated. I'm sure it's normal to eat fresh fish, but the years of Saturday morning cartoons and anti-pollution movies in school had left seeds of doubt. Even when logic told me that the fish from backwoods lakes should be safe to eat, I couldn't get the image of contamination out of my mind.

The last day of fishing, my luck ran out. In haste, I reached back to cast. Instead of letting go of the release on the reel, I let go of my rod, which sailed out of my hand and into the lake. My instinctive reaction was to dive into the lake, but Dad grabbed hold of me before I left the boat.

"Where do you think you're going?"

"My rod!"

"We can always get another one."

Thus ended my fishing experience in Minnesota. Apparently, I hadn't perfected my casting skills after all. We headed back to the resort shortly thereafter.

The Endless Road Beckons

When you're young, time seems to last longer. Time in the car also seemed to pass slower. Some stretches of road felt endless, and the new fifty-five mile-per-hour speed limit didn't help. Our '72 Catalina didn't have a tape deck or eight-track player. 1974 was still a time before CDs, ipods, or even Walkmans. Even the Mattel Electronic Football game was several years away. So, we as a family had to find other ways to entertain ourselves.

When there was some traffic, we'd play "Bug." I found out years later that some people called it "Slug Bug." In our version of the game, we played parents against kids. We scanned the road for a VW Beetle, and then called it out by color. For example, "Bug blue!" We called out the color because in the 1970s, there could be five Beetles on the road at any given time. In the Slug Bug version of the game, a person would just call out "Slug bug" while hitting the person next to them. It's probably a good thing for me that my brothers hadn't heard of the slug bug version, because it would simply have given them another reason to hit me.

Another game we played was something like car bingo. Mom had cards with pictures of items you might see when traveling. Each picture had a little window on it, so when you spotted an item, you'd close it out by sliding a red cover over the picture. The last thing we did to pass the time was sing-alongs. We'd sing songs like "99 Bottles of Beer on the Wall" or "Row, Row, Row Your Boat" or any number of folk songs, Christmas songs, and anything else we knew. Dad was the worst at remembering lyrics, so when he forgot the words to a song he'd just substitute "Da, da, da," which threw everybody off. Several hours of singing in the car was enough to drive anybody completely insane.

The long periods in the car became uncomfortable. Although the seats weren't pleasant, we did have freedom of movement because no one typically wore seat belts in those days. We'd have been hard-pressed to even find the seat belts in our back seat. I was so unencumbered in the car that if I was tired and wanted to take a nap and there wasn't any traffic, I'd climb up in the back windowsill and lie down with my pillow and blanket. We lived on the edge back then.

Our trip took us from Minnesota across the state of North Dakota. After I had played Bug and some car bingo, taken a nap, and sung until I was almost hoarse, Dad spotted a Holiday Inn where we could stay in Bismarck, and I think he was happy to stop. As soon as we arrived, my brothers and I began to explore the hotel. I grabbed the ice bucket, and we were off. Like most of the Holiday Inns, this one had a pool, so we took advantage while we could. Most of the rest of the trip was going to be more scenic than recreational, as we were going to visit national parks and forests.

The first national park on our journey was Theodore Roosevelt National Memorial Park (which later became Theodore Roosevelt National Park in 1978). The park was beautiful, and had badlands, which I'd never seen before. Before our trip was over, I had a better vision of just how beautiful our

Enjoying the view around Yellowstone.

country is, although I wouldn't truly understand just how rare and special it is to have all of our country's uniqueness in one land until much later. We continued to move westward on our way to into Montana, where Dad wanted to visit the Custer Battlefield National Monument, the site of Custer's Last Stand. When we had traveled out East, Dad's interest in history brought us to various Revolutionary and Civil War battlefields, so it wasn't anything out of the ordinary for us to visit a battlefield out West, but rather another example of the various sites stopped at on the road.

I Bet It's a Bear

Our next big destination was to see the natural wonders and wildlife of Yellowstone National Park. There are so many natural features at Yellowstone that it's overwhelming as a youngster. As a kid from the flatlands of the Chicago area, it was like I had been transported to another world. With its mountains, geysers, hot springs, mud pots, canyons, streams, rivers, and waterfalls, Yellowstone had it all. We entered Yellowstone at the northeastern entrance, which was wonderfully mountainous, and we strained our necks looking out the windows of the car as we drove along. We even stopped the car along the mountain road for an impromptu snowball fight in late July! It was incredible. We pressed on to the Old Faithful Lodge, where we were staying.

The real draw of Yellowstone for the family was the animals, especially the bears. My brothers and I were pretty excited about going to Yellowstone

National Park, mainly because of the stories Dad had told us about what to expect. We'd heard a number of tales in preparation for our trip, about how accessible the bears were and how many we'd see. The last time Mom and Dad had been to Yellowstone was in 1958. Visitors to the park during that time were notorious for feeding the bears, despite warning and fines not to do so. The result was that bear sightings were very common—the downside being the high number of human-bear encounters, sometimes ending in

Climbing into the '72 Catalina, our tour vehicle in 1974.

an attack. So, we were warned about the potential dangers, but were still excited at the prospect of seeing bears on the roadside.

During our two-night/three-day stay in Yellowstone, we drove around the park in great anticipation of glimpsing a bear, while enjoying the wonderful sights and beautiful scenery. As time passed, we didn't see any bears, but we did see all sorts of other animals, like elk, moose, deer, and coyote. We saw the natural wonders like Old Faithful and the hot springs, but still, no bears. When driving through Yellowstone National Park, it's not uncommon to come across a large number of cars stopped in the middle of the road to watch animals nearby. Each time we came across such a traffic jam, Dad got excited.

"I bet it's a bear, I bet it's a bear!" he announced gleefully, which got us all on the edge of our seats. Once he spotted the animal, he'd say in a dejected voice, "Ah, it's just a moose."

This happened so often that it became a running joke in the car. We began to believe that there were no longer any bears in Yellowstone. What we didn't know was that the park had started what the National Park Service called an "intensive bear management program" in 1970, with the goal of getting the bears to eat their natural food supply by eliminating contact with human food. Stricter enforcement against feeding the bears and eliminating garbage scavenging by "bear-proofing" garbage cans were some of the steps that the park took to fix the problem. By 1974, we didn't encounter any bears looking for handouts. As we were leaving on the third day, we were happy with the visit to the park, but a little disappointed that we hadn't seen a bear, when we came across another group of stopped cars. We began to joke in the car that it was probably an elk or moose, when we discovered it was, in fact, a black bear! Everyone had behaved themselves, and no one was feeding the bear, which was just lounging around, passive as can be. We drove by slowly, and got a nice view as we passed the bear. Our Yellowstone experience was a success.

Turning East

After Yellowstone National Park, we headed south through the Grand Teton National Park, then began our trip eastward toward home. Along the way we stopped in Cheyenne, Wyoming, to visit Uncle Herb and Aunt Delores and my cousins. We didn't see our Wyoming cousins too often because they were so far away, but we got along with them well when we did manage to get together. Aunt Delores was a gracious host, and was very conscientious of our well-being during our visit. We were traveling with Grandma and Grandpa Hinesley, which probably added

Me and Mom enjoy a ski lift ride in Jackson, Wyoming.

to Delores's stress levels. Delores was a high-spirited woman, and quite theatrical. Among her various extroverted activities, she enjoyed being the witch at the haunted house they organized annually for the local Jaycees. I don't exaggerate when I say her cackle could send a chill down your spine, as I'm sure the children of Cheyenne who saw her at the haunted house learned firsthand. Normally I would have thought our visit to Cheyenne was an excuse to play cards, but as it turns out, my cousins didn't play pinochle, which I found incredulous Our stay in Cheyenne was only a brief three days, and then we resumed our trip northeast to the Black Hills of South Dakota.

As we wound our way through the tight roads of the Black Hills, we stopped to admire Mount Rushmore. The long trip was beginning to wear us out. We continued eastward to the Badlands and Wall Drug, where we managed to get away without having to share our ice cream. As we closed in on home, we stopped at a hotel on the Mississippi River at the border of Minnesota and Wisconsin. It was the 8th of August, 1974, and that evening. President Nixon held a news conference in which he announced his resignation from the office of the President of the United States. The following day, we watched the news as he boarded the presidential helicopter and took off. Gerald Ford was our new President, and our vacation was over as we headed home.

Over the next several years, our family didn't travel. Summers had become busy for me. In 1975 I started swimming for the Arlington Heights swim team, the Arlington Alligators, which meant I swam year round. During the summers, I spent most of my hours in a pool. Mom had gone back to work in anticipation of Steve's upcoming college tuition. The economy was struggling as interest rates soared in the second half of the 1970s, and Dad's business slowed, along with many other businesses. Steve was entering his final year of high school, and would be soon going off to college. If we were ever going to take another trip, it would have to be the summer of 1978. The way things were financially, we couldn't take the type of long vacation we had in the past anyway, so Dad planned a family fishing trip.

Yours truly, displaying one of the many fish we caught while in Canada (although it wasn't a trophy fish, it sure felt good on the line).

Oh, Canada

I'm not sure if we realized it or not, but this would be our final trip as a family—in the summer of 1978. The family funds would be tied up in paying Steve's college tuition, and after Steve went off to school, another trip never seemed to be in the cards. For our last trip, Dad chose Lake of the Woods as our destination. The Lake of the Woods borders Minnesota and Ontario and Manitoba in Canada. The resort we were going was in Ontario. We packed up the now aging '72 Catalina and hit the road.

Even though it was a fishing trip, we couldn't resist the lure of the Wisconsin Dells as we drove north. We stayed at the Star Motel, but it didn't have the same appeal as it did four years before. My brothers had outgrown the playground equipment we always used to play on, and their lack of interest rubbed off on me. There was a new attraction at Riverview that we really enjoyed—water slides. In years to come, Wisconsin Dells would proclaim itself the waterpark capital of the world, but in 1978 it was something new. Some traditions just don't die, like breakfast at Paul Bunyan's. Our stomachs full, we continued our journey north.

The car ride was more of a challenge on this trip than on the previous one, because the three of us had grown so much. Now there was next to no room in the back seat, and the days of me crawling up to the rear windowsill were gone. If the drive wasn't uncomfortable enough already, driving through the city of Duluth, Minnesota, would fix that. It was somewhere on the hilly streets of Duluth that the muffler of the Catalina got damaged—now, along with the discomfort, we had to deal with traveling in a car that sounded like a tank rumbling down the highway.

Although it was a fishing trip and Canada is a great place to fish, there seemed to be some irony in that our last trip involved something we'd never even considered on earlier trips—leaving the country. It may seem silly, but I was excited to leave the country. It seemed like a really big deal to travel internationally. Ok, it was Canada, but I was eleven years old and to me, it was a huge event. We went through customs at International Falls, which turned out to be uneventful, to my great disappointment. I had pictured something with a little more intrigue, like the border crossing between East and West Germany. Once we got through customs, we entered the mysterious world of the metric system, which was supposedly in our future.

As it turns out, when you're in the middle of a lake fishing, it's doesn't matter much which country you find yourself in. Everyone had a good time on the trip—the fishing was good, and Dad didn't have to teach us how to fish this time around. We spent quality time together as a family, but that time was slipping away. Although it was the last vacation we took together as a family, I did get a chance to go on another fishing trip with Dad, but I had to wait fourteen years.

Rites of Passage

On the day we left Ontario, we stopped at the local convenience store one last time. Steve, Scott, and I wandered over to the magazine rack. I guess Canadian culture was a little more open than our own when it came to sex, because there was a selection of men's magazines that my brothers and I perused as covertly as possible. Mom and Dad noticed what we were doing.

Knowing we'd been busted Steve and I looked away. Scott, however, holding the magazine in his hand spoke up, "Hey Dad will you get this for us?"

I had to hand it to Scott, he had absolutely no shame.

"You guys don't need that."

Now we all chimed in with our, "It's no big deal. We've seen it before." and our most convincing argument, "Come on!"

Steve was just about eighteen and would be able to buy any number of magazines soon enough. After some discussion, Dad relented. Perhaps he saw it as a rite of passage for Steve—although he knew Scott and I would eventually see the magazine. Actually, we'd already reviewed most of the content at the store already. The fact that Dad bought the magazine was more symbolic in a coming-of-age sense than it was 'leading us down the path to hell.' What I mean is, Dad knew it wasn't the first time we'd seen a men's magazine. Actually, the biggest stash of magazines we ever came across was over at Grandpa Hinesley's house. They either belonged to Grandpa or had been left behind by my uncle. It really wasn't a big deal even if they were Grandpa's, because although Grandpa Hinesley was very "proper," he was, at the end of the day, a man. And like all men, he was cursed (or blessed depending how you look at it) with the hormones that have perpetuated the human species. And it was those very same hormones that began to plague me as I entered junior high school that fall.

CHAPTER 8

Days of Coke and Pizza

Taking the Plunge

With a yawn and a stretch, I walked out the front door, unaccustomed to leaving the house so early in the morning. I walked nervously to the corner of Champlain Street and Verde Drive, arms filled with folders, pencils, pens, loose-leaf notebook paper, and one or two spiral notebooks. It was the first day of junior high school, and I was now privileged enough to take the school bus. While having older brothers made me aware of what to expect, they were already in high school. This journey was going to be my own. I had an uncomfortable feeling, like I was entering the world of the unknown. Life throws you a curveball when you begin to feel too comfortable with your surroundings. I felt like the king of the world as a fifth grader at Greenbrier School, but now here I was, the newbie, at the bottom of the ladder once again. I didn't know it at the time, but this scenario would repeat itself with every life transition. The uneasy feeling I had when being placed in a new situation over which I had little or no control was like going up on the high dive to take the plunge into a pool of cold water. The drop was scary and potentially painful, and the water waiting for me meant misery. I resigned myself each time to take the plunge, accepting the suffering that awaited me, only to find that the pain was bearable and that I'd adjust to the temperature of the water. Once I found myself accustomed to the water in the pool, leaving it brought on a new wave of discomfort.

I stood in line with the kids from my street and surrounding area. Most of them were older than me and took advantage of my first-day jitters by cutting in front of me in line. I looked left down Verde and saw the headlights of the school bus coming toward us. As the bus approached our stop, it let out a low whine as the brakes squealed to a halt. Then the bus exhaled, "Shhh," as if the stop required an extra effort. The bus driver, who wore an expression of wretchedness that could only come from being a junior high school bus driver, pushed the lever that opened the door. With a little shoving and fighting for position, we climbed aboard.

When I stepped onto the bus that morning, I was entering the new world of Rand Junior High School for the next three years. Over the course of those three years, much was changing around me, even if I didn't know it. The community was changing before my eyes, as the kids of the neighborhood grew older and left home. Soon there would be a boom in video games, which would bewitch my generation. Yet there was still time before technology began to replace face-to-face human interaction. All of my family lived at home, for the time being, but that too would change. Mom was working full-time now, solidifying my role as a latchkey kid. It was during these times as my brothers and I grew older and became more independent that we'd have to fend for ourselves while Mom was at work. These were the days of Coke and pizza.

Alpha, Beta, Gamma, Delta, It's All Greek to Me

I believe my junior high school experience was common of the time; rushing to my locker between classes, playing intramural sports, and enjoying the comedy hour that sex ed provided. There were some aspects that made Rand Junior High School different from the other schools in the district. At Rand, the teachers weren't organized by department, but rather into teaching teams. Each team of teachers represented four core subject areas: language arts (English), science, social science, and math. The idea was that the team of teachers would be better equipped to assess an individual student's needs and get the most out of each student. The teams at Rand were named after the first six letters in the Greek alphabet. The sixth graders were split up into Alpha and Beta teams, seventh graders were Gamma and Delta teams, and eighth graders represented the Epsilon and Zeta teams. Suffice it to say, that's about as much Greek as I was interested in knowing. Rand was also the district's home for mainstreaming special-needs students into the standard classroom setting. But it wasn't just the pedagogical differences or the mainstreaming that made it seem different to the students, it was the school itself.

From the time it opened during the 1969-70 school year, the school had a futuristic feel about it. The building itself was unique. When plans were drawn up for the school, the district wanted the new design to match its experimental function. It looked like a building that would have appeared on the TV series *Space 1999*, with its hexagonal sections, which they called "pods." Each of these pods—

there were five—extended out from a giant hexagonal resource center. Inside each pod were five hexagonal classrooms, which surrounded a common hexagonal workspace. One side of the resource center fed into a long hallway that led to the cafeteria, two gyms, and the classrooms for the creative arts subjects, as well as various administrative offices. How the design of the school was supposed to match function, exactly, remains a mystery to me to this very day. But it did give the school a singularity which made the students feel they were part of something special.

That first day we waited outside as the time drew closer to 8:00 a.m. I took out my special Rand folder to get my bearings straight. When Mom registered me for school, she received a white folder with the school mascot (The Rand Raider) on the front, and a map on the back. I looked on my map to find my homeroom, so that as soon as the doors opened I'd know exactly where to go. The inside of the folder was filled with the rules and propaganda of the school. My favorite line in the folder dealt with vandalism against the school, buses, or books, but could be applied to any other mischief: "Remember, most trouble starts as fun!" Boy, truer words were never spoken. That could have been our household motto, but it still wouldn't have stopped us from breaking a window or two.

When the bell rang, we entered the building through the science pod, and I saw right away that this wasn't going to be like Greenbrier school. The classroom walls facing the inside of the pod had large windows, starting from about three-and-a-half feet up from the ground, making each classroom look like a giant fishbowl. There was a doorway to each classroom but no door, leaving each room open to the pod. I continued walking through this strange new world. I made my way out of the science pod and ventured onward to the language arts pod. I knew exactly which room was mine, and I met my first homeroom teacher, Mrs. Hager.

Mrs. Hager welcomed us into the classroom, and we received assigned seats. I sat down at my new desk. The desks, too, were different—they were one piece, with the seat attached to the desk. I wouldn't have to worry about any desk inspections here! I stowed my belongings in a wire storage space under the seat and waited to see what would happen next. We were supposed to go to our homeroom first thing every morning for attendance, announcements, and the Pledge of Allegiance. I was one of the first kids to arrive in the classroom, so I watched with curiosity as new stu-

R A N D

JR. HIGH

Cover of the Rand School Folder.

dents entered the room. All of the students seemed strange to me, but, over the course of the coming days, they became very familiar.

Another feature of school that I'd never seen before was the odd material on the ceilings. The ceilings of the pods and hallways were covered in acoustic plaster. I believe the idea was to keep the ambient noise to a minimum because of the open classrooms. The white material was somewhat soft and spongy. Kids threw pencils up at the ceiling, where they stuck for a while before coming loose and dropping. When a teacher left the room, some kids whipped pennies at an over-hanging area by the clock, and they became embedded in the wall (probably until a janitor felt like collecting some loose change). The worst places were the hallways around the pod areas, where the ceilings were low enough to scrape with your fingers or a folder. Between classes, when the halls were full of students, pranksters would scrape the ceiling. The result was that the acoustic plaster would rain down upon the surrounding students. I wonder if I still have some particles of the acoustic plaster in my lungs as a souvenir from Rand. As it turns out, when the district did testing years later for asbestos, they discovered the acoustic plaster contained around eighteen percent asbestos. "Remember, most trouble starts as fun!" Words to live by, apparently. I guess you can't say we weren't warned.

The Conformity of Uniformity

Physical education at Rand was significantly different from gym at Greenbrier. And by that I mean they actually expected us to exercise. The only true exercise I remember doing at Greenbrier was testing for the Presidential Physical Fitness Award. Truth be told, I enjoyed phys ed at Rand, because we played regular sports, and I really got into it. The one downside to phys ed was that they forced you to take showers, which was torture to a junior high kid, despite its hygienic benefits. As the day wore on, regardless of all of the talk about the individual, I began to get the impression that junior high school was really about conformity. Maybe it was the folder with all the rules printed inside, or maybe it was the uniforms.

Everyone was required to wear a school gym uniform. We also had to keep the uniform at school and bring it home on the weekends to be washed. We kept our gym uniform and shoes in specially assigned wire-cage baskets. Each student had to bring a combination lock to lock up the basket. The idea seemed to be that by always having a uniform at school, you couldn't avoid participating. I couldn't complain about the boys' uniforms, they were actually pretty cool as far as gym uniforms go. Rand had the same colors as my favorite alternate football team, the Los Angeles Rams—blue and gold. The shirt was reversible, with blue on one side and bright gold on the other. It was heavy, too, like two shirts sewn together. That had advantages in the wintertime when the gym was freezing, but in the early fall and late spring it could get pretty nasty. The blue side was printed with the school name in gold lettering and had a gold box where you could print your name with a marker. The uniform had blue shorts with yellow lettering.

As cool as the boys' uniforms were, the girls' uniforms looked terrible. Maybe the idea was to keep the boys' newly found hormones in check, because Charlie's Angels couldn't make these uniforms look good. OK, maybe Cheryl Ladd could, but that's still a stretch. The girls' uniforms consisted of a T-shirt that looked like something I'd imagine the female prisoners at Cook County Jail might wear, with thin, light blue, tightly spaced horizontal stripes, and light blue shorts that extended up to around the mid-abdomen. The poor girls, you couldn't help but feel sorry for them.

Puppy Love

It wasn't long before I began to get accustomed to my new school. Getting up early became less of a problem over time. The social life was completely different from that at elementary school. There were clubs to join, intramurals, and school- and PTA-sponsored activities. The biggest of these events was the Halloween party, which was usually the culmination of Spirit Week. It was at junior high school that the term "school spirit" first entered the students' vocabulary. We had a mascot, school colors, seventh- and eighth-grade basketball teams (both boys and girls), cheerleaders, and a pom-pom squad. We even had a school store that sold Rand items. A rivalry developed between Rand and the other junior high schools in the district. I too found myself swept up in the almost patriotic atmosphere that school spirit evoked.

Spirit Week consisted of themed days of the week designed to let students show their school spirit. Themes were things like '50s Day, '60s Day, Button Day, and Blue and Gold Day. It seemed to me that spirit week had the effect of a hormone injection on the students. As a young man going through puberty, I, like the rest of my friends, hadn't mastered my feelings on the opposite sex.

It was an unusual time. I began to have mini-crushes on girls. Never knowing what to do to get attention, boys can be mean or annoying, trying to get noticed. An odd way to flirt, no doubt, but when it's all new territory, it's hard to know what works and what doesn't. There was a scale as far as annoying someone was concerned. The more comfortable you felt with a girl, the more likely you felt that being annoying was acceptable. However, there were pretty girls that I didn't want to annoy, because I was almost too awed to talk to them in the first place. There were some kids who "went steady," but generally junior high school was more about the mystery of the opposite sex than it was about relationships. In the case of the more pretty girls, infatuation was more intriguing to me than reality. In other words, there was a danger knowing the girl I admired from afar too well, because there was no way she could be as perfect as my mind made her out to be.

Once I was under the spell of the ideal girl, there were several different stages of infatuation. One stage was where every little thing she did was like a sign from the gods that needed to be interpreted: a smile in the hallway, saying "hi" in the lunch line, or possibly (if I were lucky enough) an actual verbal exchange. "At lunch she saw me ask for a Nutty Buddy and then told me she loves Nutty Buddies too! Soon she'll be mine!" When yearbook time came around and she signed my book, half the summer was spent trying to decode the hidden message, like a CIA agent trying to break a difficult foreign code. "I wish I could have gotten to know you better, hope to see you this summer. Love, Jenny." Wish, hope, and love? Hmm...I'm still working on that one. The last stage was trying to go places that she might frequent in the hopes of a brief glimpse or serendipitous encounter. I'd hang around after baseball practice or bike with a friend to a park in the area where she lived. Mostly it was a complete waste of time, but it was worth a try. The one place where there was a high likelihood of seeing and meeting someone of interest socially was at the Halloween party during Spirit Week. Technically it was a school dance with a band, but I don't remember anyone actually dancing. It was a place to socialize and to bump into those girls I was trying so hard to encounter outside of school.

It was always the same for me. I'd spot the girl of my dreams talking to a couple of her friends. I'd admire her beauty from afar, with all of my friends gawking along with me at her perfect long brown hair in a ponytail, tan complexion, and chestnut eyes that could melt any boy's heart. She was definitely different from the others. When I saw her in class, she always greeted me with a warm smile. Even though she could have easily been stuck up, she always seemed nice and would even flirt and joke around with me. I enjoyed those playful moments, and wound up placing her on a pedestal, like a chivalrous knight would a lady of the court. In my eyes she could do no wrong—that is, until she went steady with someone else.

Of course there were times when I'd ask such a girl out, with Dad's words ringing in my ears, "Devil hates a coward."

"Would you like to go out?"

"No."

The curse of my glasses strikes again!

After the Halloween party and Spirit Week, things settled down into the humdrum world of junior high school. Each morning I headed out early to make sure I made it to the bus stop on time. Each afternoon I rode the bus home and got off at the corner of Champlain and Verde, walking the last hundred yards or so to the sanctuary of home.

Splitting the Difference

I searched my pocket for my key, as I stood on the front porch with my tattered school folders under my arm. Finally I withdrew my key (along with a few balls of lint) and entered the house. I could hear the muffled sounds of music coming from Steve's room just up the stairs. Frisky was happy to see me, as always, as he began to run around the house. I went down the hallway and into the kitchen to get him a biscuit. Scott walked in, grabbed a bottle of Coke, and reached for the bottle opener.

"Split!" I yelled.

Scott poured the Coke into his glass and stopped at the precise moment when the cola in the bottle reached the agreed-upon halfway point. He reached out to hand me the remaining contents in the bottle.

This scene repeated itself about a million times in our house. While it may have seemed odd to an outsider, one mustn't underestimate the importance of Coca-Cola in the Price household. The caramel-colored sweetness was the fuel that drove us. Coke was a highly desired and valuable commodity, especially during the hot days of the summer in a house without air conditioning. When supplies got low, tempers got hot. Our standard Coca-Cola supply came in cartons of eight sixteen-ounce glass bottles, although an acceptable alternative was cartons of four thirty-two-ounce bottles. My brothers and I became heavily addicted to Coca-Cola around 1975, when Mom and Dad began to buy it regularly. To keep our consumption somewhat in check, Dad enacted a "no cola before noon" law. But that only acted as a minor speed bump on the road to cola consumption. The cartons of glass bottles required a deposit, which meant that when you returned the bottles, you got money back. At the volume of Coke we drank, it didn't take long for us to assemble quite a number of cartons. Once Steve was able to drive, we turned the bottles in during the week and bought more Coke. By the time the weekend came around, Mom and Dad went grocery shopping again, replenishing our stock. By the 1978-

My Coca-Cola habit began at an early age.

79 school year, we had become fully conscious of what the other brothers had consumed. That's where the Coca-Cola etiquette of "splitting" originated. Any time someone opened a bottle, if a person called for a "split," the pourer was obligated to split the contents of the bottle evenly and fairly. Like something straight out of the Wild West, an uneven split could result in an all-out brawl on a hot summer day, or someone might stick their fingers in the other's drink if he'd been shorted. The bottom line was, it didn't pay to be greedy, no matter who you were. One hot summer day Scott shorted Steve, and, in a rage, Steve threw a thirty-two-ounce bottle at Scott, missing him and embedding the bottle in the drywall. The message was always the same: Don't mess with my Coca-Cola.

Mom's Burden

I took the bottle from Scott and shrewdly assessed its volume. Satisfied, I procured a glass from the kitchen cabinet and poured the Coke into the glass, getting out every last drop.

I sat down at the kitchen table, turned on the TV, and watched the after-school movie, *Westworld* starring Yul Brynner. Around five o'clock, Mom came home. By then, Scott and I had split four bottles of Coke. When Mom entered the kitchen, she looked worn out from the day. Almost immediately, she began to make dinner. In the fall of 1976, Mom started working part-time at the headquarters of Ben Franklin as a secretary for a buyer. By the fall of 1978, Mom's part-time job had turned into a full-time endeavor. For tonight's dinner she decided to make salmon patties. Pausing from mixing the salmon meat with crushed saltine crackers, she reached into a cabinet under the kitchen sink, removed a large jug of wine, and poured herself a glass.

As the salmon patties cooked, Mom set the table and finally sat down to relax. She lit her second cigarette of the evening. Although it was a lot of work, I think Mom was driven to give Steve every opportunity for success by helping to pay his college tuition. It wasn't going to come cheaply, as Steve had been accepted to Northwestern University. As a private university, Northwestern was one of the most expensive schools in the country, and we weren't exactly the Rockefellers. You can't say Steve didn't earn his opportunity to shine. He achieved in school just as every good first-born child should, by getting good grades and comments on his report cards like, "Work consistently outstanding." Outside of driver's ed, Steve got practically straight A's. Granted, some of the classes, like art and film study, showcased his artistic talent and creativity, but many of his classes were top-level science and math classes. Steve didn't shy away from an academic challenge. When most students chose Spanish for a foreign language, he chose Latin. You couldn't take anything away from his work ethic. Although my parents helped him along the way, he wasn't pushed—he pushed himself. Steve maintained an independent streak—he seemed to know where he wanted to go, and was stubbornly determined to get there.

Mom reading to a young Steve.

At first, Steve wanted to attend the University of Southern California. My parents shot that idea down pretty quickly. Steve's goal was to work in the film industry, and he looked to California as the place to make that goal a reality. Dad thought that was more of a pipe dream than a realistic plan. There are many good reasons to choose Northwestern University, but I'm not one hundred percent sure which of those reasons sold Steve and everyone else on the idea. I believe Steve and my parents had different reasons for believing why Northwestern was the best choice. Steve must have thought the Northwestern film department would be a good one, with a strong reputation. Dad may have felt a connection to Northwestern because his sister Nancy went there, as well as her husband Bill. I think Mom was most proud of the good reputation the school's name carried, and that Steve deserved to go there if he could. I'm sure the fact that Steve went to such a good school made her proud of herself, too, to some extent. Mom wasn't the kind of person to brag, but the unstated fact that "my son goes to Northwestern" may have been enough for her. That Steve would eventually make the Dean's List was just icing on the cake, and even Grandpa Hinesley couldn't find fault there. But of course that was still a few years away.

The Mighty Bison

Soon Dad arrived home, and from the kitchen I could hear him talking to Frisky, who was going crazy, in the hallway. "OK, OK, OK, buddy, I'm happy to see you, too. Yes, I am."

Once Dad had settled in, we all sat down for dinner. A beam of light shone down on the plate of salmon patties, bowl of mashed potatoes, and dish of corn. The six o'clock news blared in the background, reporting a mass suicide at Jonestown in Guyana. I halfway listened to the story about Jim Jones and his followers. To me, it was just another weird news story that didn't make sense. Everyone shared a similar view at the kitchen table as we ate, thankfully far away from Guyana. Dad turned to Steve.

"Is Bentley nervous about the game?" We all turned to Steve for his reaction.

"I don't know," Steve answered, with an expression that said, "How should I know?"

Steve and Bentley were close friends. During the fall of 1978, our family began to follow the success of the Buffalo Grove High School varsity football team. Steve didn't play football—he'd played tennis for a number of years to earn his school letters. But Steve's friend Bentley Patterson, who lived across the street, was having a great year as a starting middle linebacker. It was one of those high school football seasons where things seemed to work out right. As the team made it into the playoffs, it got really exciting. In

Steve's rendition of the Buffalo Grove mascot for the 1979 Buffalo Grove High School yearbook.

many of those games, the Buffalo Grove Bison had to come from behind to win the game, giving the team a feeling of destiny. When the team beat Forest View High School to advance to the championship game against the Chicago Catholic high school St. Rita, Buffalo Grove school spirit was running high at our house.

While the Greenbrier community didn't typically go crazy over high school football, this year was a little different. It was the first time that a school in the Mid Suburban League, which was made up of local Northwest Suburban schools, made it to the semifinals and, later, the finals. A number of the starting players lived in Greenbrier, and many residents had kids in high school. It's funny: As Steve's little brother, I felt a connection to the team and the school. It may have been the fact that a number of Steve's friends and other Greenbrier kids I knew personally were on the team that made it seem so cool. I admired their success and felt more pride in Buffalo Grove at that time than I did after I graduated. It wasn't going to be an easy game though; St. Rita had been rated number one in the state since the season began. As turns out, the rating was well deserved, as they were undefeated in their regular season and rolled through the playoffs. If there wasn't enough pressure on the "Mighty Bison" players for playing a seemingly unbeatable team, the game was going to be televised that Saturday after Thanksgiving at seven o'clock on WGN. It was a real life, made-for-TV moment-a local, upstart, suburban underdog team with players who were friends living literally on our street, coming off of a Cinderella season, facing the number one Chicago high school team. Scott managed to go to the game with a friend who was making the long journey downstate. The rest of the family was glued to the TV set that Saturday, but the glass slipper broke and Buffalo Grove lost to St. Rita fifteen to nine. Even though they lost, the team left an impression on me, and I knew I wanted to play football when I went to Buffalo Grove.

A Day with Steve

As Memorial Day approached, the end of my first year of junior high school was in sight. I had become accustomed to changing classrooms every fifty minutes, eating lunch at school, and showering after phys ed, and I had even become adept at sewing in home economics. At the same time, Steve was almost finished with high school, and would be graduating in a several weeks. Steve had recently started working at a local department store called Goldblatt's. Not long after starting there he was moved to the deli, located in the small grocery section of the department store, where he almost cut off his finger. That would be the first and last time Steve worked in a deli.

Memorial Day was more than just another three-day weekend: It was the weekend that Mom and Dad celebrated their anniversary. As on most Memorial Days, Mom and Dad went downtown in the afternoon. That day, as they drove down I-90 toward the city, they witnessed one of the worst airline disasters in U.S. history, when American Airlines flight 191 crashed shortly after take off. Dad described the disaster in detail: how the plane went into a turn as many planes do when taking off, but it soon became apparent the plane wasn't going to stop turning, and it rolled and crashed. When they saw the huge explosion, they knew how bad it was. Dad's story caused me to white-knuckle my first-ever flight, which happened to be a long flight to Europe. It was a sad and shocking way to start their weekend.

The trauma of the airplane crash was short lived at the house, because when Mom and Dad left home, we celebrated in our own way. Since 1977, when Steve got his drivers' license, we'd go to Marriott's Great America over Memorial Day weekend. When Mom and Dad headed downtown to a hotel, they left us some spending money, along with tickets to the park. Sometimes Steve brought a friend, and Scott and I would go on rides together, or Scott would bring a friend and I'd ride with Steve. In 1979, I spent the day with Steve, but we all stayed together for the most part.

Marriot's Great America Amusement Park opened in the Bicentennial year of 1976 in Gurnee, Illinois. At the time, Gurnee seemed like it was in the deep woods, because it was about twenty-five miles north of our house, which was already twenty-five or more miles northwest of Chicago. The park opened with a bicentennial flair, and, as the name indicated, Great America celebrated Americana with themed sections of the park. In 1979 the park was new, clean, and affordable—especially when Mom and Dad were footing the bill. Even if they didn't pay, it wasn't unusual for us to wait until the Coke bottles had piled up during the summer months to collect the deposit money to pay for tickets, which were only $9.75 each, plus a dollar for parking. We went often in those days, but the season always opened for us on Memorial Day weekend when Mom and Dad hit the road. Each year our goal was to stay from when the park opened at 10:00 a.m. until the park closed at 10:00 p.m. We had gone so often that we created a routine as to which rides to hit and when.

Before we left for Gurnee in the morning, we returned the bottles we had at the house for whatever extra spending money we could gather. Mom and Dad left enough money for us to go for two days, because you could return the next day for a reduced price. Steve was made responsible for the finances, so I never knew the exact amount he was given, but Scott and I were pretty good at keeping him honest. Soon we were ready for a day of fun on roller coasters and thrill rides. Half the thrill of going to Great America was driving there with Steve behind the wheel, which could be as exciting as some of the rides we'd ride later in the day. And, like those rides, you were always grateful to have survived when all was said and done. Steve didn't have bad luck behind the wheel, nor did he get in many accidents, but he was a scary driver just the same. To put things in perspective, Steve was an "A" student who worked hard at every class he took. He was a perfectionist. In all likelihood, he was something of a brown-noser. In driver's ed, he got a "C," and that's saying something.

After we arrived, we stayed together as a group at first, making our typical rounds. The natural flow of the park first led to Hometown Square, which was reminiscent of Main Street in "Anytown, America." It was here that we always made our first stop, at the Triple Play and Willard's Whizzer. Before we separated, we set a time to meet for dinner, and went our separate ways. Steve and I wandered the park for a long day of rides, junk food, and shows. In 1979, there were only three roller coasters at Great America, and the result was that we spent more time going to the sweet shops, arcades, and shows. There was also a new attraction at Great America that year, which was a hugely popular show: the Pictorium seven-story IMAX theater, and the movie *To Fly*. Like many of the more popular rides, the Pictorium had a long wait, but after being out in the hot sun for hours, the prospect of air conditioning and sitting down in front of a giant movie screen appealed to me enough that I could tolerate the line. About forty minutes later, Steve and I sat in the gigantic movie theater with seats set on an incredible incline. I don't think there was a bad seat in the house. The Pictorium was touted as the largest indoor movie screen, and sitting in front of it, I believed it.

After the Pictorium, Steve and I made our way to Orleans Place. As we passed through the gate, we entered Great America's version of the French Quarter during the mid-nineteenth century. I deferred to Steve as to what he wanted to do. Although I'd been to Great America before, there were still a few rides that I hadn't yet ridden, out of fear. Steve would test my limits.

"There's a ride up here I'd like you to go on with me."

"Which one?"

"The Orleans Orbit."

"Sure, why not?"

I was game. Much like on that summer day when Steve took me to the carnival in Greenbrier, I let him lead the way. It wasn't until we came to the ride that I realized what I was in for.

"You want to go on that? Are you crazy?"

"Come on, it'll be fun," he said, wearing an evil smirk like an inquisitor racking a heretic.

The words of the Rand folder once again rang out in my head, "Remember, most trouble starts as fun!"

"I guess if you want to vomit it'd be a fun ride," I thought to myself, as I watched the ride and heard the screams of the people inside. The Orleans Orbit was very much like a Ferris wheel on its side. Each car sat two riders—one in front of the other. The cars could swivel so that when the wheel began to spin at high speeds, the centrifugal force leveled out the cars with the wheel. Then the wheel moved slowly from a horizontal position to a vertical one, causing the rider to do high-speed loops. I relented to Steve's pressure, figuring if he could do it, so could I. Next thing I knew, I was climbing into the padded car, and the ride operator ran over to pull down the cage-like top to lock us inside.

"Hey, why do you think they have a pad on the top of the car?"

"Don't worry about it. Just pretend it's like *Star Wars* and we're in a Tie Fighter trying to shoot down the fighter in front of us."

Oddly enough, Steve's advice helped as we sailed around in circles. When I got out of the car I couldn't walk straight, but I wasn't sick. I turned to Steve and asked, "Want to go again?"

We rode the Orleans Orbit several more times, along with two or three other rides that I had previously lacked the courage to attempt, including the Tidal Wave roller coaster, which was one giant seventy-six-foot-high loop. The Tidal Wave was a breeze after the Orleans Orbit. Now the only danger the Tidal Wave presented was the outrageously long wait in line. Around dinner time, Steve and I met up with Scott and his friend, and we went to the County Fair area to grab a burger from Burger on the Run.

Each time we went to Great America, we employed our own version of the Dick Price method by waiting until the last hour of the day to hit the water rides over and over again, because most people were either leaving or going to the roller coasters. The two water rides at Great America in 1979 were Logger's Run and the Yankee Clipper. They were both the same type of water-coaster ride, except one ride used logs while the other used boats. Many times we were able to just hop into the next open log and ride again right away, without having to wait. As ten o'clock came around, we were exhausted from the long day. As the employees began to close down the rides, we walked through the dark park to the parking lot, only to return the next day.

After Memorial Day weekend, life went back to normal. With June came Steve's high school graduation and with it the beginning of a big transition in his life, while I finished my first year of junior high school, ending, if only temporarily, one of my life's transitions. Thank God for summertime.

Steve Goes to Northwestern

As the summer came to an end, I don't think I appreciated that it would be the last summer Steve would live at home. Once he started going to Northwestern, his status changed from resident to houseguest whenever he returned. He had moved on to the next stage of his life, although I think part of him would have liked it if home hadn't changed in his absence. Once he was gone I was no longer able to sneak into his room and play his records (very risky), or look at the cool things he had in his room, like his Frank Frazetta books, his sword from India, his Hot Wheels collection, or his Super Fuzzy comic books. I'd miss hearing the wide variety of music he'd play, and watching *Monty Python's Flying Circus* or *Fawlty Towers* with him. Most of all, I'd miss his dry, dark sense of humor around the house. He came back occasionally over the holidays or for other special occasions, but mostly I visited him with Scott, and then later, by myself.

I helped Steve move into his new dorm room in the Foster-Walker complex at the university. It was small, but at least it was a single room, so he didn't have to worry about a roommate as he unloaded his belongings. We stayed a while, helping him get settled into his new surroundings. Once he had everything unpacked, we talked briefly, but the cramped space made us feel like we were intruding, and it seemed like Steve wanted to wander around and meet people on his own. We left him to become more acquainted with the dorm and the other students. And with that, the first son flew the coop.

Steve's love for Frank Frazetta's artwork inspired Steve to do a rendition of Frazetta's *Death Dealer* on his dorm room wall—In the upper left-hand corner, you can see the pipes coming out of the wall and in the lower right-hand corner is Steve's Frazetta-like signature. When Steve moved out, I believe he had to pay a fine because they had to repaint the room. Ouch! I guess even at Northwestern there are people who don't appreciate

Home life changed after Steve left. Scott and I continued to share a room, even though Steve was gone. This went on for over a year. I hoped the entire time that Scott would move into Steve's old room. But Scott, as it's his habit to do, couldn't decide between moving into Steve's old room and having me move. So we did nothing, and the room stayed vacant for a while. It was after Steve moved out that we began to play four-handed pinochle very regularly. Scott and I played as partners and became quite a team, frustrating Mom and Dad on many occasions. Mom's erratic play gave us a bit of an edge—that and the fact that they drank Scotch and wine during many of the games. On those occasions, the longer we played, the more our luck improved.

A Subdivision in Transition

The bell rang, signaling the end of another school day, and, more importantly, the end of another week. I fumbled with the combination on my locker and unlatched the door. I dropped off the books and folders I didn't need, grabbed my jacket and homework, and made my way to the bus. While the weather wasn't the best, I did have some things to look forward to that gray October Friday. One was the weekend, and the other was Grandma and Grandpa Hinesley's 50th wedding anniversary party. While I looked out the window daydreaming about pouring myself a nice icy cold Coca-Cola, Doug flopped down on the seat in front of me.

"What're you doing this weekend?"

"It's my grandparents' 50th wedding anniversary, so they're coming over and my uncles from out of town are coming."

"Oh, sounds like fun. Do you think you're going to the Halloween party this year?"

"I don't know yet," I lied. I really planned on going because there was a girl in my language arts class that I hoped to "bump into."

The bus came to a screeching halt at Doug's stop. "Maybe I'll see you this weekend," Doug said, as he got up to exit the bus.

"Yeah, I'll give you a call if I can do something."

I stayed on the bus until the next stop. As the bus approached the corner of Champlain and Verde, I stood up to leave. I held on tightly to the padded bus seat as the bus stopped with a jerk. The drizzling had stopped, leaving a miserable gray day as I walked home. When I arrived home I could hear Frisky jumping up against the door as I searched for my house key. I opened the door, and Frisky practically knocked me down, as always. Nobody was home, Steve was at Northwestern now, and Scott had probably stayed after school to play basketball with his friends.

I went into the kitchen and took a bottle of Coke from the refrigerator. I took advantage of the fact that there wasn't anyone home to split the bottle with, and poured a generous amount into my glass. I searched the kitchen drawer for a bottle stopper to put in the bottle before placing it back in the refrigerator. I quickly flipped through the TV listings to find there was nothing on worth watching. Out of boredom, I decided to shoot some hoops out in front of the house. We had a basketball net set up on our roof, which allowed me to go out periodically and do my part in destroying the gutters with every missed shot. (When I was shooting, that was often.)

In between two missed shots (and two associated crashes), I heard the Greenbrier School bell ring out, signaling the end of the school day. When I went to Greenbrier School, the bell signaled the rush of swarms of kids running through the streets of Greenbrier. While there used to be many kids who walked home, now there were only a handful. When I entered kindergarten in 1972, there were 442 students at Greenbrier. By the time I entered eighth grade, there were only 256 students at Greenbrier. This trend wasn't unique to Greenbrier, but was common to the district as a whole. The district had 9,508 students when I entered, and 4,762 when I left it. My class represented the last large number of kids from the great expansion of Arlington Heights in the 1960s and early '70s. With the change in the number of kids in the neighborhood came a dramatic change in the neighborhood itself. Residents became less involved in the Greenbrier Civic Association, and as those numbers dropped, things like the Greenbrier Boys' Softball League and the Fourth of July Bike Parade disappeared. With each passing year, the streets became devoid of the kids that had been so commonplace in the past.

There were several reasons for the change. There were many families who came in the early '60s, like ours, whose kids were now in high school or going off to college. The kids my age were at the tail end of those types of families. The result was an ever-increasing number of "empty nesters" in the neighborhood and throughout Arlington Heights and the northwest suburbs. Another reason the neighborhood didn't rejuvenate with younger families was that the late '70s were plagued by an economic crisis and burdened by double-digit inflation, high unemployment, and high interest rates. Those few families that did move into the neighborhood at that time had a tendency to have fewer kids than previous families. About the time that Steve went off to college, the transition was becoming apparent, although there were still a healthy number of older kids in the neighborhood. In five years, they too would be mostly gone.

The Anniversary

When Grandma and Grandpa Hinesley got married, it was the eve of another economic crisis, the Great Depression. As we got the house ready for everyone to come over and celebrate their 50th wedding anniversary, I don't think I truly appreciated what an achievement it really was. They had to go through some real tough times together. They endured the Great Depression, raised three kids (with ten years separating the first and third children), did what they could for the war effort, rented an apartment for years before buying their own home in the suburbs, and, above all, had to deal with each other.

While it may sound like a cliché, they made it fifty years because they loved each other. Their love may have been reinforced by the hard times they went through, or it may have just been one of those things that was meant to be. The Hinesleys had traveled from far and wide to be at our house that evening. Uncle Herb came in from Wyoming, while Uncle Jerry drove in from Michigan, where he lived at the time. Even though it was a simple family party, it felt like Christmas, with the little pile of anniversary gifts and Mom's large dinner preparation. As the center of attention, Grandpa Hinesley beamed with pride and was in great spirits, as was Grandma Hinesley. That Grandpa was happy came as no surprise to me, that was just the Grandpa Hinesley I knew. He was the outgoing and happy man who talked with strangers while out shopping, as if he'd known them for years. I don't think it ever occurred to me how happy he must have been at home in his marriage

Fifty years of happiness represented in two pictures: (left) Grandma and Grandpa Hinesley shortly after they married in 1929 and (right) their 50th wedding anniversary.

to keep him in such good spirits, but I'd find out later. As it was on that October night in 1979, I saw firsthand what long-lasting love was, and it wasn't in a movie.

Discovering "Real" Pizza

As the 1980s began, change was in the air. Technology, music, and politics were all changing rapidly. Change was something I'd grown accustomed to since entering junior high school. In addition to the differences in school itself, some kids' personalities changed because of puberty or modifications in the social structure. Additionally, I'd met a number of new people at Rand, and I found myself making new friends along the way. Some of them were from Greenbrier and lived close by, but for whatever reason I hadn't befriended them in elementary school. One such friend was Mike Gannon. While at Greenbrier School, Mike and I never shared the same teacher. However, in seventh grade we were in the same academic team, and in eighth grade we were in the same homeroom. As I got to know Mike, it became apparent that we shared some common interests, such as history and politics. Mike's family was a few steps ahead of ours when it came to the new technologies of the day. They had a microwave before we did, and a VCR. But when I visited

Mike's house, we spent most of our time with the most important new technology of the 1980s: the home video game console.

The early 1970s saw the emergence of video games, although most of the games were primitive games, like Pong or Breakout. But by the end of the '70s and early '80s, video games began to take off and become more imaginative. Although Magnavox's Odyssey was the first home video game console, released in 1972, it wasn't much of a system. We actually owned an Odyssey system, but I don't recall it ever working very well. It had Pong and some other games that used plastic overlays that stuck to the TV with static electricity or tape. So while Odyssey may fit the historical criterion of being the first video game console, it wasn't the kind of system you had to worry about becoming addicted to playing. The real video game movement started with the stand-up video games found in bowling alleys, restaurants, and arcades. Then, in 1977, Atari came out with a cartridge-based home video game system. The first time I saw the Atari game system was at a friend of Scott's house, probably around 1979. The graphics weren't the best, but it was still amazingly cool, and something a kid could sink his teeth into. In 1980, Mattel came out with their own video game console, called Intellivision. Intellivision also used a game cartridge system, but they bumped up the graphics a couple of notches, so, for example, a car looked kind of like a car instead of a blob. We just had to use our imagination in those days. Who says video games weren't educational?

Mike had the newest Intellivision game console, meaning our imaginations didn't have to work quite so hard. There we sat, in his basement, playing NFL football, or at least Intellivision's version of it. The players in that game looked like Rock 'Em Sock 'Em Robots as they moved across the screen. They even had similar colors. While I pondered the resemblance between the players on the screen and the robots in the plastic boxing game, it was getting to be about dinner time, and my world was about to change.

"Do you want to get a pizza?"

"I don't know. I need to call home and make sure it's OK."

"You can use the phone over there if you want."

I cleared it with Mom but didn't realize the significance of the day or that moment.

Chicago is known for its pizza—specifically its deep-dish pizza. There are a number of famous pizza places, all of which have earned their established reputations. With all that top-notch pizza to choose from, there is a gem that lies among them, hidden, of all places, at the very entrance into the Greenbrier subdivision—La Roman Kitchens.

Ever since they opened in 1972, La Roman Kitchens had been strictly a delivery/take-out pizza place, which may be one reason it had escaped my family's notice up to that point. It was a family-owned business, and the home of the best pizza on the planet in my opinion. That may seem like an outlandish claim, and everyone's taste is different, but I have never been addicted to anything like I am to their pizza. There have been summer weeks where Scott and I would order pizza from La Roman Kitchens four or five days out of the week and never get sick of it. I was unaware of just how good it was when Mike ordered it that night.

When the pizza arrived, we went up to the kitchen to eat. The package sat on the table waiting to be opened. The pizza was delivered in a large white paper pouch, with a sketch of a chef holding a pizza on it. The pouch swelled, and, as Mike tore it open in the middle, steam burst forth, driving scents of cheese, sausage, pepperoni, and tomatoes toward me. It was intoxicating from the very first whiff. I will never forget that first taste of La Roman Kitchens's pizza. Soon the news was spread at my house, and my world hasn't been the same since.

A Fresh Wind

During the late 1970s, there was a general feeling of melancholy in the country, as well as a sense of pessimism that surrounded life as an American. It wasn't so much a conscious feeling of negativity toward the country, but rather a feeling like that of belonging to a struggling sports team having a bad season. This impression came from the stories and images I saw on the news and in the local newspaper. It was quite a different atmosphere than what my parents experienced at the same age, following the U.S. victory in World War II.

During Jimmy Carter's presidency, economic issues like high interest rates (with the prime rate going as high as twenty-one percent), double-digit inflation, and high unemployment were killing the economy, and with it, the morale of the people. U.S. manufacturing was slumped and became less competitive than that in countries like Japan, which threatened the steel and automotive markets. President Carter himself didn't inspire much confidence. Because of his inability to take the bull by the horns while the Democrats held Congress, he seemed weak and ineffective. That image affected foreign policy as well, with the Iranian hostage crisis and the invasion of Afghanistan by the Soviet Union in 1979. To add to those problems, the image and reputation of the military were at an all-time low after Vietnam and President Carter's amnesty for the people who left the country to avoid the draft. Then there was the botched hostage rescue attempt, which seemed as brilliant as sending a base runner home on a ground ball hit to the pitcher. Even a Cubs fan can see when it's time for a change in leadership. Things seemed dismal. But 1980 was an election year, which offered an opportunity for the fresh winds of change.

I entered eighth grade during that election year, which coincided with my social studies class that was focused on U.S. history and the Constitution. The timing couldn't have been better. By September, when school began, the presidential candidates had already been chosen. The Democrats stood behind incumbent President Jimmy Carter, while the Republicans picked the conservative former California Governor Ronald Reagan as their candidate. There was an independent in the election mix as well, a congressman from Illinois, John Anderson. John Anderson started his quest for the presidency in the Republican primary. After losing to Ronald Reagan in the primary, he threw his hat into the race as an independent candidate to offer an alternative to voters who believed Reagan was too conservative and Carter too ineffective.

Although the state of the union was terrible, Ronald Reagan didn't get a free ride from the press. He was often portrayed as a warmonger, who was too old to serve as president. Because Reagan's message was a simple one, the press often accused him of not comprehending the complexities of the economy and foreign policy. However, keeping his message simple and communicating it effectively was one of Reagan's strengths. Reagan spoke of traditional American virtues in a positive light, in contrast to years of mass media negativity relating to Vietnam, Watergate, and the economy. His message, as it related to the Cold War, was to negotiate from a position of strength, which meant reinvesting in the military after years of neglect. When it came to the economy, Reagan borrowed ideas from people like the acclaimed economist Milton Friedman, which included reducing government involvement in the economy, reducing income and capital gains taxes to increase public spending and investment, and reducing corporate taxes to encourage businesses to reinvest in people and in the revitalization of their companies.

My September and October were filled with election fever. As an eighth grader, I was simply a bystander to the whole process. What I couldn't avoid was the frustration every night before going to bed in watching what would become the regular news program Nightline, with the tag line "America Held Hostage Day 170," then the next day 171, then 172, and so on. Each evening we'd receive the reminder of how ineffective the Carter administration had been at solving the crisis. The day of the election, November 4th, was the one-year anniversary of the hostages being taken. While the hostage crisis had to hurt Carter's reputation and chances for reelection, I think Reagan hurt Carter's chances even more when he asked the American public, "Are you better off now than you were four years ago?" The answer to that question was clear the evening of the election, when Reagan won in a landslide. On January 20th, 1981, Ronald Reagan was sworn in as the 40th

President of the United States. The hostages were released the same day, after four hundred and forty-four days in captivity, and America was finally able to move on.

Losing a Friend

My fever finally broke around lunch time, but I still wasn't hungry. I rolled over in bed just in time to see the time flip on Scott's alarm clock from 11:52 to 11:53. I slowly got up and went to the bathroom to brush my teeth and at the same time purge the awful sickly taste of three days of the flu. I looked at my miserable reflection. My bed head and pale face stared back at me. After three days of sickness, I was finally able to see the light at the end of the tunnel. I wasn't the only one who wasn't feeling well in the Price household—Frisky had been very lethargic the previous week, and he wasn't eating his food. Dad brought him to the veterinarian over the weekend, and the night before, when he returned from the vet, he was in his old peppy spirits, running around the house and wagging his tail nonstop. As I stepped into the shower, I could do nothing but envy his recovery. The one benefit of being sick was that I had missed school. However, I didn't think it was much of a trade-off this time around. It was a Wednesday, and I knew I'd be back in school the next day. Feeling a little better from the shower, I went downstairs to watch some TV.

Sometime shortly after 2:00 p.m., after the start of the Beverly Hillbillies, I heard an unusual sound, like a handsaw cutting wood, coming from the hallway. I got up to see what was making such an odd sound. As I reached the hallway, I saw the source of the noise. Frisky was spread-eagle on the hallway floor, too weak to lift his head. When his eyes looked up, he let out a low whine and tried to move, but he couldn't. His breathing was labored and the cause of the handsaw sound. I knelt by him, trying to comfort him and see if I could help him, but he couldn't be roused. I went to the phone and called Mom to see if she could help me get him to the vet. After clarifying that I thought he was about to die at any moment, she left work. I waited with Frisky until Mom got home. When she arrived, poor Frisky tried to get up, but he couldn't. I did my best to comfort him during the ride to the vet. As I walked into the vet's reception area with Frisky's limp body, I could feel the eyes of the people in the waiting room fall upon Frisky and me, taking our last steps together as a boy and his dog. The veterinarian came out of a back room to meet me at the front desk, where I handed Frisky over to him. As the vet took him away from me, Frisky looked back at me sadly, for the last time. Then he disappeared with the veterinarian.

A Trip to Mother's

Frisky died on February 4th, 1981, eight days before his thirteenth birthday. While we were all sad about Frisky's death, we knew he had lived a full life. As a matter of fact, he lived a remarkably long time, considering the life span of every other pet we had owned. Frisky outlived a dozen goldfish, three or four hamsters, two parakeets, and every other creature that had the misfortune of coming into our care.

Several months after Frisky's death, I walked home from the bus stop, reached my front door, and struggled with my folders while I dug in my pocket for my key. Just then the door opened. Scott had seen me outside and had opened the door. As I walked inside, it still seemed odd not to be greeted at the door by an overly excited dog. It was almost equally odd to see Scott, because he usually stayed after school to play basketball. Scott had recently finished his varsity season on the Buffalo Grove basketball team, which captured the Mid Suburban League title. I was somewhat impressed, but would have been more impressed had he been a starter. I entered the kitchen and tossed my books and folders on the table.

"Split."

Scott poured half of the bottle and handed me the rest.

"Nice split," I said sarcastically, looking at the bottle's contents, which were just slightly less than half.

"What? That's about half."

"Hmm."

I grabbed the TV Guide on the table and began to leaf through it. There wasn't much on TV, so I turned back to Scott.

"Are you guys going to Mother's today?"

"Yeah, we can go, I'll give Bob a call."

Mother's was a video arcade in the neighboring village of Mount Prospect. Its official name was Mother's Pinball. During 1981 and 1982, the heyday of coin-operated video games, Mother's was the place to be. It had become a teen hangout, staying open on Fridays and Saturdays until 1:30 a.m., to the pleasure of parents in the area. We'd go there with some regularity, but we weren't as addicted as some of our contemporaries, who'd go through a hundred dollars of quarters trying to master Defender or Pac Man. By the latter half of 1982, I went to Mother's with decreasing frequency. But the night I went with Scott and Bob Berg, it was the first time my eyes were opened to the world of the arcade. We all packed into the car and drove to Mount Prospect.

Steve poked fun at Scott because Scott spent most of his time as a basketball player on the bench, despite his best effort. Always the supportive brother, Steve named Scott President of the American Bencher's Association.

After we arrived, we exited the car into the cool April evening and walked briskly to the entrance of Mother's. As we turned the corner of the old red brick building, I could hear the sound of rock music coming from the arcade. We reached the door just as a small group of teenage girls walked out, and I began to understand why Scott and Bob had made a habit of going there. As I passed through the door, my senses were welcomed by an atmosphere that was more like a night club than a game room. The dimly lit room was packed with teenagers, most of whom were older than me. Girls were dressed to impress, with their Calvin Klein jeans and silk jackets. Big hair dominated the scene as far as the girls were concerned, while the guys resembled a casting call from Fast Times at Ridgemont High.

"Do you see the change girl?" Scott practically screamed, so he could be heard over AC/DC's "Black in Black."

I didn't know who he was referring to, but I glanced around the room in an effort to find someone changing bills, and then I spotted her. She was hard to miss. She was tall and blonde and dressed almost like a stripper, with hot pants, a tight black shirt advertising a local radio station, thigh-high stockings, and the all-important change belt.

We fought our way through the crowd to where she stood, and Scott handed her several bills. He gave me several dollars worth of quarters, and I went off on my own for a while. I searched for a game to play. Mother's had two floors of games and about fifty machines in all, including pinball machines. Although they had many games, they didn't have a great deal of space, and if I were claustrophobic I most certainly would have suffered a breakdown in the room of wall-to-wall people. I worked my way through the crowd amid the flashing game lights and sounds. Mother's had all the newest and most popular games of the time. Recently released games like Donkey Kong were hard to get a turn with because of the number of kids lined up to play. There was the coin-operated game etiquette of placing a quarter on the machine to establish your place in line or indicate that you wanted the next game. I saw that Scott was playing Missile Command and looked around for an open game that I'd like to play. I walked past the games Berserk, Tempest, and Galaga, when I spotted a guy leaving the Battlezone game. I quickly took over the game before someone else could pounce on it. I dropped the quarter in the slot and began cruising the green wire-framed landscape in search of enemy tanks and what seemed to be a flying saucer. I'm not sure how the two go together, but I didn't care, and shot everything that moved. It wasn't long before we were out of quarters and once again seated in the car for the drive home.

Over the next several years, a number of arcades like Mother's closed down, as the newness of the fad and the appeal of spending hundreds of dollars in quarters to play a game that could never be beaten wore off. Besides, if we wanted to waste hours at a time playing a game, we could do it at home on our newly acquired Intellivision.

Climbing the Ladder

The time ticked away to my next life transition, as the day of my graduation neared. I wasn't alone: Scott too would be graduating high school, and would be faced with the next stage of his life. The weather was changing as May began. It was a familiar time that was marked by one of Rand Junior High School's end-of-the-school-year rituals, Track and Field Day. Track and Field Day was a special intramural event in several ways. It was held during the school day, to ensure student participation, and between events, you could wander among your schoolmates and socialize. I stood with Doug in a crowd of students, dressed in my now-faded gym uniform, which I supplemented with blue sweatpants. We were watching a girls' relay race while waiting to compete in the next event.

"How's your section doing?" I asked.

"We're in the middle of the pack somewhere. What about you guys?"

"About the same, I think."

"Do you know what classes you're signing up for next year?"

"I'm not sure. Aren't they supposed to have counselors here next week to give us advice?"

"I think so, but what about the people going to Arlington?"

"I don't know, that's a good question."

After our grand day of competition, I began to ponder what classes I was going to take in high school. I also wondered about Doug's question. Not all of Rand's students were going to Buffalo Grove High School. While all of the Green-brier students went to Buffalo Grove, the students who lived south of Palatine Road would go to Arlington High School. It was a shame, really, to have to go to two different high schools after finally getting to know the other students. It was bad enough to have to adjust to a new school, but now we'd have to go back to almost square one in the game of social status. As it turns out, I was luckier than my classmates south of the Palatine Road line, because Arlington High School was closed after their junior year, forcing them to attend another high school for their senior year. That's an "I-gotcha!"

The end-of-the-year process was in full motion during the last days of school. Whereas earlier in the school year every minute seemed to pass slowly, the last days of school seemed rushed and chaotic. Summer was closing in fast, and a feeling of the coming freedom hung in the air. Students ran through the hallways, scraping the acoustic plaster from the ceiling. I have to admit I was guilty of having thrown a coin or two into the wall by the clock in those final days before I left Rand for good. In social studies I helped take down history posters and decorations while a door propped open by a plastic school chair let a warm spring breeze fill the classroom. The breeze caused some of the papers held in place by a thumb tack to flap on the wall. Large gray garbage cans overflowed in the main hallway, and loose papers were strewn on the floor by kids cleaning out their lockers. It looked like the American Embassy minutes before the Fall of Saigon. We received our yearbooks and were allotted time for gathering signatures from our classmates, many of whom we wouldn't see again as they moved on to a different high school. The final step was graduation—those last steps as an elementary school student were like climbing the ladder of the high dive once again. Except this time, it would be a little higher. To make the transition even more apparent, the graduation ceremony wasn't held at Rand, but at what would become my new home, Buffalo Grove High School.

The Missing Ice Cream Sandwich

It had been about three months since Frisky died, and the house just wasn't the same. Dad figured the best time to get and train a new puppy would be during the summertime. At the very end of the school year, Mom and Dad bought a little German shepherd puppy. We named him Caesar. One day Dad called out to me from the dining room as I sat in the kitchen watching TV while keeping an eye on our new little puppy, who was taking a nap by the back door.

"Do we need any dog food?"

I got up from where I was sitting and looked in the end cabinet Dad had built from scratch when we got our first dishwasher, because the old cabinet would no longer fit.

"Looks like we could use some cans. I know I need lunch meat, too."

"You better come with me then if you want it. Misery loves company."

"Hmm...OK, let me see what else we need."

Going to the grocery store with Dad was a pretty good deal, actually. He was a speed shopper, and if you went along for the ride, you could usually choose whatever your heart desired. It was like going shopping with another kid, except he had money. When it came to picking out junk food, there were times he could put me to shame. Because there were occasions when he worked late and missed dinner, Dad developed some unusual eating habits. He'd eat peanut butter and jelly sandwiches until he wasn't hungry anymore—the result was he'd end up eating about five sandwiches. If it wasn't sandwiches, he'd sit down with a large block of Kraft American cheese and a sleeve of saltine crackers. It was pretty surprising what he could put away.

I loaded eight of the twelve cartons of bottles into the trunk and the remaining four into the back seat. Once he finished the shopping list, we hopped in the car and drove to the local Jewel store with the clinking sounds of Coke bottles rattling in their cartons. On the way to Jewel, I looked out the window, and it occurred to me how much had changed just over the course of a few years, as the familiar landscape changed with new developments. Korvettes had left, only to be replaced by Goldblatt's, which also struggled and went out of business. A whole new shopping mall called Town and Country was built on what had been a large undeveloped field where Palatine Road meets Arlington Heights Road and Rand Road. There was a new Dominick's grocery store to compete with Jewel. Jewel, too, had gone through some changes. Attached to Jewel was a department store called Turn-Style. Apparently the combination of the two stores didn't work out, and Jewel sold all of the Turn-Style stores, which were taken over by a similar department store, Venture. As we drove into the parking lot, I looked over at Venture and remembered how convenient it was to be able to walk into Turn-Style from Jewel, as opposed to leaving the store and walking all the way down to the new entrance. It began to occur to me that it wasn't just people who went through life transitions.

I pushed the cart full of bottles toward the store in the midday heat. Dad was one or two strides ahead of me, maintaining his speed-shopper pace. The huge pile of empty bottle cartons in the cart shifted dangerously, but I was able to prevent any from falling as I made my way to the service counter.

"We've got twelve cartons, sweetheart," Dad quipped, when he saw the woman behind the counter struggling to get a proper count.

"That's OK, you can just leave the rest in the cart," she told me, as she came from behind the counter to take the cart.

I was only too happy to comply. I thought it might be kind of funny to say, "Thank you, sweetheart." But I didn't want to push my luck, so I kept that thought to myself. I obtained a new shopping cart and prepared myself for the mission before me.

As the representative of the Price brothers, it was always the responsibility of the one who went to the store with Dad to be sure we were set for the coming week with an ample supply of snacks and Coca-Cola. I don't recall Dad ever objecting to anything we placed in the shopping cart. I guess Dad's method wore off on me when it comes to grocery shopping. The key aisles for me were the cookie aisle, the snack aisle, and the soft drink aisle. I had most of the store mapped out in my head and knew where all of the "standard items" were. As far as junk food was concerned, my shopping requirements weren't outrageous. They didn't have to be. I could count on Dad to pick up a box of Hostess doughnuts, as well as a box of Ding-Dongs, Ho-Hos, or Twinkies. Then there were the ice cream snacks. Dad was a sucker for ice cream sandwiches and Eskimo Pie ice cream bars, so we usually bought a box of each. Of course we bought all types of regular groceries, along with the salty snacks and the sweet treats.

I came across an aisle that made me think I'd just walked into either an army supply depot or a store behind the Iron Curtain: the generic brands aisle. These were plainly labeled basic commodity products that were sold at lower prices than their popular brand counterparts. I glanced down the aisle and spotted the plain white cans with only the word "Cola" printed on them. It made me shiver with fear—it seemed so un-American. Wasn't this the whole reason we were fighting the Cold War?! Thank God the generic brand concept didn't really take off. Instead, the concept evolved into store-branded products, which seemed more acceptable. Being the brand-conscious kid I was, I always skipped that aisle.

By the time we were done shopping, the cart was overflowing. I was pretty satisfied, as long as Dad made it out without getting too frustrated at how the bagger bagged our groceries. It was smooth sailing from here on out, and we did it in record time. As we made our way out to the car and began loading the trunk and back seat with groceries, Dad separated the ice cream sandwiches and handed them to me to bring up front. We polished off several before we got home, leaving the package short a few ice cream sandwiches. As we packed away all of the sweets and snacks at home, I knew I wasn't in the best shape, and I wanted to try out for football in high school. Mom was smoking away, as was Dad as he put away the Oreos. Not long thereafter, Scott came into the kitchen and wanted to order a pizza, which no one could turn down. In a few short months, I would learn that it's possible to have too much of a good thing.

CHAPTER 9

Too Much of a Good Thing

Self-Discipline

"Well, I'm not going to sign the form just yet. If you lose ten pounds and get your blood pressure down, I'll sign it, but until then you'll just have to change your habits," my doctor told me seriously. "Come back in two weeks and we'll see."

I couldn't believe it. I was ten pounds overweight, with high blood pressure at the age of fourteen. OK, I'd let myself go a little over the past year after I stopped swimming, but not that badly! It was late summer of 1981, and I was entering high school. I needed a medical release form signed by my doctor before I'd be allowed to play football. I was really looking forward to playing, but now the doctor wouldn't sign the release. For a freshman I was a good-sized kid, being essentially full grown. Apparently, I was too big for my own good, and in some unwanted ways. Too much fast food, too many Cokes, and too many sweets had all taken their toll. Moderation wasn't a family motto in the Price household.

That was going to have to change. My days of carefree eating would have to stop—at least until I got a handle on the problem. It wasn't going to be easy. The first issue was that I was surrounded by family members with bad habits. Whether it started with genetics or my environment, I had become a creature of habit when it came to food. I had a sweet tooth that wouldn't stop. I loved fatty foods. I was in heaven growing up in the Chicago area, which is known for its deep dish pizza, Chicago-style hot dogs, Italian beef, great steaks, and ribs. Now I had to challenge my willpower, change my bad eating habits overnight, and somehow lose ten pounds in two weeks or I couldn't play. I could already hear the question, "Hey, Price, why aren't you playing football?"

"Well, let's see, I'm a fat pig and I have high blood pressure."

Good God, I just had to lose that weight! My addiction to Coca-Cola and ice cream in a house without air conditioning was going to make the two weeks a challenge. I believed I had to lose weight without exercising, mainly because of my high blood pressure. It'd be just my luck to run out and try jogging and die of some weird heart condition. I imagined the doctor saying to my parents, "What the hell was he jogging for when I didn't sign his medical release form?"

I started to really worry that if I didn't fix this blood pressure thing, I might have a serious problem. It was a good thing that I had that attitude. But I was still stuck with the quandary of how to lose weight. I couldn't look to Mom or Dad—they were the enablers who had gotten me here in the first place. As it turns out, I didn't have to look too far for some dieting inspiration.

At the time, Scott was in shape and jogging every day. The previous school year, Scott had won four hundred dollars in a bet that he could lose twenty pounds in less than a month. During that time, Scott employed self-discipline and willpower to reach his goal. Unlike me, Scott exercised and was in shape before he started the bet. But my inspiration came from his ability to be disciplined about what he ate. Each day during his extreme diet, Scott ate one beef patty and a bag of M&M's. OK, it wasn't the kind of diet any doctor would prescribe, but as Dad would say, "What the hell do they know?" Well, they knew I had high blood pressure, and that was enough for me. I didn't want to follow Scott's diet because red meat was not the typical cure for high blood pressure, and if I didn't burn off the sugar it would go straight to fat. Dad had gone on a several diets in the past and had bought a book that had a calorie chart for just about everything under the sun. I began to look up all types of foods and check the packaging on products we had at home. The first day I started the diet I didn't eat anything at all. I did this so that on the second day when I ate a little food, I would feel full. I started a routine of eating about sixteen ounces of low-fat cottage cheese each day, which was about four hundred calories. The second week I ate other foods, but kept my caloric intake to about four to six hundred calories a day.

The two weeks seemed like an eternity. Temptation surrounded me everywhere I went—at the White Hen with the candy island, whenever the family ordered La Roman's pizza, and when Dad ate an Eskimo Pie before we played pinochle. My biggest challenge came when Scott opened an icy cold bottle of Coca-Cola, and I heard that sweet smooching sound as the carbonation escaped from the bottle. My biggest addiction, Coca-Cola, was begging me to call for a split. I knew I couldn't break down. As much as I thought it would kill me, I switched to diet drinks. Well, at least for the time being.

In the late summer of 1981, diet drinks were few and far between. As luck would have it, Diet Coke wasn't released until the summer of 1982. Mom drank Tab on occasion, but I didn't like it, as I had to resort to drinking it during periodic cola shortages at the house. I chose Diet RC Cola out of the few choices available. Diet RC actually made the transition bearable. Each morning I checked my weight on our trusty bathroom scale. After two miserable weeks of diet and starvation, I actually dropped the ten pounds. Two weeks to the day, I found myself once again in the waiting room at the doctor's office. A short while later, I was given a clean bill of health. That was the easy part. Now I had to deal with football practice twice a day, known as double sessions.

No Pain, No Gain

After the first week of double sessions, I understood the need for the medical release form. I thought swimming was bad, but double sessions in the ninety-degree heat just about killed me. For the first time since kindergarten, I was actually looking forward to the first day of school. I got up early and prepared to bike with Doug to practice. The ride was only about three miles, but when you're half asleep that can seem like a long way, especially with aching muscles from the previous day's practice. I looked out the front window to see if Doug was there yet. I figured he could show up at any second. Caesar kept me company.

"Are you hungry, buddy?"

Caesar looked up and gave a little whine, so I opened a can of dog food for him. There was a light knock at the front door. I picked up my small duffle bag and went outside.

"Hey, you ready for practice?" I asked the all-too-awake Doug as I opened the garage door to get to my bike.

"No, but it doesn't really matter."

"Well, we better get going."

The question was, was football worth all this trouble? I was betting on it. Although it wasn't easy, it was a way to meet new people before school started. It also provided a positive connection to the school, while offering a great way to get into shape. There was also a bond with the older football players, even though you didn't play on the same team. Since I was starting at the bottom of the totem pole, I could use all the help I could get. After twenty minutes or so, we arrived at the school, locked up our bikes, and went into the locker room to change.

Somehow, there seemed to be more football padding in high school than in the pros. With the hip pads and tail-bone pads in addition to the standard shoulder pads, thigh pads, and knee pads, it's amazing I was able to run at all. Maybe that's why they ran us so much, so that we'd get used to running with all of those prohibitive pads. I swept up my helmet. Across the front was a strip of worn athletic tape with my name written in bold letters with a black marker. I put it on over my glasses, which I'm sure added to my intimidating appearance. Once dressed, we made our way out to the practice field to the sound of our cleats clacking on the tile floor.

Here I am on the bus for an away game, senior year.

I don't believe the field we practiced on was ever maintained. Most of the grass had been torn away by the cleats while the grass was wet. When the ground dried after being baked several days in the hot sun, it turned the field rock hard. Most of our double sessions were spent running laps around the football field and then running more laps. I was constantly pushing up my glasses, which slid down my nose as I ran. The worst part was that my glasses prevented me from wiping the sweat out of my eyes, causing them to burn. It was enough to drive anyone crazy. Just when I thought I was going to lose it, Coach Garcia whistled for a water break.

"Thank God," I said, as I removed my helmet to wipe off my face.

"How much time to you think we have left?" asked a teammate.

"I don't know."

A second teammate seemed amused about something, "Hey, look at that guy—busted!" he laughed.

I turned to see that a driver had been pulled over by the Buffalo Grove Police Department, which had set up a speed trap on Arlington Heights Road close to our practice field. It was a common sight.

The first teammate turned to me and asked, "Are you ready for classes next week?"

"I'm ready for double sessions to be over."

A whistle sounded, followed by Coach Garcia yelling, "All right, line up!"

"So am I," he muttered.

We put our helmets back on and joined the line of players.

Where the Buffalo Roam

The day I entered its doors, Buffalo Grove High School was still a relatively new school and had around 2,100 students. Built in 1973, the school looked more like a municipal building. The interior had a modern and businesslike feel to it, giving it a serious tone, but in the end it was still a high school.

I was entering a high school world different from that which my parents had entered thirty-two years earlier. A lot had changed since then. Absent were the social clubs like Delta and Delta Chi Alpha that Dad and Mom had joined. For Mom and Dad's generation, a high-school diploma might signal the end of the line in terms of education. For most kids my age, high school was a stepping stone to college, whether you knew what you wanted to do with your life or not. Previously, many girls had been steered in the direction of a domestic education, whereas now they were being pushed toward college. Times had definitely changed.

I would have thought there was little more that needed changing. The gender-based curriculum of Mom and Dad's time was the stuff of ancient history. There were as many girls' sports teams as boys' sports teams, and all of the non-sports related activities were gender neutral, except for cheerleading. There had been great strides in civil rights, and it seemed to me at the time that many racial issues were things of the past. Perhaps I was delusional when it came to racism, but I never put much thought into someone's ethnic or racial background. As a whole, the student body was an ethnically diverse group. There were students of French, German, Greek, Italian, Lithuanian, and Polish descent (now, most students with these backgrounds would just be termed "white"). We had students of Chinese, Korean, and Japanese descent, as well as Indian, Iranian, Mexican, and African American. We had every major religion covered, too. But it didn't seem to matter where someone's parents, grandparents, or distant ancestors came from, because we were all

Always the happy student.

Americans, and for the next four years, we were collectively known as "The Mighty Bison."

This is not to say that we were all one happy herd grazing lazily under the sun of contentment in a utopian school. Even though ethnicity may not have been a divisive factor in a student's life, students still found a way of segregating themselves into social groups. At that time, the social groups were very much similar to the stereotypes represented in the John Hughes movie *The Breakfast Club*, which ironically happened to be filmed in the Chicago area while I was a student at Buffalo Grove. I never fit squarely into any one social group, so I guess I bounced between them.

For some people, high school was a special time in their lives. It was a time you could play sports and feel like a pro, complete with cheering crowds and newspaper coverage. It wasn't just sports that got outside attention, but other school activities as well, with competitions and performances going on all the time. The quality of education at Buffalo Grove, as with any school, varied from class to class and from teacher to teacher. If you got a bad teacher, it could put you off a subject completely. However, you might get lucky enough to have a good teacher who inspired you to want learn their subject, as I did when I finally signed up for German my sophomore year. Regardless of what teachers you had or if you played a sport or participated in a club, it seemed like high school always stuck with you.

You're Under the Gun

I had looked forward to the fall of 1981 not because of high school or even football, but because I was finally going to have my own room! I should have had it much sooner, but Scott's indecision kept that dream at bay. Now that was all in the past, I thought, because Scott was off to college at Western Illinois University. I thought wrong. Apparently unable to separate himself from his younger brother for great stretches of time, Scott dropped out of Western and decided to take a year off of school to work. So my elation over my own room lasted only about a week. I didn't even have enough time to personalize the room before Scott walked right back through the door. It was at this point that I decided to take Steve's old room once and for all. However, having Scott around the house had its benefits. For example, I didn't need to worry about getting a new stereo, since I could use Scott's. We were also able to get in more games of four-handed pinochle on weeknights.

Scott and I had been on a winning streak lately, and I believe it was starting to bother Dad. The family kept a number of pinochle decks around the house. Scott and I had been particularly lucky with one red deck that week, so, as we sat down in the downstairs family room to play cards, Scott quickly grabbed the lucky red deck and began shuffling. Dad set his drink on a coaster and picked up a pad of paper to keep score. Scott handed Mom the cards to cut, after which he dealt out the cards three at a time. Dad quickly wrote down our names with a cigarette dangling from his lips.

Everyone started picking up the cards when Dad said, "Where's the blue deck?"

"I'm not sure, but these cards are fine," Scott answered with a smile.

The lucky deck continued its spell, as Scott and I took an early lead after the first three hands. With each hand we got more meld points than with the previous one, while Mom and Dad hit a dry spell. It wasn't long before Dad grew annoyed with Scott's braggadocio. When it was Mom's turn to deal for the fourth hand, we led, sixty-eight points to forty. The first team to reach a hundred points or more wins the game, and we were only thirty-two points away, although a thirty-two point hand isn't common in four-handed pinochle. The three of us watched patiently as Mom shuffled the cards and dealt them out slowly.

Once everyone picked up their cards, Dad said to Scott, "You're under the gun."

Bidding in pinochle can be a tricky thing. Remember, there are two ways to get points: with meld or by taking tricks during game play. When you bid in a four-handed game, you're counting how much meld you have, plus the amount of tricks you think you can take, as well as what points your partner might have.

"I open," said Scott, and the bidding continued clockwise around the table to Dad.

"Sixteen."

Then it was my bid. As it turns out, I didn't have a good playing hand, but I had a fair amount of meld points. In order to communicate this to Scott so that he'd know he could count on me for points, I skipped a bid to the next number and gave Scott a jump bid. But a simple jump bid might make him think that I didn't have much extra meld, so I did a theatrical pause.

"Eighteen!"

"All right!" Scott said happily, having caught my message.

All eyes turn to Mom.

"Pass."

"Nineteen," Scott bid confidently.

"Twenty."

"I guess I'll pass," I said.

"Twenty-one," Scott bid again.

Dad finally gave in. "I'm going to have to pass, what's trump?"

"Clubs," Scott said, as he began to lay down his meld.

After Scott laid his meld down, we all did the same. Dad quickly counted it all up. "OK, you guys got seventeen points and only need to take four to make your bid. It's like falling off a log." He then said to Mom, "We've got to stop them from taking fifteen or they'll go out."

We had a slim chance to make fifteen from where I was sitting, since my hand was full of losers except an ace of trump, unless, of course, we got lucky. As the hand was played out, we took more tricks than I expected. Whoever gets the last trick gets an extra point, and it might be just enough to put us over the edge. It seemed like there was a good chance to get it, the way the cards were falling, but Mom was able to force Scott to play his last trump card, and Dad took the last trick. Both Scott and Dad started counting their respective tricks.

Suddenly Scott's hands shot up in the air. "We're out!"

"Time to change decks!" said Dad, and he ripped the cards in two, which settled the matter.

What seemed like the reaction of a sore loser turned out to be exactly the luck-changing strategy that Dad had hoped for, as Scott and I lost the next two games. Scott's bragging was enough to get Gandhi to lose his temper, but Mom and Dad weren't without their own methods of getting under our skins. Mom was the best at it. Anytime Mom was dealt a good hand, she hummed "Amazing Grace." It was an effective tactic, because with each lost game it became more distracting. Dad was now in great spirits, joking in a cocky way, as they began to win games. He knew the game well, and many times knew the cards I was looking for or needed for my hand. Before I would even lead my next card, Dad, anticipating my lead, would select his card and hold it face down on the table in his outstretched arm. While the other players

Dad looking over his hand.

were deciding what cards to play, before the play came around to him, Dad would turn the card slightly so that only I could see what it was, then give me a knowing smirk as if to say, "Is this what you're looking for?" The worst part was that he was almost always right.

As Dad played over Scott's card, he said, "Never send a boy."

After our third straight loss, Scott said, "These cards are getting sticky, I think we should change decks."

"I agree," I said quickly.

"You think they're sticky?" Dad inquired.

"Yeah."

"Hold on, I think I have a solution."

Dad stood up, walked into the downstairs bathroom, and returned with a container of baby powder.

"Here we go," he said, as he spread the deck of cards on the table. Then he doused the cards with baby powder, resulting in a mushroom cloud of powder that wafted through the room, mixing with the smoke of Mom's cigarettes. He then proceeded to mix the cards and the baby powder together.

"How's that?" he asked, and sat back down.

The cards didn't stick for a while, but everything was covered with a thin layer of powder, giving the room the appearance of a construction zone.

"Well, I think I need a new Coke," I said, noticing baby powder floating on top.

"Split."

After that night of losing at cards, when everyone left the room, I got rid of that blue deck.

The Best Things in Life Are Free

The evenings I didn't play cards or do homework, I looked through the TV listings to see if there was a late night movie I'd like to watch. If I was lucky, Humphrey Bogart or Clint Eastwood movies would be showcased that week on WGN. But sometimes there could be slim pickings. As the 1980s began, the sacred world of television was changing. The transition from having free TV to paying for it started before cable TV arrived on the scene in Chicago, with two subscription TV stations. The biggest one was channel 44, which I'd watch for things like reruns of Speed Racer and the 1960s Spiderman cartoons. It was called On-TV. The station ran some of its older programming up until about 7:00 p.m., then switch to a scrambled signal. During the hours pay TV was on the air, they'd play some popular uncut movies, some sports events, and, late at night, some adult movies. Every now and then we'd sit and watch the late-night scrambled adult movies, trying to figure out what was going on. Well, we knew what was going on, we just couldn't see it. Then the screen would unscramble for a brief moment or two, which was just long enough to keep us fiddling with the tuning dial a little longer.

The whole concept of paying for TV was a hard pill to swallow for many people. There was also a general feeling that if you could pick up a signal with an antenna and unscramble it, why not? It seemed logical that if they broadcast it freely into the atmosphere, it was fair game. Soon you could find devices that could unscramble the signals at the local electronics store. The subscription pay channels didn't take off, and most people stuck to watching network TV and shows like *Dallas* and *Dynasty*. Then, in the late summer of 1982, cable TV came to Chicago suburbs, including Arlington Heights, and this time pay TV was here to stay.

Cable TV didn't alter my TV viewing habits during the early 1980s because we didn't get cable until much later, and by that time, that was all right with me. So the new world of pay TV still eluded me, but I couldn't ignore its influence on American culture, even if we didn't have cable. The most profound effect cable TV had on a high schooler's life that I witnessed was its effect on popular music. The addition of cable TV to the Chicago suburbs brought MTV along with it. The newness and perceived "hipness" of the still relatively new channel gave MTV a power over popular music that no radio station could match. The result was that music videos began to determine the success of a band as much as or more than the music itself did. If a song had a terrible video, chances were it would achieve limited success, but if a song had an awesome video, it got people's attention. For some reason, whenever I watched MTV I got the impression that I was being told a band or song was hot, and not drawing that conclusion myself. If something wasn't on MTV at all, it must not be good. This phenomenon was lost on me to some extent, because I didn't have cable TV. Every now and then I'd visit a friend who had cable and we'd watch some MTV. I wasn't all that impressed. The format was enticing, but when I watched a rock band, I wanted to see real rock and roll, not some lip sync nonsense. I wanted to see great guitar solos and other examples of exceptional musicianship, not people pretending to play. In some cases, the videos had nothing to do with a band playing at all, but were rather a video director's vision of the music. Some videos were entertaining, but for the most part they lacked substance. I wasn't sold. While many high schoolers tuned into the Flock of Seagulls,

Madonna, and Michael Jackson, I went in a different direction to find good music. I looked backward to "rediscover" music from the late 1960s.

The reason I was disappointed with the videos on MTV was because of an experience I had in the spring of 1982. One spring night, I went out with Scott and Bob Berg to the Plitt theaters at Woodfield and saw the midnight movie *The Song Remains the Same.*

Midnight Movie

I guess it all began in 1969, when Scott bought his first Led Zeppelin album, *Led Zeppelin II,* at the age of seven. Scott first heard the album because Uncle Jerry had bought it when it first came out, and Scott fell in love with it. Not too long after Scott got the album, we became roommates. Throughout the '70s I heard many of the band's songs, but I wasn't as big a fan as Scott was. In 1980, Scott became excited at the prospect of seeing Led Zeppelin live. I didn't quite understand how big of a deal a Led Zeppelin tour was at the time. Then, on a brisk September day, I was walking by Doug's house when a beat-up light blue Monte Carlo pulled up to me and a guy with long dark hair, a thin beard, and sunglasses called out to me from the window of his car.

"Have you heard the news, man? The greatest drummer in the world is dead. Bonzo, Zeppelin's drummer, is dead."

"What? How?" I asked, thinking I hadn't heard him correctly.

He mumbled something incoherent and drove off, leaving me there in stunned silence. I rushed home to tell Scott what I'd heard and figure out if it was true. I found a melancholy Scott, who confirmed the news, saying he'd heard it at school earlier that day. Well, you might think that was all she wrote for our interest in Led Zeppelin, but it actually had the opposite effect. Outside their regular albums, there was very little someone with an interest in the band at that time could sink his teeth into. Most important were the rumored live performances. I knew the music from the albums and was aware of some unflattering images painted by the media, but knew next to nothing about their live performances. That is, until the midnight movie at Woodfield Theater. The movie *The Song Remains the Same* mostly highlighted the band's 1973 performances at Madison Square Garden over three nights. The movie was released in 1976, but later became a cult film with Led Zeppelin fans. On the weekends during the early '80s, various Chicago-area theaters were rented out to a third-party organization that promoted cult films like *The Rocky Horror Picture Show* and *The Song Remains the Same*, which were shown at midnight.

Going to see *The Song Remains the Same* was like going to a live concert, except that the band appeared on celluloid rather than on a stage. As I sat in the theater that night, I finally saw what it was that drove these people insane. The best way to describe it was no-nonsense rock and roll with power and passion. It was like watching no other band. Each of the band members was a master of his craft who thrived on improvisation, which made the live versions of their songs seem fresh and unique, yet maintained the feel of the studio versions. I was most impressed with Jimmy Page, who seemed to play his guitar effortlessly, yet better than other guitar players I'd seen (certainly more entertaining). After the movie I became hooked on Led Zeppelin, with a new appreciation for their live music. But the band broke up after their drummer, John Bonham, died in 1980. So Scott and I became obsessed in the coming years with finding more material, from books to bootlegs, and everything Zeppelin related. That passion led me to drive Mom's car seven hours one-way to pick Scott up from school to see Jimmy Page in concert. He was appearing with his band The Firm during my senior year in high school, and we had second-row seats. Well I couldn't just leave him stranded, could I?

Culture Shock

Scott's first brush with college wasn't to his liking, so he took a year off and got some of the wildness out of his system. By the summer of 1982, he knew he had to get things back on track and go to college. Money was an issue. Scott found a school that was acceptable to him, while also being affordable. Best of all, one of his close friends was studying there, so he would be able to meet people easily. The school he chose was Murray State University. Although Scott had researched the qualifications of the school, he hadn't research the area at all. All he knew was that the university was in a town called Murray, Kentucky. The first time he set foot on campus was the day he moved into his dorm room.

Since neither Scott nor I owned a car during the majority of our time in college, Dad maintained his role as Mr. Dependable when it came to picking us up or dropping us off. Dad was happy to drive Scott down to Kentucky. I think he enjoyed the whole road-trip feel of driving there. He had his road atlas ready, with his route already highlighted. Dad rented a van for the trip. I helped Dad and Scott pack the van with all of Scott's belongings. Since my school didn't start

Mr. Dependable, driving back home from Kentucky.

for another week, I asked if I could tag along for the trip. I believe it was when we stopped for gas at a Huck's that I knew Scott was in for an adjustment.

While Murray was a nice little university town, it was significantly different from the Chicago metropolitan area, and getting used to it would take some time. Things had a tendency to move a little slower, as well as some of the people. Out of the three brothers, Scott was the partier. I guess you could say he made up for what Steve and I didn't drink. But what he didn't know was that Murray was located in a dry county (and I don't mean arid). Scott would have plenty of time to figure out what dry meant while he was there. I would visit periodically and actually liked the area, and wound up studying there myself. I, too, would learn that visiting a place is different from living in it. Scott would get that lesson first, however, as Dad and I left him stranded without a car when we returned home the following day.

Trouble in Texas

It was an evening in February when we got the call. Mom answered the phone. These were the days before rampant telemarketing, when you could still answer your phone confident that you knew the person on the other end and that the call came from inside the country. It did come from inside the country, if just barely. Grandma and Grandpa Hinesley had taken a trip to Brownsville, Texas. My other grandparents, Grandma Artie and Grandpa George, had moved down to Brownsville several years earlier. Grandma and Grandpa Hinesley headed down there to pay them a visit, and vacation in the warmer climate. However, instead of responding to cheerful news of sunny weather and beautiful beaches, Mom seemed stressed on the phone, talking in quiet tones and waving her arm to shush me if I spoke, as she concentrated on what was being said on the other end. When she finally got off the phone, she said that Grandma Hinesley had had a massive stroke.

The early 1980s hadn't been kind to Grandma Hinesley. In 1980, she and Grandpa Hinesley were involved in major car accident that left them hospitalized for a week. In 1981, she was diagnosed with breast cancer and had undergone a mastectomy, but seemed to recover well.

Grandma and Grandpa Hinesley, shortly before their trip to Texas.

As a matter of fact, I would have never noticed her struggle with cancer at all if someone hadn't told me about it. She had high blood pressure and was on medication for it. Apparently the dosage of the medication wasn't enough to prevent her stroke. Doctors are only human. Although she had seemed to overcome her bout with cancer, the stroke would present a different set of challenges.

When Grandpa Hinesley called Mom, Grandma's condition was too poor for her to return to Chicago with the airline. As weeks passed, the urgency to move Grandma up to a local hospital in the Chicago area increased, as Grandpa feared she wasn't receiving proper care in the border town, and her physical status seemed to worsen. With her condition still too poor to allow her to take a commercial flight, Grandpa was forced to charter a private plane, while Uncle Jerry drove Grandpa's car back up to Illinois. After Grandma and Grandpa arrived, Grandma was placed in a nursing home.

Shortly after Grandma returned, Mom and I drove to the nursing home to visit her. Mom signed us in, and we got into the elevator even though it was only one floor up.

"What room is she in?" I whispered.

"209."

We walked down the hallway. Two or three elderly patients sat out in the hallway in their white hospital gowns. A mixed smell of sickness and cleaner hung in the air. I just knew I wasn't going to like this place. I'd been in hospitals before, like when Dad broke his finger or when Scott broke his shoulder. It didn't seem that long ago that I was visiting Grandma and Grandpa after their car accident. I never enjoyed going to the hospital, but the nursing home made the hospital seem like a funhouse. It had a gloomy feeling about it that reminded me of a phrase in old Roach Motel ads: "Once they check in...they don't check out." When we reached Grandma's room, Mom entered first, and I followed behind. Grandma was in the far bed next to the window, and a curtain divider blocked my view when I first entered. As we came around the curtain, I got my first glimpse of Grandma. Grandpa Hinesley sat by her side, and he announced to Grandma who had come to visit. Grandma's eyes seemed to light up at the news, and she attempted to talk, but the words wouldn't come out.

It was the first time I'd ever seen the results of a stroke, and was faced with the full realization of what it meant. Grandma was paralyzed on most of her right side, and her speech was affected. It was difficult to tell if she could understand what I was saying when I spoke to her. Either way, she couldn't communicate back to me. As I would do many times over the coming months, I gripped her left hand in mine while I looked in her eyes. She squeezed back. I spoke words of encouragement, and she would squeeze my hand, giving me the impression that she understood at least that I loved her.

At first her status seemed to improve, but it wasn't long before she plateaued and became increasingly tired when we visited. Grandpa was constantly by her side and tried his best to raise her spirits. He was grateful anytime we visited. After her condition stabilized, the nursing home didn't seem to offer much hope in terms of further improvement, and there was always the risk her status could worsen if care slackened, as Grandpa believed had happened in Texas. Seeing the writing on the wall, Grandpa decided the best place for her was at home. He rented a hospital bed and arranged for a nursing service to visit twice a day. At home, he could always keep her company while making sure the care was consistent. It was at that time I witnessed Grandpa's devotion to Grandma. He tried so hard to help her improve. As Grandpa sat alone with Grandma, he began to grow increasingly bitter. He was bitter toward the doctors for not giving her enough blood thinners before their trip, he regretted the treatment Grandma received at the hospital in Texas, and he resented Grandma's friends at the senior center who seemed to desert her after her stroke. Without Grandma's soothing influence, he became more critical of Dad. His world view darkened with each passing day.

Because I was a newly licensed driver, there were times when I was able to visit Grandpa on my own. Sometimes I helped him with chores, for which Mom had so nicely volunteered my service. I tried to keep Grandpa in a positive mood by playing gin with him or ask him to tell me stories from his past. I think it helped somewhat. As time went on, it wasn't easy watching Grandma's condition worsen. It seemed that every forward step she took toward improvement brought her two steps back. But, I wasn't there every day like Grandpa. I can only imagine how he felt watching her slow decline.

The Heart of the Matter

Crash! The basketball slammed into the gutter.

"Are you going to chance it?"

"Yeah," said Jim Kluka, as he bounced the basketball in front of him on the pitted surface of the concrete driveway. It was a beautiful spring day in mid-May 1983 that marked the opening of our driveway basketball season. Jim had to concentrate to avoid some protruding branches of our Norwegian pine tree off to his left and to ignore the three of us trying to distract him off to his right. He put up a shot that hit the dead rim, rolled around, and dropped in the basket.

"You lucky bastard!"

Jim advanced to the next spot on the driveway, slowly catching up to Scott, who had arrived home from college the week before. I was losing to Scott, Jim, and Doug in a game of Around the World. Our crack-lined driveway was ideal for playing games like Horse or Around the World because of all the clearly defined spots to shoot from. Doug and Jim came over to play basketball regularly in those days, as long as the weather was good. Jim was also a Greenbrier native and lived on Champlain Street. I didn't have many classes with Jim at Greenbrier School, although he had been in my kindergarten class. I remember he was the only one to wear a suit and tie on picture day. Show-off. He was also the one I had distracted in the fifth-grade choir all those years before.

Not long after sophomore year started, Jim began spending many hours at my house. So many hours, in fact, it was like having another brother. Jim wanted to get out of his house when he had the chance. He had lost his dad some years earlier to multiple sclerosis, and his mother could be a little demanding on his time. So between chores, he came over to play basketball, video games, or cards, watch TV, or participate in our daily speculation about a Led Zeppelin reunion. During the summer, we'd play basketball late at night by the light of a flood lamp, order La Roman's pizza, and drink more Coca-Cola than should be allowed. Between football seasons, I fell back into my old habits. On this day in May, I got a lesson as to the dangers of not having more self-discipline. It began, as it always did, with Jim knocking at the front door.

"Hey, you want to play some hoops?"

"Sure, I'll be out in a minute."

It wasn't long before Doug came over, Scott came outside to join us, and all of us were playing Around the World. Nothing in particular seemed different that day. Mom came home at the regular time and started dinner. I missed most of my shots, as always. The night before I had stayed up late watching David Letterman, and I was a little more tired than usual. I was considering quitting after the game and taking a nap before dinner. It was Doug's turn, and he was on a roll when Dad's car pulled in the driveway. Dad got out and watched Doug take his turn. Doug ended up winning the game, and Scott suggested a game of two on two. I bowed out, so Dad joined the game while I went inside.

"Ah, I should really quit smoking, I'm having a little trouble catching my breath," Dad said, as he struggled to keep up with the other players.

"You got to play a little more defense!" Scott yelled, in the heat of the game.

Dad and Scott came out ahead, but Dad decided he'd had enough.

"I need to catch my breath for a minute," he said, and went inside.

Meanwhile, I woke up from my brief nap and heard odd noises in the house. I heard the sounds of a CB radio. From the upstairs hallway I saw an ambulance in our driveway, and I realized why I heard the radio sounds. I ran downstairs to see Dad on the couch with his shirt off, being checked out by a paramedic. Mom stood on the other side of the coffee table looking scared and apparently at a loss for words.

"What's going on?"

"They think it's a heart attack," said Scott.

The paramedics brought in a stretcher, put Dad on it, and off they went. I was still half awake, so everything seemed like a dream. We were all a little shocked. Like Grandma, Dad smoked and didn't concern himself too much with what he ate. Didn't anyone tell him that too much of a good thing can kill you?

Too Much of a Good Thing

We drove out to St. Francis Hospital in Evanston, which was well known for their cardiac care, to visit Dad. Dad was a pretty robust individual, and seeing him in this fragile state was a little unsettling. As I looked at him sitting up in his hospital bed in the intensive care unit, I wondered if he'd be able to turn things around. It wasn't going to be easy.

Dad's brush with death was a result of years of excessive eating and smoking. His self-indulgence wasn't a unique trait during the 1980s—it was beginning to become a standard flaw of American society. The term "yuppie" wasn't a term of endearment for those young urban professionals of the day who had experienced the upswing of the 1980s economy. Instead, the term reflected an aspect of avarice that was fast becoming the norm in the country. Despite the negative overtone of the term "yuppie," the lax habits the term reflected were swallowed up by the mass media.

Greed and self-indulgence weren't traits limited to individuals, but could be found in communities as well. Urban sprawl began to eat up many of the free spaces, like the nursery where we played as kids. Property taxes continued to rise, even though there were significantly fewer children in the school district and the park district. When open space wasn't available to swallow up, the avarice of some towns wasn't curbed at all. Instead, "best use" studies would be done with the goal of "revitalizing" a town. Areas that were not generating the expected tax dollars were bought using eminent domain and resold to developers. I guess in many ways, it was much like Dad's weight problem. As he got older and his body used less energy, he didn't cut back on eating. If anything, he ate more, but instead of being satisfied, he gradually increased his appetite. The problem is that once the weight is on, it's a bitch to get it off (especially at his age).

Uptight

Dad's recovery took some time. It also took him about two months to get back in the swing of things at work. For someone who'd just survived a heart attack, the added stress of getting his business back up and running was not exactly what the doctor ordered, but he had no choice. As to the things he could choose to correct, he was having a little more success. Dad stopped smoking. He quit after the heart attack and never looked back. This was quite an achievement, since he hadn't been successful in the past. His battle against overeating wasn't going quite as well. Dad felt that once he recovered, he didn't need to be as concerned with what he ate, and he believed smoking was probably the main cause of his heart attack. So he went on diets for several weeks, then broke down and went out to eat. If I visited him downtown, we almost always went out to eat.

I began to visit Dad downtown more regularly after the fall of 1981 when Dad moved his office to the new, more modern location at Columbus Plaza. There were times on the weekends or when I was out of school that I drove downtown to visit Dad or hang out at the apartment. We became spoiled by the location, especially during the summer, when festivals, Chicago Fest, and, later, the Taste of Chicago, were only a stone's throw away. It was on one such summer day in 1984 that Doug and I drove into the city to wander around downtown.

It's funny how political correctness seeps into one's personality without one being fully conscious of it. How judgmental, elitist opinions and standards gain a foothold in one's mind. I was guilty of it and didn't even realize how badly. It didn't come from home, so it must have come from school or from some form of mass media, but wherever it came from, it was certainly present the day Doug and I went downtown. Dad was working

Mom relaxing at Columbus Plaza during the early '80s.

alone that day, and while we were in the apartment he asked Doug and me if we'd like to go to lunch at Scampi's, an Italian restaurant in the neighboring Hyatt Regency Hotel. We gladly accepted Dad's offer of a free meal. Soon we were following Dad's fast-paced walk through the concourse level's corridor to the Hyatt Regency, as if the food was already getting cold. We reached the escalators leading into the Hyatt's lobby in record time. As we rode the escalator upward, I could hear the sound of piano music and rushing water. As we came to the top, I saw a pianist sitting at a white baby grand piano in the lounge area of the lobby. The lobby, which was encased by glass, resembled a giant greenhouse. The glass walls and ceiling provided an open atmosphere, allowing visitors to enjoy the view of the city. Scampi's was located in the middle of the lobby. There were potted trees and other plants, adding to the greenhouse feel. The restaurant was set out like an island amid shallow pools of water. There were small fountains in the pools. Luckily, we beat the lunch crowd and didn't have to wait very long for a table. Once we were seated, a young waiter of Middle Eastern descent took our order. As we looked through the menu, Doug and I noticed that the prices seemed a little hefty. Dad was quick to notice.

"Order whatever you want, don't worry about it."

Those words put us at ease, and we placed our orders without feeling like we were overstepping our bounds. We chatted away about school and football while we enjoyed our meals. As is my habit, I put away my third glass of Coke in record time. Dad, wanting to be a good host, saw my dilemma as I struggled to get the waiter's attention.

"Do you want me to get the waiter?"

"Yeah, if you can. Good luck."

Dad turned to our waiter, who stood ten feet away at another table, and boomed,

"Hey, Muhammad, can we get another Coke over here?"

The waiter acknowledged Dad's request and walked off. "Muhammad," I thought. "I can't believe he just said that." I wanted to crawl under the table, I was so embarrassed. Doug seemed to look uncomfortable as well. Maybe Dad thought it was funny. I was imagining the waiter spitting in my drink. I was embarrassed, but I was also disappointed in Dad. I held him in higher regard than to think he'd utter some jingoistic slur at a poor waiter busting his butt to get our food. I just had to say something.

"I can't believe you just called that guy Muhammad."

Dad looked at me strangely and said, "Why? That's his name."

Just then the waiter walked up and set the glass of Coke down in front of me. My eyes scanned his red jacket for a name tag, and sure enough, it said "Muhammad" in bold black letters.

"Oh, well then, never mind."

Now I was embarrassed for myself. Dad and Doug, however, had a good laugh at my misunderstanding.

A Family Reunion

My cleats sank into the soft, sodden grass of late fall. I never noticed the essence of fall until I started playing football. Ever since that time, the smell of a misty fall day, along with the deep shades of the green grass and autumn leaves, take me right back to football season. My black Adidas cleats were caked with mud as I ran at practice that afternoon with the rest of the defensive squad. It was the middle of November, 1984, and our hard work over the past four years had paid off. Much like the fall of 1978 with those other Greenbrier kids I admired, our team had had a great season and made the state playoffs. As the MSL North champions, our first challenge was against the MSL South champions, Prospect High School, for the MSL title. It was a strange year because Arlington High School had closed the year before, and the then-juniors had had to select nearby high schools to attend for their final year. Many picked Prospect High School. The result was that I found myself face to face with former classmates from Rand. We managed to win that day and move on to the next round, which we also won. As I ran that afternoon, we were preparing for the semifinals against the previous year's state champions, East St. Louis. As our practice came to a close, I ran up to my coach.

"Coach, I'm going to have to miss practice tomorrow because I'm going to a funeral."

"I'm sorry to hear that, whose funeral is it?"

"My Grandma's."

Grandma Artie died of pancreatic cancer several days earlier. The next day we drove to the town of West Chicago for the funeral. I looked out the window of the moving car that rainy afternoon and thought back to a summer day in 1977, when we had driven out to Aunt Nancy's house for a large family gathering. I went with Mom and Dad, while Scott and Steve played in a baseball game. Soon after we arrived, Dad and Uncle Milt went to pick up Steve and Scott, leaving Mom and me with (for me) a group of strangers. I searched out a quiet place to be by myself. I thought I found one too, until a voice suddenly came out of nowhere.

"Hello, Tommy."

I was a little startled, and turned to see Grandma Artie sitting in a chair in the living room of my aunt's house.

"Hi, Grandma."

"I hear you're doing real well at swimming."

"Yes, I'm swimming for two teams now."

"Dick never learned how to swim."

Grandma Artie related a story about various relatives I didn't know, and my eyes glazed over. Normally I was curious about our family's history, but Artie would forget that I didn't even know half of my first cousins by name, much less a great uncle or second cousin twice removed. So I looked for a way out of the conversation while Artie talked on.

"And Claude, George's half brother, or was it Vernon?"

"Are they going to cut the cake soon?"

"Oh, I don't know, Tommy, you can ask your aunt Nancy."

"OK."

The occasion for the family gathering was Grandma and Grandpa Price's 50th wedding anniversary. Unlike Grandma and Grandpa Hinesley's party two years later, this one wasn't a small get-together. It seemed like there were as least a hundred people there, ninety percent of whom I didn't know. My little chat with Grandma Artie was about as much as I talked to her that day. Luckily, it was Scott who got most of the attention that afternoon. Apparently, right as Dad and Uncle Milt were getting out of the car to watch the game, Scott had a few choice words for the umpire, who, in Scott's opinion, missed one too many calls. Much to Dad's embarrassment, Scott got tossed from the game. Getting tossed from a Little League game—only Scott could manage that. I chuckled to myself and came out of my stupor.

"Are we almost there?"

Steve sat on the other side of me. Dad had picked him up earlier that day. Scott wasn't with us. He was still down in Murray, without a car or any means of getting to Chicago in a hurry. This was my first funeral, and I wasn't sure how to feel. I learned that I dealt with tragedy with a dark sense of humor. Actually, my brothers, as it turns out, are the same way. To those around us we might seem callous and cold, but I think it was just a way for us to disassociate ourselves from our sadness. I wasn't that close to Grandma Artie—I just didn't see her very often. Sometime around 1973, Grandma and Grandpa Price moved further away, and we didn't see them all too often after that. Previously, they'd come over during the holidays and I'd watch them play pinochle, but after 1973, the only time I saw them was usually at a family get together—which I dreaded. This made me uneasy about the funeral. I was thankful Steve was there. As Dad would say, "Misery loves company." In this case, it was true. Steve was dressed stylishly and casually, yet gloomily enough to be mournful. He had a sense for that kind of thing. I wasn't so stylish in my charcoal gray suit that I had worn for my eighth-grade graduation. As it turns out, Mom was wise to make sure it was a little big when we got it so I could grow into it later. We entered the parlor and I scanned the crowd to see if there was a face I could recognize. Just as I was thinking we were in the wrong place, I spotted my aunt Nancy among the sea of strange faces.

We made our way to the casket before sitting down. The strange music was beginning to annoy me. An organist was playing background music that sounded like something out of an old horror movie on late night TV. The experience was surreal and would have been comical, if the situation hadn't been so serious. We reached the casket, and Steve and I looked inside. Artie wasn't exactly a pretty woman when she was alive, but she looked like a wax figure in the casket.

"You'd think they could do a better job," Steve said, with a slight grin. We went to sit down, and Steve continued, "What's with the organ?"

"I know, I'm waiting for Grandma to sit up any minute like something straight out of *Creature Features*."

After that comment, Steve and I got the giggles at the most inappropriate time. I was biting my lip so hard to keep from laughing, I'm surprised I didn't bite through it. I was half-expecting Dad to clock me, but he didn't seem to notice. I'm sure he was lost in his own thoughts, although he never showed his sadness. I noticed many years later on old calendars Dad kept, I assume for work records, that Artie's was the only birthday he always seemed to write down. Somewhere in the back of my mind was the realization that I'd never see her again, and while that was a sad thought, I knew I was lucky to have ever met her at all.

That night, our house was toilet papered, and a gigantic sign wishing me good luck in our semifinals against East St. Louis was draped over the front of the house. At least I had football to take my mind off of the funeral. Unfortunately, we lost our game, and worse still, my funeral experience was only a sign of things to come. It was almost as if it were a dress rehearsal, because a little over two months later, I'd once again be sitting in a funeral home.

A Cold Day in January

When I heard, I wasn't sure if I felt sad or relieved. Grandma Hinesley died on the evening of January 21st, 1985. The 21st was a Monday, and I had just visited her over the weekend. Her condition never improved since her stroke. When I visited her for the last time, it seemed like she was exhausted. Without anyone to dye her hair red, the color faded from her hair over time, much like her energy to fight off the inevitable end. It was such a shame to watch her suffer such a long and miserable death. That's why, despite the fact that I loved her so much, I felt it was a mercy that she had finally died. For Grandpa, it was significantly harder. They had been together so long and had experienced so much together that her death left him empty and bitter. Much of his lively personality was placed high up on a back shelf, only to be brought down on special occasions, of which there would be few. Mom seemed to be without words. It was a tough time for her, but as with most of us, Grandma's condition left little doubt as to what the eventual outcome was going to be. Her reaction seemed a little empty and confused, since she had really lost her mother almost two years before.

It was a dreary January day that matched the overall mood for the funeral. The funeral itself was a small affair, as Grandpa didn't want anyone coming who had neglected to visit her after her stroke. He would let them know by and by. My uncles were both there, as was Aunt Delores and two of my cousins. Scott was still in Kentucky and couldn't be there. So it was that Steve and I once again found ourselves seated next to each other at a funeral as the horror-movie organ music began to play.

I turned to him and said in a quiet voice, "This is getting to be a habit."

"Who do you think will be next?"

I looked over at Grandpa, Mom, and Dad, then over to Uncle Herb and Uncle Jerry and said, "Hell, it could be any one of them. With that high blood pressure scare, I could be the next one up there."

"Well, if it's me, promise me you won't let them play this cheesy music."

"It's a deal."

First Signs of Trouble

The early 1980s were hard on Mom. Grandma, who had been her confidant, seemed to have one bad turn of luck after another. During the years following Grandma's stroke, Mom had difficulty dealing with Grandma's condition. Grandma liked my dad and was able to keep Dad in somewhat good relations with Grandpa Hinesley. Following her stroke, Grandma was no longer able to shield Mom from Grandpa's negativity toward Dad. As the role of confidant slowly switched over to Grandpa, Mom began to see things a little blacker. Her stress levels regarding money and security started to rise. It was first after Grandma's stroke and, later, her death that the positive influence Grandma had over the upbeat personalities of Mom and Grandpa became evident.

Mom wasn't made to handle great amounts of stress. In addition to Grandma's problems came Dad's heart attack and recovery. Along with Dad's heart attack came the need for him to rebuild his business. During that time, Mom kept on working. The stress of money, work, and Grandma's and Dad's health problems began to reveal itself in several different ways. One way was that Mom developed a skin condition that became worse during stress. She participated in a bowling league at work and drank socially, but nothing crazy. There was a slow but subtle change from drinking socially to drinking alone. The habit of drinking may have started as sharing a nightcap with Dad while we played cards. But she wasn't just having a nightcap. I guess I first took notice when Mom started drinking a glass or two of wine after she came home from work. By itself, that may not be a big deal. I didn't find it strange when she and Dad drank a glass or two of alcohol while we played pinochle. But I began to notice that alcohol was disappearing from the liquor cabinet even when we weren't playing cards. I figured someone was sneaking it. I pointed it out to Scott, who also thought it was unusual. Both of us mentioned it to Dad, who said we were making a big deal out of nothing. He'd change his tune over time.

In the meantime, subtle changes in Mom's personality began to surface. Normally even-tempered, she'd get snappish for no reason, or she'd become overly dramatic over the littlest things. After I called Dad's attention to the bottles in the liquor cabinet, I noticed

Mother and Daughter.

that the volume of vodka in the bottle didn't seem to change. But the instances of peculiar behavior didn't disappear. Then, I began to notice that Mom didn't come straight into the kitchen, as she always did, but instead she went up to her room. I pretended not to notice, but one day I checked her room and found a half-empty bottle of vodka in her nightstand. Well, I didn't need a high-school health class to tell me she had a problem. Bringing the problem out into the open didn't solve it. Dad stayed in denial for a while, until it was apparent to him as well. At first, her drinking would last only a day or two at a time. Even when she did drink, and there were subtle hints, she was functional. Gradually, over the years, her excessive drinking became progressively worse, and she'd call in sick to work for several days. Searching for vodka bottles became a little like an Easter egg hunt anytime Mom showed signs of drinking. By the time Dad couldn't avoid the truth any longer, she was a full-blown alcoholic.

Don't Drink, Don't Smoke

Watching Mom succumb to alcoholism while I was in high school turned me off to the idea of drinking completely. This made me a bit of an oddball whenever I went to parties. Drugs weren't in vogue at Buffalo Grove High School during my years there. There were some "burnouts," a.k.a. stoners, who smoked pot, but they were a small social group of their own. There may have been an occasional student who tried other drugs, but I wasn't aware of them. Underage drinking, however, was rampant at the various parties during the year. Although I didn't drink, it didn't mean that I was above making a buck off of those who did. That's why I played host to one of the biggest parties during the year, which we dubbed "Zep Fest." I wasn't the sole host; I had an investor in Jim and a supplier and partner in Scott. We timed Zep Fest to take place on Memorial Day weekend while Mom and Dad went downtown to celebrate their anniversary.

It was a challenging operation. One challenge of the night was going to be how to keep Caesar, our one hundred and thirty-pound German shepherd, under control. I'd figured this out the year before by having him guard my room, where we kept the stereo. Another challenge we faced was making sure that nothing got broken and no valuables were stolen. We solved this by moving anything of value up to Mom and Dad's room. We moved so much stuff that if we moved anything else, we could have painted the living room and dining room while we were at it. We knew from the previous year how the word of a party could spread like wildfire and, next thing you knew, there could be over a hundred people in your house, with the street lined with cars. We were prepared. Dad's methodology must have rubbed off somewhat, since we weren't just prepared for possible problems but also the big clean-up afterwards. During the party, everyone had a job. Scott's was easy: Get the keg and distribute the cups. Jim's job was to collect the money. As the only stone sober one, I would maintain order—constantly moving from room to room while keeping the music going. Before you knew it, the place was hopping. Unlike many of the parties I'd been to, no one got out of hand, which was a blessing. And after all was said and done, nothing was broken. Scott and Jim made most of the profit, but I still made out all right. We worked feverishly after the party to clean up and ventilate the house. We moved all of the furniture and other items back to where they belonged. We were perfectly ready for Mom and Dad to come home. When they arrived, we greeted them as if nothing had happened. Of course, that made them suspicious.

"Did you guys have a party?"

"Party?" Scott replied.

Mom pointed to a single beer can sitting behind a chair on the back patio.

"Well, we had a couple of people over."

Going Our Separate Ways

A week after the party, I graduated from high school. For many students, high school graduation brings comes a feeling of both achievement and hope. The paths people take can lead them all over the country and sometimes the world. Some students had their whole futures mapped out, including college and a career, while others found their direction during college. Some were just happy to be done with school.

Among many of my classmates, there was a feeling of entitlement when it came to college, as if their parents owed them a higher education. I didn't have that luxury. I knew my parents would help where they could, but I would have to work to pay for much of my schooling. Because of my limited funds, I joined Scott at Murray State, where we would be roommates once more.

By the time I graduated from high school, much of what I had known in my earlier life and community had changed. Greenbrier's developer, Miller Builders, had gone out of business several years earlier. Rand Junior High School had closed two years earlier, after being open only fourteen years. Much of the open space in the area had been developed, blending the old neighborhood with the new. It seemed like Greenbrier was on a new path of its own. It wouldn't be too long before the civic association was gone, and with it, the Greenbrier Boys' Softball League and the Fourth of July Bike Parade.

At home, Mom fought alcoholism while Dad struggled with weight loss. Both of them were losing their separate battles. Their paths seemed to be fixed. Steve, however, was headed in the right direction. In 1984, he joined a company called Post Effects and began his career in computer animation and postproduction effects. Computer graphics were still in their infancy, and some of the effects seem primitive by today's standards, but at the time, the work he was doing was on the cutting edge of that technology. Steve contributed his talents to the Chicago Bears' "Super Bowl Shuffle" video, which was exciting for everyone at home. Bigger and better things where waiting for Steve as he left Chicago in the fall of 1986. He first went to Florida, but eventually wound up in California, where he began working on the TV series *Star Trek: The Next Generation*, with a company called the Post Group. Scott later chose to follow Steve to California, while my direction, over time, led me to Germany. It wouldn't be until the summer of 1992 that our paths would cross again.

It's never a dull moment (this photo was taken the summer of 1986, shortly before we went our seperate ways—I'm the one on the left, Steve's in the middle, and Scott is on the right).

CHAPTER 10

All Together Now

Coming Home

I sat in my seat waiting for the 747 to taxi to the gate. Tired and feeling stale from the long flight, I was relieved the end was finally in sight. While waiting, I began to contemplate my next step in life. I had one more semester to wrap up at school, and about three-and-a-half months to earn enough money to register. Before going to Germany, I worked at a suburban nightclub called Bogie's. It was a real hot spot at the time, and I made a fair amount in tips. "Bogie's should take me back," I thought, as the plane finally reached the gate.

"Welcome to Chicago's O'Hare International Airport, the local time is..."

It had been a while since I'd left the States. I had an unusual feeling returning home after being in a foreign country for a couple of years. While overseas, I hadn't seen any American news or read any American newspapers. I didn't even speak English during that time, other than my phone calls home. I felt a little out of touch. The culture and community had moved on. I couldn't escape the feeling like I didn't belong anymore. There were new celebrities I didn't know. The Gulf War had begun and ended during my absence. The Soviet Union had been dissolved. The Chicago Bulls won their first NBA title. Everywhere I looked, something was being hyped as if to compete for my attention. The nation was revving up for the 1992 presidential election, which had a circus-like atmosphere with the addition of the on-again off-again third-party candidate, Ross Perot.

At home, some things had changed too. Mom's problem with alcohol caused her to miss great stretches of work. I imagine she must have been close to being let go when the company moved its head quarters to the far western suburbs. Mom took the opportunity to leave the company during that transition, using the move as her reason for leaving. I can hear Dad's voice, "When opportunity knocks..." Meanwhile, Grandpa George had died down in Texas and was buried in West Chicago next to Grandma Artie. I felt bad that I missed the funeral. Apparently Steve missed it too, which alleviated my guilt somewhat. While I was gone, Caesar got cancer and had to be put down. Mom and Dad bought a new German shepherd puppy and named him JB. JB was supposed to stand for "jet black," because of his black face. Being a dog person, I looked forward to meeting the new puppy.

I exited my plane and made my way down to the baggage claim and U.S. Customs. I walked the final paces to the two large sliding doors of terminal five, and, like money in the bank, there stood Dad, a little heavier than I remembered him.

"Hey, Pops! Good to see you!"

"Hey, Buddy, how was your flight?"

"Not bad, a little long, but you know..."

"Let me take that," he said, reaching for one of my suitcases.

"Thanks, so where are you parked?"

"Right over there," he gestured toward the parking lot, where a new '92 silver Ford Escort stood.

"Ah, new car?"

"Yep, just got it. You can have the black one."

"Really? Cool. Not ten minutes in the country and I've got a car!"

Dad and I put the suitcases in the trunk and started for home. While the Ford Escort could hardly be considered one of Dad's best cars over the years, he simply wanted a fairly inexpensive car on which he didn't need to make any payments.

"So, how's Mom been?" I asked hesitantly.

I wasn't really asking about her general health as much as I was asking about her "condition." Dad understood exactly what I meant.

"She's tapering off."

"I see."

"Tapering off" was code for Dad trying to get her straight. It meant she had been on a real bender recently. Dad's method for trying to sober her up was to ease her off the juice gradually. In fact, he was simply enabling her to continue. To his credit, Dad meant well. It was kind of sad to see Dad's methodical ways used on such a fruitless exercise. Sooner or later, after sobering up for a while, Mom would go out and get a bottle or two and then strategically hide it around the house. Shortly thereafter, she'd be blotto again. How Dad managed to deal with it as long as he did baffles me, but he did it. I think it became a chore that would raise its ugly head periodically. He would seem to solve it, then Mom would fall off the wagon, and the whole process would start all over again.

Different Paths

Although I sympathized with Dad, Mom's drinking was always an unpleasant subject. Dad must have sensed that, so he changed the direction of the conversation.

"Your brothers are going to be in town, and I think they might even cross paths."

"Really?

I hadn't seen either of my brothers for a long time. By 1992, both Steve and Scott were living in California and working in the field of postproduction visual effects. Steve's work on *Star Trek* earned him several Emmy nominations. Then, in 1990, Steve got the chance to work on the film *Ghost*, which earned him his first movie credit. Steve's career seemed to be on a roll. Around the time I went to Germany, Steve helped Scott with some job connections at the Post Group then, later, Digital Magic. While Steve helped Scott get settled in, Steve didn't stay put for long. He understood that his expertise on the HARRY (video animation and compositing editor made by Quantel) added to his demand in the industry. He also knew the industry was fast paced and that demand for his work would only last as long as he stayed at the forefront of his craft. And he did. In 1991, Steve got the opportunity he had been waiting for—to work for the most renowned of all visual effects companies—George Lucas's Industrial Light and Magic. If that wasn't enough of a high point for Steve, the first film he'd be working on with ILM was a Steven Spielberg film, Hook. By the time Steve arrived in Chicago, he was involved with another Steven Spielberg movie, *Jurassic Park*. Dad was excited for Steve. Once he had heard Steve was going to be working on the movie, he bought and read the Michael Crichton book, which he loved. Soon thereafter, he was proudly giving copies of the book as a gift to clients and friends.

In 1992, Scott was primarily working on TV shows and commercials, while Steve had moved on to working on motion pictures. Unlike Steve, most of Scott's work was non-credited digital clean-up, fixing flaws on the film and such. During the late 1980s, Scott took on a number of odd jobs while trying to find the right career choice. It was during that time that he worked as a pizza delivery man for La Roman Kitchens. It seems that La Roman would stick with him in more ways than just the extra pounds coming from their delicious pizza, because he met his future wife, Alison, there. I guess you could call it La Romance. It was a long-distance romance in 1992, with Scott living in California.

I turned to Dad. "When are they coming in?"

"Scott comes in at the end of June, and Steve arrives at the end of July."

It turns out Scott had five weeks of vacation, which he wanted to spend with his fiancée, and, of course, us. I was sitting in the car on the way home, happy with the thought of seeing my brothers again, when Dad brought up the topic of work.

"Do you know what you're going to do?"

"Well, I figured I'd call Bogie's and see if I could pick up where I left off. I should be able to make enough money for my last semester."

"I'd rather you not work there. What about working with me and learning some of the skills to be able to help me out? I'd pay you what you'd make at Bogie's."

"You mean an apprentice type of thing? Because I'd need training."

"Yeah, I'd train you on what we're doing. You wouldn't be working on the final product until I thought you were ready."

We arrived home. I met the puppy shortly after walking in, and he took to me quickly. Mom up and gave me a hug. I brought in all of my things and put them in my old room. I went back down to the kitchen to join Mom and Dad. After chit-chatting a while, we decided to play a game of three-handed pinochle.

Measure Twice, Cut Once

I took Dad up on his offer to work with him during the summer of 1992. Dad's work had changed somewhat from what he'd been doing all those years before. While he would still do illustrations from time to time, most of his work hours were spent on new work that came from his partner, Fred Anderson. As Fred was getting ready for retirement, he began to pass off some of his projects over to Dad. By 1992, Fred was semi-retired, and Dad had taken over the majority of the projects. The niche Fred had discovered was doing some outsource work for the large advertising company Leo Burnett in Chicago. When Leo Burnett did photo shoots or commercials for new products, they needed mock-ups of the new product as props for the advertisement. That's where Fred and Dad came in. They were given flat hi-res photo proofs of the new product packaging, and then they took those proofs and created the mock-ups. The mock-ups had to be absolutely flawless. Creating flawless mock-ups became Fred's and Dad's specialty, and they were very good at it. Apparently, from time to time, competitors tried unsuccessfully to take their business, and the work seemed too specialized for Leo Burnett to do it in-house cost-effectively. That summer, I learned some of their trade secrets.

Dad hard at work, during the summer of 1992.

Each morning we hit the road at the crack of dawn to beat the rush-hour traffic. I hopped in the car, and soon Dad was speeding along the tollway, dodging potholes as we went.

"You should probably signal before you cut a guy off like that."

"Oh, you mean like this?" he chuckled, as he signaled after passing someone.

"Something like that."

His chipper mood changed quickly when an old woman pulled in front of him and drove five miles per hour below the speed limit.

"Come on, clown!"

Now it was my turn to chuckle. Part of our morning routine was walking through the concourse level of the Illinois Center complex and buying a newspaper and a giant cinnamon roll, which by itself was probably two thousand calories. Business came in waves, so there were times when there was a lot to do and other times when things were slow. It was during one of the slow periods that Dad asked me if I'd like to take a fishing trip with him. I jumped at the chance.

Musky Haven

The last catch.

So it was that Dad and I took our first fishing trip in fourteen years. Dad got all excited at the prospect of a fishing trip. He had been planning it long before he ever asked me to go with him. He'd bought maps and acquired brochures from various locations in northern Wisconsin. Part of him wanted to go back to the Chippewa Flowage, where he fished before I was born, but instead he settled on a small resort owned by Fred's brother on a small chain of lakes near Minocqua. Bearing the name Musky Haven, the resort sounded more promising than fishing on Dead Lake. Dad and I visited a local fishing shop to get new lures, a new rod and reel for me, and new line for Dad's reel, as well as the all-important fishing license.

Before you could say "catch and release," we were on the road, with me navigating our way into the northern woods of Wisconsin for what would be our last fishing trip together. Once we arrived, Dad was ready to hit the water. With his cap pulled down low and sunglasses on, it could have been 1974 all over again, except he'd gained a few pounds since then. Otherwise, it was just like old times: the spray of water in my face, Dad fiddling with the motor, the excitement each time a fish was on the line, and searching for hot spots around the lake. All in all, it was a good trip. We caught a fair number of fish, although none of them were trophy fish. Without Mom there to fry them up, we practiced catch and release. At night we looked at the map and picked out hopeful spots to fish the next day. Even though fishing gear and gadgets had come a long way since our last trip, we continued with our old method and managed just the same. Between working with him and going on the fishing trip, the summer of 1992 offered me a chance to get to know Dad in a way I hadn't before. Maybe Dad felt I would move away like Steve and Scott and wanted to get his time in while he could. Soon we'd all be together under one roof, if only briefly.

Welcome Home

It had been a while since I'd seen or talked to Scott, so that evening as we sat in the kitchen watching TV and drinking a Diet Coke, I asked him how things were out in Los Angeles. He leaned back in his chair, sporting his L.A. attire—zebra-striped Zubaz pants—as he told me stories about LA.

"Did you have to deal with the riots at all?"

"Yeah, it's funny, one of the first nights of the riots, we're doing this video shoot for a 20 Minute Work-out exercise video with these hot chicks and it was getting late. There was a curfew so they wanted to spend the night in the studio and they wanted someone to stay in the building with them. I was responsible for making sure the alarms were set and everything was locked up, so I volunteered to stay."

"You're quite the gentleman."

"Yeah, well, what else was I going to do? While one of the girls went out for a smoke she said she heard gun fire close by. So, she asks me if I'd go out to her car with her so that she could get her purse, because she wants to get her gun."

"Nice. What kind of gun was it?"

"I don't know, the kind that shoots bullets. Anyway, it's late and we go to sleep. I'm in the lobby and they're in another room. At about 2 O'clock in the morning the fire alarm goes off, and it's loud. I get up and start feeling the doors to see if they're hot but it's a false alarm. I figure I better go tell the girls that everything is ok so they don't panic. So, I go up to the door and knock loudly and then go inside."

"To where the chick with the gun was?"

"Exactly, I didn't even think about it until I had already walked in the room. Then it hit me, she's got a gun, the alarm is going off, and I'm banging on the door. I break out in a cold sweat. I'm thinking I have to get to the girl before she goes for her purse. I reached her just as she was waking up and I told her it was a false alarm."

"You're lucky she didn't shoot you."

A scratch came from behind me and I saw that JB wanted to go outside. I got up to let the dog out.

Dad called out to me from the living room, "Hold on, Buddy. Let me check to see if there are any skunks out there."

"OK."

We had first experienced a skunk problem with Caesar, and Dad had worked out a system to keep the skunks away from our backyard. First, he put chicken wire all around the bottom two feet of the fence to keep them out of the yard. As an extra precaution, he scanned the backyard with a large flashlight. The last deterrent was a CO_2-powered BB gun that we shot at the skunk, if we ever saw one. The BB gun wasn't powerful enough to kill a skunk, but we hoped it might discourage one from coming back into the yard if we ever hit him. (In reality, if we had actually ever hit a skunk, it would probably have pissed him off more.) Tonight, Dad went through his normal routine. He scanned the backyard, holding the large flashlight at eye level, much like you would hold a camcorder. The beam of light danced across the back perimeter of our yard by the fence like a searchlight from an old prisoner-of-war movie.

"Looks OK."

I let the dog out, and he shot out the door, straight for the back fence. JB was so fast that he was growling and fighting with something before Dad could even shine the light on him. I grabbed the BB gun, and Dad tried to locate whatever it was with the light. We had only taken a few steps out of the sliding glass door onto the porch when JB came bolting back at full speed, darting right past us into the house. It wasn't until he was already past us that the stench of skunk spray hit us. The air was now heavy with the musky smell, making it difficult to breathe.

"God damn it, JB!" came Scott's voice from the kitchen.

"Stop him!" I yelled, "He's been skunked!"

"I know he's been skunked, he ran in here and rubbed his face in my crotch!"

An hour and one or two gallons of tomato juice later, the dog smelled like a soapy tomato with a hint of skunk. A dejected Scott sat in the kitchen in a new outfit, cursing the dog.

"I just got those pants."

"Welcome home," Dad said with a chuckle.

All Together Now

I saw Scott often during the five weeks he was home. We even had an opportunity to go up to Musky Haven to go fishing. Unfortunately, Dad couldn't get away with us for that trip. Although he could barely contain his excitement when he heard Scott caught a twelve-pound musky.

As Dad predicted, my brothers and I all crossed paths one day at the end of July. We hadn't all been together at the same time since 1986, so it was a special occasion. Normally we'd have seen each other over the holidays, but for some reason we weren't all able to coordinate it over those six years. We played cards while Mom

The day we were all under one roof again (Scott, Steve, and me).

made lunch. It was just like old times that afternoon, with the whole family being together. The best part was that there wasn't any special occasion to celebrate. We could all be ourselves. Steve, Scott, and I went out that evening and played pool and darts. Regrettably, the one day together as a family was short lived. The next day, Scott went back to California, and Steve went downtown for his trade show. Our reunion was over as quickly as it had begun. I saw Steve downtown during the course of the week, and we went out to eat at Gold Coast Dogs so he could have a Chicago-style hot dog. The time with Steve seemed a little pressured, and the week went by too quickly for my liking. I found myself once again saying goodbye to Steve, not knowing when I'd see him next. As it turns out, it was sooner than planned.

University of Diversity

There were only a few minutes left in the soccer game, as the other team got the ball and began its counterattack. I watched patiently from my position in the goal box, reading the play as it developed. As they closed in on me, I prepared for the pass I knew was coming. Then came the long crossing pass I had anticipated. A striker from the other team rushed the goal from the opposite side to meet the pass. As the ball sailed toward the goal box, I ran out to meet it and then made my move. Diving into what would almost certainly be a hard collision with the oncoming player, I kept my eyes focused on the ball. Just at the right moment, I punched out and knocked the ball away. A millisecond later, I collided with the other player. We both got up quickly. The ball had gone to one of my players, who brought it back down toward the other goal. I got back into position and waited for the next strike.

That fall semester, I was the sole American on the International Student Organization soccer team. It was a very diverse group of players, coming from all over the world to play soccer together on an intramural team at Murray State University. Diversity is a funny thing. There has been a push in American society for increased diversity and multiculturalism, as if it were a difficult thing to achieve. It doesn't have to be. If a person lives by the golden rule, diversity becomes normality. So normal, that you don't even think about it. At least I didn't. Yet, I was told at parties of international students that I was "different" from most Americans. I wasn't. If there was any difference, it was only that I looked for common ground with people, as opposed to differences. There were, of course, other American students who reached out specifically to be connected with the International Student Organization, like groupies interested in globalism, but I wasn't one of them. One might wonder, what I was doing at an international student party in the first place, if I wasn't searching for diversity?

I knew from the beginning that this was going to be a different semester. I felt a little odd going back to finish up at Murray after having been out of the country almost two years. My college career wasn't the smoothest. Not only had I been gone for two years, but I'd missed a couple of semesters in the past due to lack of funds. This was finally it: I'd come to wrap things up once and for all. As I drove into town on Highway 641, it appeared that little had changed in Murray since the last time I was there, but I soon learned differently. All of my friends were gone, of course. The very same professor who encouraged me to go abroad was now instrumental in recently establishing an exchange program between Murray State and the University of Regensburg in Germany. I returned during the first semester of its inception. This, however, wasn't good news for me. Now there was an official exchange program, complete with curriculum—which I didn't follow while I was in Germany. Most Americans who study in Germany through an exchange program don't take the standard courses the German students take. They might choose to go to various lectures, but for the most part they take American-style courses. These courses may, in fact, be taught by German professors, but some are taught by visiting American professors. This works well for the American students because it's an equivalent class. Getting my work from Germany accepted was a mess that would take some time to clear up.

In the meantime, the professor invited me to a party for international students, an invitation I gladly accepted, since I no longer knew anyone on campus. The result was that I befriended the German students who came to Murray. I'd like to think I helped them overcome the culture shock somewhat. Soon, I was actively involved with the International Student Organization, going to their parties and playing goalie for their soccer team. I felt bad that they were stuck in Murray, so I called Dad to see if it would be OK to invite a group of Germans up to Chicago on the weekend of October 17th. I already knew what Dad would say.

Father and Son Revisited

The night of October 17th, 1992, had been longer than I expected. After hours of drinking and dancing at the Baja Beach Club at North Pier in downtown Chicago, my German

Dad at his drawing table in Columbus Plaza—the picture was to serve as inspiration for his ongoing diet. This photo is the "after" photo to an earlier "before" photo taken in August, 1991. In this August, 1992 photo, he had actually gained weight over the previous year. At least he could laugh at himself.

friends and I decided to call it a night. Around two o'clock in the morning, we made our way back to Columbus Plaza. Once we arrived, the doorman let us in, and we boarded the elevator. Earlier that night, Dad had suggested that I stay in the apartment with him so that I could sleep in if need be. I bid my friends good night, and exited on the ninth floor, while the others continued up to the guest apartment. I entered the apartment as quietly as possible, so as not to wake Dad. I made my way through the darkness of the living room, which was illuminated slightly by the lights of the city. When I reached the futon, I lay down and drifted off to sleep.

After what seemed like a brief moment later, I was awakened by a loud knock on the apartment door. I slowly came to my senses. I looked at my watch, and it was already a few minutes after eight o'clock. There was another knock at the door, so I got up, still dressed in the clothes I had worn the night before. I opened the door, and there stood one of the German students, Harm.

"Good morning," I croaked. I was still a little groggy, as I gestured for him to come in.

"Good morning," Harm replied. "The others are still sleeping, and I thought you might be up."

"To tell you the truth, I just got up myself when you knocked on the door. It's kind of funny because I figured my Dad would be up by now," I said. "Tell you what, let me shower and get dressed, then I'll swing by and get you when I'm ready. It shouldn't be more than twenty minutes or so."

"Sounds good," said Harm, as he got up to leave.

I lead Harm out and closed the door behind him. I turned to look down the short hallway at the bedroom door. It was unusual for Dad not to have coffee going by seven or eight o'clock. I reached the door and turned the handle. I opened it slowly, and saw what I dreaded most.

Dad was lying on his back, with his left arm on his chest, and his right arm extended out from his body. He was dressed in the T-shirt and shorts he normally wore to sleep. My head was in a fog as I heard myself scream "No!"

Tom, the tour guid (left) shows off a shut-off a nonfunctioning Buckingham Fountain on October 17th, 1992.

repeatedly, at the top of my voice. I stumbled over to his body, which was already cold and somewhat stiff. I knelt next to him in shock, before before coming to the realization that there was nothing I could do for him. It was over. I was dumbfounded, and unsure of what to do next. I needed to talk to someone, so I called each of my brothers in California. Then I made a mistake I will never make again, and which was leaving a message on an answering machine, telling them the bad news. It's just not a good way to find out someone has died. Uncertain what to do, I called 9-1-1 and asked for an ambulance, but told them there was no rush, since Dad was already dead.

"Are you sure he's dead?" the 9-1-1 operator asked.

"Well, he's stiff and blue, so yes, I'm sure," I replied.

Then she said, "If he's dead, then you don't need an ambulance, you need the police."

"Send over whoever handles this kind of thing, because it's all new to me."

A rush of feelings filled my head. I felt a sense of disappointment and helplessness, because I was unable to help him. I wondered if I had come back sooner the night before, if I could have saved him. Everything seemed unreal to me, as if it were a dream. My mind hadn't yet caught up with the reality of the moment. I knew he was dead, but hadn't fully accepted it yet. Finally, I called Mom to tell her. I was really worried that my call would send her over the edge, and induce her to drink. I think she was too shocked to really even think about drinking. I then called my German friends, and they came downstairs to be with me.

It wasn't long after the Germans arrived that the police came to the door. There must have been ten officers in the apartment. At least, it seemed that way at the time. It didn't occur to me then that they had to investigate to make sure it wasn't a homicide. As they did their thing, I stared out the window. It was a nice day. I took in the beautiful view of the city, the Wrigley building, the Michigan Avenue Bridge, the Tribune tower, The John Hancock Center, the NBC building, and the Chicago river. It was a beautiful view that Dad saw almost everyday, but he'd never see again. I watched the people walking over the Michigan Avenue Bridge. Chicago was moving on, the world was moving on, life was moving on. For me, though, Chicago was different, and the world was different. It was as if suddenly, a new phase of my life had begun.

Soon I was being interviewed by one of the police officers. While telling the officer a funny anecdote about Dad, it hit me: He was really dead. I broke down.

Someone from the funeral home arrived to take the body. First the body needed to go to the coroner's office before it could be released. Although the man from the funeral home was a big guy, Dad wasn't a small package to lift, so I helped him lift Dad onto the stretcher. It was the least I could do for my coach, my role model, my Santa, my father.

And Then There Were Four

My head was in a daze as I left apartment 902 in Columbus Plaza that day. My friends took my keys and drove me home to my grieving mother. Uncle Jerry was already keeping her company by the time we arrived. It was a Sunday, and my German friends and I had planned to head back to Kentucky that day, but I needed to stay to help arrange for the funeral. They were able to rent a car on short notice, and left that afternoon without me. It was a sad ending to an otherwise fun trip.

Upon hearing my message, Scott quickly arranged a flight out of Los Angeles that same day. Steve, too, had made quick arrangements to get back to Chicago in time for the funeral. As Scott arrived later that day, it was me who greeted him at the airport.

The next day Mom, Scott, and I went to Friedrich's funeral home. We began to discuss the details of the funeral. After Dad's first heart attack and the passing of both of my grandmothers, we had discussed on several occasions what kind of funeral we'd wish to have. At the time, everyone agreed there was no need for a fancy ordeal. Now we were actually faced with making the arrangements. Steve and I didn't like either of our grandmother's funerals. I wanted to avoid cheesy music at all costs, or I wouldn't be able to look at Steve throughout the whole service without laughing. We agreed on cremation, but Mom still wanted visitation. I hate looking at an embalmed person, because it seems so artificial. But Mom was persistent.

"I have to see him, it's so hard to believe he's gone," Mom said tearfully.

"Trust me, he's gone," I said matter-of-factly, having had my fair share of time with the body.

I did respect her need for closure, although I couldn't imagine much good coming from the viewing. There's not much to see, except an embalmed body with make-up. I want to state, for the record, that there wasn't a day when my father was breathing that he had an orange tint to him. To have visitation, we had to choose a casket, even though Dad was to be cremated. We were shown a selection of caskets of all price ranges. Scott started asking all sorts of pricing questions.

"If he's being cremated anyway, why do we need to buy the casket? Don't you have one we can rent?"

Well, they didn't. I thought Scott was being outrageous, until I saw a similar question raised in the 1998 movie, *The Big Lebowski*. The movie instantly became one of my all-time favorites. After much consideration, Mom settled on a model that had an elegant appearance. The funeral was set for 7:30 p.m. the next day.

Steve flew in early the day of the funeral, and I volunteered to pick him up at the airport. As we drove home, we talked about Dad. Steve started the conversation in an unusual serious tone.

"How are you doing? When I heard your message I was a little worried for you."

"I bet, I honestly don't remember what I said."

"Well, you seemed out of it."

"I guess my mind was elsewhere," I said with a hint of sarcasm. "Anyway I wish I could be picking you up for a different reason."

"He knew better, it was his own fault."

"True, he could have lain off the ice cream sandwiches, but at least he quit smoking."

We shared the feeling that Dad had pushed his luck by remaining dangerously overweight after his first heart attack. Steve's attitude seemed to be closer to disappointment in Dad's self-neglect than sorrow for his passing. We drove around for a while, sharing funny stories about Dad, like our Christmas shopping days. Those days were already long behind us, and now we were burying our connection to them.

Amazing Grace

The funeral was an emotional roller coaster from start to finish. We, as a family, were poorly prepared for these types of events. The funeral had a churchlike atmosphere that made my brothers and me feel out of place. As people I barely knew extended their sympathy, it was difficult to know how to act. I felt a sense of resentment that Dad had died early, and didn't feel that people knew what kind of gap his absence would leave. Sitting right up in front of the casket, I realized the night was going to be a tough one to get through. If the experience wasn't miserable enough, it went a step further when the cheesy horror-movie organ music started up with "Amazing Grace."

I couldn't bear to look at Steve. But, like a moth to flame, I couldn't avoid sparing a glance in his direction. Steve, who was sitting upright and facing forward, had a slight smirk on his face. His eyes turned toward me, and we made eye contact. I broke out instantly in a cold sweat. I looked away, but it was too late. I bit my lip hard to avoid laughing. I bent forward and rubbed my eyes with my left hand, holding my laughter in while bouncing in my chair. My emotions were in a weird state of hysteria, where I could find myself crying one minute and laughing the next. I thought I was ripe for the funny farm, because I was losing it. Red-faced and watery-eyed, I sat back up and took a deep breath.

Aunt Nancy, who was Dad's older sister, brought a female minister from her church and asked Mom if it'd be all right for her to say a few words. Because Mom hadn't arranged for anyone to speak except the funeral director, she agreed. I was able to regain my normal emotional condition as the minister, who had never met Dad, spoke of his salvation and the love shared by all those around him. After the minister was done speaking, the funeral director invited anyone who wanted to speak to come up to the podium and say a few words. There were so many great things I would have loved to have gone up and said, but I was in no emotional state to even get a sentence out of my mouth. Each time I even thought of something I'd consider saying, I teared up. Scott, who was sitting next to me, also struggled with wanting to say something, but he too was too shaken. I think Steve was secretly hoping the whole thing would end soon so he could get out of there. Just when it seemed like the end was near, Uncle Milt stepped up to the podium.

Uncle Milt and Dad had a similar relationship to that of Scott and me. Milt was the older middle brother, and Dad was the youngest. While they were similar in appearance and sense of humor, they had slightly different personalities. Milt was a little more outgoing, not unlike Scott. All in all, he and Dad were very close. They grew up together, got into mischief together, and experienced many of the same things in life. Maybe he was the perfect person to speak about Dad. Milt began to tell funny and serious stories about his life with Dad, which had me both laughing and crying. He did justice to Dad that night by sharing with everyone, including people who maybe only knew Dad as a commercial artist, neighbor, or an uncle they rarely saw, the personal side of Dick Price.

After Milt finished his words about Dad, the funeral director made a last request for a speaker, which no one answered. At that

Mom and Dad celebrate Grandpa Hinesley's eighty-fifth birthday on October 9th, 1992.

point, he invited the various rows of people to go up and pay their last respects. Everyone made their way past, and Steve, Mom, Scott, and I brought up the rear. Steve went first, then Mom, who seemed heartbroken and lost. Scott and I approached the casket as the last two viewers. It was hard to say goodbye.

I'm Sorry

I walked downstairs and into the kitchen to get a cup of coffee. As I entered the kitchen, I was startled to see Dad sitting at the table, drinking a cup of coffee and reading the newspaper.

"Hey Pop! How's it going?" I asked, obviously surprised to see him. "You know, I'm sorry, I thought you were dead. Where have you been?"

"I just had to do some things."

"We moved all your stuff out of the apartment, and everyone still thinks you're gone."

"I'm going to work out of here for a few days until things are settled."

"If you need any help getting settled, I'm here. I'm glad you're back. Does Mom know you're here yet?"

"No, not yet."

"I'll go get her."

I awoke with a start to the beeping of my alarm clock. I hit the snooze button and lay in bed for several moments. It had been another dream. I'd had several weird dreams over the past several months. Dad's business died with him. My apprenticeship, of sorts, was too brief for me to continue where he left off— besides, I still had to finish school. After wrapping up my classes, I came back home to try to move my life forward. It wasn't progressing as much as I'd hoped. I was still held up slightly by the university about accepting some of the hours I had earned over in Germany. It was more red tape than anything else. During the early months of 1993, I spent a number of days down in Kentucky trying to get it resolved. Ultimately I worked it out, but they dragged it out long enough that I didn't get my degree until August instead of January or May, as it should have been. It made for a fun job search, in any case. But that was only a small part of my stress at the moment.

CHAPTER 11

Last Hand

Hide the Bottle

Mom sat at the kitchen table in the dark, smoke-filled kitchen, lit only by a solitary spotlight that shined down on the table as if it were an empty stage. A deep depression had taken hold of Mom's joyful personality, and turned it bitterly sour. She played with the ice cubes in her tumbler, which contained about ninety percent ice and ten percent Diet Coke. Hair unkempt, she sat in terrycloth pajamas, staring blankly at the glass next to the ashtray, which held a half-finished cigarette.

It was a scene that repeated itself on a nightly basis. During some late-night rants, she would discuss many of the painful thoughts swimming around in her mind, weighing her down with a burden she struggled to bear. Sadness filled her brown eyes as she spoke of her heartbreaking loneliness at having lost Dad. She periodically spoke of a feeling of guilt that her drinking may have contributed to his early death. Those feelings changed to fear that tied her insides in knots when she spoke of money and her uncertain future. Lastly, I think she also felt the shame of being an alcoholic, and that everyone she loved knew her weakness, although she'd never admit to it herself. It was hard to tell for certain how deeply she felt about her issues, because

Mom struggling to cope with life without Dad.

she looked for any excuse to drink. Her spirit seemed to be in a downward spiral, like a plane spinning out of control. I believe, psychologically, she had hit rock bottom. She tried to use alcohol as a parachute in an attempt to escape. While alcohol wasn't the solution, she acted as if she knew of no other way. There were even times she'd talk of suicide.

As much as I loved her, it was hard to feel pity for Mom. I recognized the fact that things were more difficult now that Dad was gone, but her long bout with alcoholism left me with little empathy for her. Much of her sadness resulted from the way her life had played out. As a young mother, she never saw herself going back into the workforce. When she went back to work, she thought it would be temporary, while Steve went to school. Dad's heart attack and an increase in the cost of living solidified the fact that she had to keep working. Her position as an administrative assistant wasn't glamorous or highly paid, but since she hadn't planned on a working life, she hadn't prepared or studied for it. In her mind, the rules of life changed around her, and she was left holding the bag. Her drinking eventually solved that problem, as she became unable to function well enough to work. Even though that excuse was gone, she'd always find another one. As I walked into the kitchen, I knew I was in for some mental grief.

"Tom, can you go to the store for me?"

"What do you need?"

"I need another bottle; I'll give you the money."

"You can't be serious? Are you kidding me? You want me to go out and get you another bottle? I think you've had a little too much if you think I'm going to do that for you."

"Don't do this to me. Just get it this one time."

There is nothing sadder than a mother sitting across from her youngest son, begging him, with tears in her eyes, to go out and buy some alcohol for her, as if her very existence depended on it.

It would be one thing if I had barely known my mother, or if she had always had a substance abuse problem, but that wasn't the case. This was the same Mom who had practically been the perfect mother—the one whose name I'd call out in the night if I had a fever. The one who planned my birthday parties, volunteered at my school, made my favorite foods, sewed my Halloween costume, and helped me

Dark Times.

make Christmas ornaments. The one who seemed to know where everything was, and was always there if I needed her. Now that same woman sat across from me, a shell of her former self, begging me to go and get her a bottle of alcohol. I knew I was walking into trouble the moment I entered the kitchen. There's no easy answer when you're dealing with an alcoholic. You're damned if you do, and damned if you don't. For an alcoholic, stopping cold-turkey could result in some serious health problems, as I discovered one summer day in 1988.

After binging for over a week, Mom attempted to stop cold. On that day, I was sitting at the kitchen table watching TV when Mom staggered into the kitchen as if she were in a trance. I hadn't seen her for a couple of days, so I asked her how she was doing. She sat down and just stared straight ahead. I asked her again, and then asked if she could hear me at all. She continued to look straight ahead with soulless eyes, like Queequeg in *Moby Dick* after he predicted his own death. If she had dropped dead that very moment, I wouldn't have been the least surprised. I called 9-1-1, and an ambulance came. After a week in the hospital, she seemed OK once again. She managed to stay on the wagon for a while after that, but not for too long. I learned quickly that an alcoholic can't be helped until she takes the first step to help herself, and Mom wasn't there yet. After about an hour of begging and my refusing, she broke me down, and I went out and got the bottle. It wasn't my proudest moment.

Many people after college settle for a job that may not be directly related to their career goals and aspirations. As time went on, I began to face that possibility. My career goal was to find a marketing position where I could use my German background either for a U.S. company trying to market products in Germany or for a German company marketing products in the United States. I felt that with my skills, I could fill such a void. I didn't care which industry I worked for, since no matter where I started, it would be new to me and I would have to learn about the company and its products. I wasn't having any luck on the U.S. side of the Atlantic, and I was just about ready to settle for anything applicable. It was around that time that I decided to at least attempt looking for a position from the European side. I talked with Mom, and she agreed to lend me enough money to give me a three-month job search and see what came of it. I planned to leave in late August, finally with my degree in hand. The chances of getting a job without a work visa seemed slim, but I figured I had to risk it. Previously I was able to obtain a student visa and was accepted to a university there after my arrival, so perhaps I could find work the same way. I bid Mom farewell. She was sad to see me go. I reminded her that I'd probably be back in three months, but that I had to at least try my luck. Soon, I was once again sitting in a plane, dreading the long flight. During my brief time in Germany, I wouldn't land a job, but Mom would break her smoking and drinking habits once and for all.

Breathe Deep

It had been almost a year since Dad died when I walked down Hofstallstraße in Würzburg that early October evening, carrying a few items in my tan canvas shopping bag. Among them were a few one-liter glass bottles of Coca-Cola Light, which was the German equivalent of Diet Coke. The funny thing was that I actually preferred Coca-Cola Light to Diet Coke, because I thought it tasted more like regular Coke than Diet Coke did. I don't think the Germans fully understood what kind of treasure they possessed. If they didn't, I did, and to the amazement of all of the Germans around me, I went through it at about the same rate that I used to go through regular Coke, without any brothers to help me. I also carried a jar of Nutella and some butter, ham, and dark bread. (OK, with my diet, I don't have any illusions about living as long as Grandpa Hinesley—I'm the first one to admit it.) I arrived at my place of residence during my three months' stay: the Thomas-Morus-Burse.

The Thomas-Morus-Burse was a Catholic dormitory built in the early 1950s and was where I lived while I was a student in Würzburg. Although I was no longer a student, I was able to stay as a guest during the break until school started later in the month. My job search, while a learning experience, didn't produce the desired results, and my three-month time was coming to an end, with one week left to go.

I walked through the lobby to the old Schindler elevator, also from the early 1950s. The elevator comfortably fit two persons but held a maximum of four—four underfed postwar Germans, no doubt. I stepped inside, and pressed the little black button for the seventh floor. The elevator began to slowly rise. If I walked quickly, I probably could have beaten the elevator to my floor, but after walking to the market, I wasn't in the mood to test my endurance. When I reached my room, there was a note attached to the door that read, "Your brother called." "Which brother?" I wondered. There was one telephone on my floor, and it only took incoming calls. If I wanted to call someone, I had to go down to the lobby, where there was a pay phone. I called both Steve and Scott, but didn't get ahold of either of them. There was a community TV room on the ground floor, where I could watch the news until I could try again. I was watching a report on Boris Yeltsin struggling for power in the midst of a revolt in Russia when I ran out of Coca-Cola Light, and went upstairs for a refill.

When I got upstairs, I was told that Uncle Jerry had called to say that Mom wasn't well. Once again I found myself at the pay phone in the lobby. Residents looked at me strangely as they walked by, as I was speaking English to Uncle Jerry on the phone. He told me that Mom had gone to the doctor because she was having trouble breathing. She started to turn blue on the examination table and was rushed to the hospital, where she was intubated and placed on oxygen in the intensive care unit. Jerry's tone was grim. I was due to fly back to Chicago in one week. I asked Jerry how serious he estimated it to be, and whether he thought I should try to arrange to come home right away or wait out the week.

"Well, the doctor said the last time he saw someone with such a low blood-oxygen level, they didn't make it a week."

"I guess that answers my question."

I called the hospital and was able to speak to one of Mom's nurses. When I asked if it was as serious as Jerry had described, I was told they couldn't guarantee anything. There was really only one thing to do, and that was to return home immediately. It was getting late by then, so I went to bed wondering how I'd get back. Luckily, I had just over four hundred dollars left in my German bank account, in case I needed to pay to change my flight. The next morning, I rushed off to the local ticket office. I explained my dilemma to the pretty blonde ticket agent, and hoped she'd be able to help me. When she looked at the tickets, she informed me that I shouldn't have that ticket at all, because it was an employee ticket. The truth was that I had responded to a newspaper ad for cheap round-trip tickets to Europe. The round-trip tickets to Frankfurt were three hundred and fifty dollars. I knew they were nonrefundable, and I knew I was going to have a problem changing them, but I didn't think anything was wrong with them. Then, in a very German way, she went about getting me the correct ticket in the proper manner. Four hundred dollars later, I had my return ticket. After the whole fiasco, I was happy to have a ticket at all.

I went back to the dorm and packed my things. My ticket was for the next day. I didn't have enough money for a train ticket, so I asked everyone I knew with a car if they would drive me seventy-five miles to the airport. Fortunately, I found someone willing to help me out. With that weight off my mind, I called Scott to see what was going on. Talking to Scott, I discovered that Steve had decided not to fly home, but instead, to continue with vacation plans, which totally baffled me. Scott explained that he didn't know the exact reason Steve was going on vacation, other than that Steve must have felt Mom was OK.

Scott picked me at the airport after my long flight, and we drove to the hospital to see Mom. When we arrived, she wasn't the picture of perfect health. We weren't allowed to visit too long while she was in intensive care, but she seemed happy to see us and was recovering nicely. Over the next several days, I finally spoke to Steve. It turns out that around the same time I had spoken to one of Mom's nurses who wouldn't guarantee Mom's recovery, Steve had spoken to another of her nurses, who told him she was doing better and should get out of intensive care shortly. I guess that made his choice to go on vacation a little more understandable.

I was still a little surprised at Steve's blind trust in the nurse's assessment. Fortunately for everyone, Steve's nurse was the more reliable source of information.

Mom was diagnosed with chronic obstructive pulmonary disease and would have to receive oxygen for the rest of her life. This was unpleasant for Mom, who now wore an air hose attached to an oxygen machine the entire day. The oxygen machine in the house sounded like Darth Vader as it compressed the oxygen, but after a while you got used to it. The best thing to come from this tragic event was that Mom never took another drink again, nor smoked another cigarette from that day forward. Although she needed help getting around, she was a much more pleasant person.

Happy Birthday

By January of 1995, about a year and a half had passed since Mom's near-death experience. Not long after returning home from Germany, I finally began my career as a director of a school for foreign languages. It was a great experience because it was like running my own business. I managed a team of instructors, obtained new clients, and dealt with the profits and losses. Now, I was getting ready for another one of my life's transitions, and intended to get engaged the weekend after my birthday to my longtime girlfriend Vikki. We met at Murray and had maintained a long-distance relationship for several years. It seemed to be the right time for me to make the next move. Scott was the first of the three of us to get married, but, ironically, he wasn't living with his wife at the moment. Alison and Scott were married during my three-month stint in Germany, a fact that Scott never lets me forget. Alison had moved out to L.A. with Scott, but preferred the flat land of Illinois to the earthquakes of California. I figured, having lived with Scott for a long time myself, that she just wanted to get away from him. They agreed to move back to Chicago, but Scott stayed out in California until he got a job back home. As a result, he constantly flew back and forth.

Steve was in a relationship at the time, which I really didn't know much about, until I received a call on my birthday. Steve called to wish me a "happy birthday," and then said he wanted to share some urgent news with Mom and me.

"I'm getting married this Friday," Steve said nonchalantly, as if telling us he was going to the store. There wasn't the expected emotion in his voice, so I assumed I heard him wrong.

"You're doing what?"

"I'm getting married this Friday," he repeated.

Mom seemed dumbstruck. I said, "What a coincidence, I plan to get engaged on Friday. But what's the rush in getting married? Were you already engaged?"

"No, I have cancer."

A Career Cut Short

I didn't know what to think after Steve told me he had cancer. Different questions entered my mind: "Are you positive?" "How did you find out?" "Did you get a second opinion?" Steve wasn't in a talkative mood. I found out over the course of the next several days that his first symptoms were feeling nauseated when he ate. I remember talking to him after he went on a trip to the Czech Republic to scout locations for the movie *Dragon Heart*, and he complained about how he couldn't stomach the food. I thought he was simply being picky. Back in the U.S., he continued to feel ill, and assumed he might be lactose intolerant or something of that nature. Doctors did tests, and didn't find anything until they tested for cancer. That's when they found out he had pancreatic cancer. Worse still, the cancer had spread to his liver and other organs.

At 34 years of age, Steve had already accomplished many things in his career in visual effects. His uncanny artistic skills had made him a standout in computer animation at ILM. This came as no surprise to me, because it always seemed that everything Steve did artistically had a touch of excellence about it. Dating back to the time of Super Fuzzy, Steve put his passion and intellect into his work, giving it a uniqueness that's difficult to describe.

When he started working on major films like *Jurassic Park*, I enjoyed telling friends about his accomplishments. Even so, I never could convey just how talented he really was. After *Jurassic Park*, Steve became visual effects supervisor on another Spielberg movie, Schindler's List. He was working on the film *Jumanji* when he was diagnosed with cancer. The movie was to be a visual-effects extravaganza, breaking new ground in CGI animals. With much of the project already set in motion, Steve's condition forced him to hand over the remaining duties to Ken Ral-

Steve on location for the filming of *Jumanji*.

ston. It was about that time, in April 1995, that Steve came home for Easter.

Last Homecoming

I looked out the upstairs window, waiting for Steve's car to arrive. It had been two and a half years since I had seen him. I was looking forward to talking to him face to face. I knew that he had started treatment and was waiting for some news about its effectiveness. The last time I spoke with him, prior to his trip to Chicago, he didn't seem too optimistic. I spoke words of encouragement to him, hoping I could lift his spirits so that he wouldn't give up. On his trip to Chicago, Steve was also bringing his new wife, Patty. It would be the first time I met

Steve, getting ready to battle cancer.

her. I had actually never spoken to her, and wasn't sure what to expect. Steve had met her while working at ILM. I kept an open mind. Patty turned out to be not only one of the nicest people I have ever met, but a great wife for Steve, and probably the best thing that ever happened to him. As I looked out the window that day, it didn't seem that long ago that my brothers and I were eating chocolate Easter bunnies and hunting for Easter eggs while enjoying spring break from school.

My trance of looking out the window was broken suddenly by a Mom's voice.

"Can you run to the store for a couple of things?"

Mom was out of breath, having walked into the hallway from the kitchen, clutching a long, rolled-up bundle of air tubing with one end connected to an air compressor that supplied her with oxygen.

"Sure, what do we need?"

"I made a list."

"OK, I'll try to get back before Steve gets here."

I was both nervous and excited to see Steve again. I wasn't sure what to expect. I knew he had shaved his head before undergoing chemotherapy. Patty and Steve had some photos taken shortly after he had his head shaved and sent them to us before heading to Chicago. I thought he looked pretty good with a shaved head, but still, it was going to be a little different seeing him in person. As it turns out, it was even more different than I expected.

As I arrived home, I noticed a rental car parked in front of the house. I walked in, carrying several bags of groceries. From the foyer, I could see Steve sitting at the dining room table. He sat upright, with a smile that seemed sadly forced. The drugs he was taking made his eyes look big and black, and his movements were very slow. There are not many people more optimistic than me, who can put a positive spin on a bad situation like I can, but when I saw Steve, my instant thought was "Holy Moses, he's a goner."

Steve and I stepout into the fresh air on Easter Sunday, 1995.

"I just need to put this stuff away real quick, and I'll be right out," I said, smiling back at him.

I made my way to the kitchen. I hoped he hadn't noticed my shock and sadness at seeing him in that condition. I tried to regain my composure as quickly as possible. I tried to wrap my mind around what I'd just seen. Mom came into the kitchen, dragging her air tubing and puffing as she went.

"He doesn't look so good," she said, with a worried look on her face.

"That's an understatement," I replied in a low voice.

I must have looked like I had just had the wind knocked out of me, because that's exactly how I felt. I took a deep breath, calmed myself, and made my way into the dining room.

"How's it going?" Steve asked, still moving like someone had turned a switch on his movement control settings to a quarter of his normal speed.

"I'm doing fine, are you OK?"

From that point on, we began to catch up with each other. It wasn't long before Grandpa Hinesley arrived with Uncle Jerry. Grandpa Hinesley was 87 years old, and had some difficulty getting around—the result of one or two minor strokes. The strokes caused him to lose some of the sensation in his hands, as well as limited his mobility. At the same table sat Steve, who was only 34 years old and was having about the same difficulty getting around as Grandpa Hinesley. It was good to see Steve again, although I couldn't help feeling like it was the last place in the world he wanted to be.

During his visit, Steve seemed absolutely miserable. It reminded me of our collective misery when my brothers and I were dragged off to some family gathering. It was a bonding experience for us, because we all shared torturous boredom during such visits. We would search out things to do to entertain ourselves. Since there were no video games or cable TV yet, we'd find a deck of cards, a board game, a ball, or something with which we could make a game. If we were lucky enough to be at Aunt Nancy's house, we made a beeline for the pool table or ping-pong table. Best of all, Aunt Nancy had a bar in the game room that was stocked with plenty of soft drinks. If you had to be stuck in a house full of people you didn't know, what better way to spend your time than drinking Coke and playing ping-pong or pool? Although Steve was having a tough time that Easter, I think deep down he felt he had to be there. He knew it was most likely going to be the last time he'd come home to Greenbrier.

All in all, it was a strange visit. Even Grandpa Hinesley didn't really know what to say to Steve. I didn't get to talk to Steve much on my own. He was mostly there to visit Mom. He hadn't seen her since Dad's funeral two and a half years earlier. I did enjoy meeting Patty and talking with Steve as much as I could. The visit was brief, and I'm sure Mom wished he could have stayed longer. I wasn't as upset as Mom, because I had already planned to head out to California to see Steve in mid-May. Seeing Steve's condition over Easter made me conscious of the urgency of that trip.

Going to California

I had mixed emotions about my first-ever trip to California. I wanted to see Steve again, I wanted to visit Scott, and California was also a place I had never traveled, but I couldn't get the purpose of the visit out of my mind. My plan was to fly to Los Angeles and stay with Scott for a few days. On the weekend, Scott and I would travel together to visit Steve in the San Francisco area. After spending several days there, Scott and I would return to L.A. and I would fly back to Chicago. The whole trip would last one week. Knowing I was going to travel California to visit Steve, Scott recommended that I come to L.A. at the same time as the Jimmy Page-Robert Plant tour in mid-May, and he would get tickets. So that's what I did.

I found myself cramped in coach once again on a long, four-and-a-half-hour flight. For someone who doesn't like to be cramped up in a plane for more than an hour, I always seem to pick faraway destinations. I suppose it could have been a lot worse—Steve could have lived in Tokyo or something. Sitting in the very rear of the plane, I waited for my turn to get up and gather my belongings. Then it was my turn to join the line of happy travelers walking slowly down the aisle to exit the plane. I walked down the corridor to the arrival gate. As I came out, there was a little crowd of people waiting for friends and family. There, waiting for me, was...no one. Scott wasn't Mr. Dependable. Instead, I scanned the signs for the baggage claim and decided to pick up my suitcase.

Instead of picking me up, Scott told me to catch a shuttle to where he worked. Little did I know what the day had in store for me. After sitting on the plane for more than four hours, I spent another four hours standing at Scott's work, while he ran around attending to various projects. I was glad when it was finally time to leave, because I needed to sit down. I carried my heavy suitcase to Scott's sporty Mitsubishi Eclipse. I heaved the suitcase into the hatchback and went to sit down in the front seat. As I bent down awkwardly to fit into his car, a searing pain hit me in the back, as if I had I sat on a knife. The stress of worrying about Steve, the long flight, the long hours of standing, and schlepping that heavy suitcase, caused my back to give way, and I dropped to the pavement as if hit with a blast from a Taser gun.

I should have probably gone to the emergency room, because I couldn't walk five feet without having a major back spasm that brought me to the ground, but we had twentieth-row seats for the Page-Plant show, and Scott was insistent that we go. So I found myself lying face down in the parking lot of the L.A. Forum that night several times before the show's security crew took pity on me and sent a cart to transport me up to the stadium. Somehow I made it through the show, but I didn't sleep much that night. The next day I saw a doctor who prescribed the best muscle relaxers and pain killers I've ever had. I spent most of the rest of my time in L.A. in bed.

If You're Going to San Francisco

On Saturday, when Scott and I climbed into his tiny Mitsubishi Eclipse, I was heavily sedated with pain killers and muscle relaxers. We didn't know exactly what was in store for us in San Francisco, but we knew it wasn't going to be good. We took the scenic Highway 1 from Los Angeles to the San Francisco area. As we drove along the coast that day, as amazing as the view was, it wasn't enough to shake the somber feeling of what awaited me when we got there. After my experience at Easter, I wasn't going to be caught off guard by Steve's condition. Sometimes, regardless of how prepared you think you are, life still manages to surprise you. Scott and I drove across the Golden Gate Bridge, and, although I'd never been to San Francisco before, I scarcely took in the sights as we passed them. Scott and I checked into our hotel before heading over to Steve's place.

Steve was under hospice care at home when we visited him. We arrived late in the afternoon that Saturday. Steve lived in a town northeast of San Francisco called San Rafael. Since Scott had visited a number of times before, he knew the way, and it wasn't long before we parked the car in the street and were walking up the pathway to the front door of Steve's house.

Patty greeted us at the front door. Although I'd only met Patty in Chicago about a month before, I felt like I'd known her for years. As we entered the house, Steve was lying propped up, with some pillows and a blanket on his lap, on a black sofa. His condition had worsened since I'd seen him last. Jaundice had set in, giving him a yellow tinge, as if I were looking at him through a pair of yellow-tinted sunglasses. I noticed that his feet, which were peeking out from underneath his blanket, were swollen and puffy, which I took to be the reason he was on the couch. Although his appearance didn't inspire any chance of rebounding back to full health, his mind was clearer than when he was in Greenbrier the last time.

He gave me one of his sly smirks and said, with an air of irony, "Welcome to California."

I returned his smirk. "Thanks, I wish I could have come under better circumstances."

I would have continued talking, but, as was his habit, Scott took over the conversation, rambling on about nothing of great importance. Steve wasn't up for a great deal of small talk, however, because it wasn't long before he asked us to leave. Scott and I went off to find someplace to eat.

Over the course of my visit, Steve would ask us to leave if he felt particularly bad, so we came and went throughout the next day. Finally, in the evening he was too tired to have us around, so he recommended a Thai restaurant he had enjoyed when he was still able to hold down his food. Scott and I ate at the restaurant, then went out to play some pool and find some other distractions from the depressing reality that faced us. I was beginning to feel uneasy because we were driving back to L.A. the following day, and my time with Steve was running out.

Scott and I stayed out past one o'clock in the morning. An hour later, around two o'clock, we received a call from Patty, asking us to come over because Steve wanted to see us. We drove to his house, in the middle of the night. When we joined Steve, he was in his bedroom. The bedroom was dimly lit, giving the room an orange glow. An owl hooted from somewhere in the backyard. We had two white buckets with us, because Steve would periodically cough up dark coffee ground-like blood. Steve was beginning to hallucinate, perhaps as a result of the medication or just the severity of his condition.

For the first time, Steve seemed scared as he said, "Everyone keep breathing, don't hold your breath."

It felt like he needed us to breathe for him—that if just one of us held our breath for a second, he might stop breathing himself. After a while, Steve calmed down and slept. I, too, needed some rest. I lay down on the couch, only to be awakened around eight o'clock in the morning. Steve was up again, coughing up more blood. Scott went to rinse out a bucket as Steve lay back in the bed. Then, suddenly, came a violent cough, like an explosion spraying outward. Patty and I sat Steve up in our arms, as Steve exhaled one last time, and slowly faded from us. At that moment, I lost my brother.

The rest of the day seemed like a blur, with Scott and I driving back to L.A. later in the day. I flew back home the following day, while Scott went back to San Francisco to participate in a service held for ILM employees and friends of Steve's, including George Lucas. Scott picked up Steve's remains and flew to Chicago.

A Promise Made Good

I walked into Memory Gardens with Mom, and joined the group gathered for the service. We had arranged for a room at the cemetery, for us to have a service according to Steve's wishes. Up to that point, every funeral I had attended had been with Steve. This one was no different, except this time he wasn't sitting next to me to help me get through it. As promised ten years before on that cold day in January, there would be no cheesy horror-movie organ music. Like the previous funerals, this one was like a family reunion, with one exception. Grandpa Hinesley opted not to go. He didn't like the fact that there wasn't going to be a religious portion to the funeral.

Here's where I'd like to say that we were a model Christian family. But that would be a lie. I'm not a hundred percent sure why. My par-

Patty's artistic rendition of the day Steve died, titled, *Who Dies*? (*Who Dies*? © 1995 Patricia Blau)

ents both came from families that went to church, but for some reason we drifted away from going. But it wasn't always that way.

When I was little, we attended the First Presbyterian Church, on Dunton Street, in the heart of downtown Arlington Heights. It's a beautiful church made of red brick, with a distinguished white-pillared entrance and white steeple. It was founded in 1855, providing a long and involved history in our community. We always dressed in our Sunday best, which included a little suit, a white shirt, a clip-on tie, and buckled dress shoes. I didn't enjoy church too much. When we arrived, the family split up, with Steve, Scott, and I shuttled over to Sunday school while Mom and Dad attended the regular service.

To keep us enthusiastic about going to church, Mom and Dad worked in a choice breakfast incentive: Each week, one

The three of us pose for a picture before going off to church (I'm in the middle, with Scott on the left, and Steve on the right). Steve appears to be the happiest of the three of us—it must have been his week to choose our breakfast spot.

of us got to pick where we would eat breakfast afterward. I almost always picked the Dunton House restaurant, which was just down the street, because they had the best pancakes around. But no matter where we went, we all had fun, and it was a good incentive to get us into church on Sundays.

As time went on, we attended church less regularly. I already felt like I didn't know anyone in my Sunday school class, because other kids missed church every so often, as well. The less frequently I went, the more I felt out of place, and the more I didn't want to go. I think everyone else in the family started to feel the same way; we felt bad that we missed so often. By late 1976, we had quit going to church altogether. So Steve had become more or less atheist over the years, and didn't want any religious ceremony. The format of the service was therefore different from the previous funerals I'd been to, in that it was set up more as a memorial to Steve than as a traditional funeral. Steve had been cremated, and there was no visitation. Instead, there was a montage of photographs celebrating Steve's life. There before me was a man's whole life, summed up by a collection of photographs.

At some point, people were asked if they wanted to say something about their memories of Steve. Various friends and relatives spoke. Scott even spoke. I, once again, couldn't. It was too painful, and my words couldn't convey how I felt about what I had lost. The unspoken connection to my brothers made me feel like a part of me died that day in May. To this day, I miss him terribly. There are times I forget that my son, who never met my brother, only knows him from old photographs, family stories, and the dedication to his memory in the closing credits of *Jumanji*.

The End of an Era

After my brother's death, over the course of the next three years, Mom's health deteriorated further. Grandma Artie's words about how she could never get over the loss of her son came back to haunt her. I was married the August after Steve's death. We decided to stay with Mom in Greenbrier as Mom's condition worsened. Mom helped watch my seven-year-old step-daughter while my wife and I worked. We helped Mom with her various errands and medical needs. Plagued by years of smoking, Mom developed breast cancer, on top of the emphysema she developed. Her poor health began to depress her. I feared she would once again turn to alcohol. However, in the summer of 1996, something happened that seemed to give her a new outlook on life. It was the birth of her first grandchild, my son, Spencer.

Despite her poor health, she seemed to come alive after Spencer was born. With her spirits raised, she battled cancer the best she could. Following a mastectomy and chemotherapy, she seemed to have a leg up on the disease. Mom met regularly with her longtime friend Gayle. She began to pursue old hobbies, such as ceramics, and even added some new ones. She continued to see her various doctors and her cancer specialist, even though she felt like her condition had stabilized. Then, in the summer of 1998, she started to have trouble breathing. By July, she found herself back in the hospital.

Mom and her newly born grandson, Spencer.

She underwent a number of tests to see if her emphysema had worsened. The doctors told my brother and me that her lungs seemed clear enough that she shouldn't have breathing problems like those she complained about. After several days, she was released. Less than a month later, she entered the hospital once again, complaining of difficulty breathing. This time she began to act oddly. She began talking about how the doctors and nurses were trying to kill her. Again she was tested. Again they couldn't find an issue with her lungs that should cause her breathing trouble. They considered releasing her from the hospital, when they finally found something. Scott and I were told they had discovered a tumor on her liver that was pressing against her lungs. It was the tumor, they now believed, that was causing her difficulty breathing. Scott and I were informed that her chances of survival were slim at best. They recommended chemotherapy. I was skeptical. After witnessing Steve's condition, I felt that if her chances were slim, why torture her with chemotherapy? We debated, and decided that a slim chance was better than no chance, so we opted for chemotherapy.

The same night they were going to start Mom's chemotherapy, I went to a going-away party for a work colleague, while Scott attended a concert. When I came home, I received a message from my Uncle Jerry that Mom had gone into a coma that night.

The next morning, Scott and I sat in Mom's hospital room. We knew the drill. We'd been through it before with Steve. This time was less messy. We were told that we could expect her to die sometime that morning. Scott and I must have seemed like a pair of cold-hearted sons, as we sat there and waited for Mom to die. At 10:10 a.m. on August 16th, Mom passed away. I remember the time distinctly because of something Dad taught me when I was little. He pointed out to me an ad for watches and clocks in which the time was always set to 10:10. He explained that they showed the time this way because when the hands are set to 10:10, it makes people subconsciously think of a smile. It's tough to see it that way now.

You Can Please Some of the People Some of the Time

When it came time for Mom's funeral, Scott and I were a little more prepared for what to expect. Mom had liked Steve's low-key funeral, and wanted hers to be kept simple. While Mom wasn't an atheist, she simply didn't want a reverend who didn't know her to speak about her at her own funeral. To cover our bases with Grandpa Hinesley, we made sure that Mom's wishes would be OK with him, since Steve's funeral seemed to bother him. Despite saying he was fine with the plans; we found out later that he was disappointed with the service. Well, we tried. For some reason, he blamed Scott, and I was in the clear. We southpaws have to stick together. I would have thought life is too short to hold a grudge. Of course, when you've reached your nineties, as Grandpa Hinesley had, you might see it differently.

Again there was the gathering of relatives, a couple of whom I now recognized from the flurry of funerals. Once again people spoke, and once again I couldn't. Scott and I met up after the service was over.

"I guess this just leaves you and me," said Scott.

"It would appear that way."

"If I'm next, are you finally going to have the guts to stand up and say something?"

"Well, considering there isn't anyone else left, I guess I'll have to."

With those words, we parted. After I said goodbye to Scott, it dawned on me that after Mom died, we had played our last hand of pinochle as a family—only the two partners remained. Our time as a family is but a memory now, as is the community where I grew up. Daily, I adjust to the new world and await its next transition.

Rejuvenation

It's been over seven years since my business trip to Germany in November of 2000, and this country has continued to evolve. Unfortunately for me, my marriage wasn't the type of marriage Grandma and Grandpa Hinesley had. My marriage lasted only eleven years, and ended in divorce. Scott's marriage fared better—I think it's the La Roman's connection. I've remained in Greenbrier over the years. The changes here in recent years have been subtle, yet noticeable. Some younger families have begun to move into the neighborhood, and even though the families are smaller than they were in the past, they have attributed to a general feeling of rejuvenation. The face of Greenbrier also continues to change, but in a new way. The most recognizable change is the new trend of tear-downs, as new mansion-sized houses replace some three-bedroom ranch houses of old. It seems that there has also been an increased pace of life in the neighborhood, giving it a similar hectic frenzy to that of the floor of the New York Stock Exchange. A daily swarm of minivans surrounds the remodeled and enlarged Greenbrier School, from which Spencer recently graduated. His experience was significantly different than my own, having escaped the multi-age classrooms. Changes in the school culture have inspired a parent handbook of rules and policies longer than that of the Constitution of the United States. I guess it's just another sign of the times. Even though Greenbrier may no longer be the place of my youth, it remains a great place to live.

Everyone needs a break from the stresses of modern day life, and my son is no exception. I knew just the place to bring him to relax, too—Musky Haven. We've been lucky enough to make the trip up there to fish together a couple of times. The last time, we were joined by Scott and two of his children (he has four!). It felt good to be out on the lake, with the spray of the water in our faces as the boat skimmed along the surface. We shared the universal excitement of a fish on the line, and the thrill of the hunt.

I have taught Spencer how to play pinochle. Even though he doesn't have great teachers like Dad and Grandpa Hinesley, Scott and I do our best. On the last night of our fishing trip, we played a game of three-handed pinochle, while Scott's kids played with toys. Once and a while, Scott's kids would watch us play a hand or two, the way I did so long ago.

"Whose deal is it?"

"Mine. You're at ninety-two, Spencer is at fifty-four, and I'm at eighty-six. This should be the last hand," Scott announced.

"OK, we need to wrap this up because we have to get out early tomorrow."

As luck would have it, Scott won the game, after which everyone went to sleep. The following morning, we quickly packed our things in anticipation of eating breakfast at Paul Bunyan's Restaurant on our way home. I paid for the cabin while Spencer finished packing our car. Scott loaded the last of his fishing gear into the trunk, climbed into the driver's seat, and we drove off separately to the restaurant.

Following a filling breakfast that reminded me of years past, Scott said his good-byes from the rolled-down window of his minivan.

"We had fun; I think the kids were starting to get the hang of fishing. We should think about coming back next year, and I'll try to bring Kevin."

"I'm up for it, if you are."

"It's too bad the others aren't around any longer to join us."

"Yeah, I was thinking the same thing."

Scott and I wrapped up our conversation while his kids made a racket in the back of the van, secured tightly in their car seats. Scott looked at them in the rear view mirror and said, "Guys, give it a rest!"

Suddenly, there was silence. Ryan, who looked like Scott in miniature, raised his eyebrows and looked at me with a mischievous grin, which I reciprocated. I thought to myself, "Some things don't change after all."

Scott turned to the kids and said, "Say goodbye to Uncle Tommy."

"Goodbye Uncle Tommy."

"Goodbye."

Acknowledgments

A Little Help from My Friends

My inspiration for the book came from my children, Heather and Spencer Price, who never had the chance of knowing all of the members of my family. For them the story must seem like a tale from the very distant past.

While writing the book, I dwelled many hours on reconstructing and confirming my memory of events. To make sure I wasn't remembering things wrong, I enlisted the help of friends and family. I'd like to thank a number of people who helped me in this regard, most of all, my brother and pinochle partner, Scott Price. My memory was also aided with help from old friends; Tom Berg, Doug Brooks, Brian Carey and Jim Kluka.

There were other family topics and events relating to my parents before I was born that I based on stories told to me over the years as well as interviews conducted for the book. I'd like to thank those who helped me. They include: my uncle Jerry Hinesley, uncle Herb and aunt Delores Hinesley, Joel and Gail Schimpf, my uncle Milt and aunt Joy Price, my aunt Nancy (Price) Hime. On a sad note, my aunt Delores passed away while I was writing the book. Her constant enthusiasm in life and spirit was an inspiration.

Keith Betti, Orlando Devillia and Lorna Torrez helped and supported me while I struggled along with the book. Their kind words of encouragement pushed me along to the finish line.

Lastly, I'd like to thank those who contributed directly to the book in some way. My sister in-law Patty Blau contributed the painting for the cover of the book. I know she put more than paint on the canvas when she painted it. And a special thanks to Alyssa Popowitch and Heather Babiar, who helped me make the book come alive.

Historical Information

While writing the book I added historical details relating to the Chicago area and businesses. For general information I frequently used two local newspapers, the Chicago Tribune and Daily Herald. I've listed some specific articles that I used relating to the various topics I covered. Information regarding Arlington Heights Elementary School District 25 was obtained from copies of the school board meeting minutes spanning the years 1964-83.

The photos for the book come mostly from my personal collection. Every reasonable effort has been made to identify owners of copyright. Errors or omissions will be corrected in subsequent editions.

7146981R0

Made in the USA
Lexington, KY
25 October 2010